Beyond the Blockade

CARIBBEAN ARCHAEOLOGY AND ETHNOHISTORY

L. Antonio Curet, Series Editor

Beyond the Blockade

New Currents in Cuban Archaeology

Edited by
SUSAN KEPECS, L. ANTONIO CURET,
and GABINO LA ROSA CORZO

Chapters by Cuban authors
translated from Spanish by
SUSAN KEPECS

THE UNIVERSITY OF ALABAMA PRESS
Tuscaloosa

Copyright © 2010
The University of Alabama Press
Tuscaloosa, Alabama 35487-0380
All rights reserved
Manufactured in the United States of America

Typeface: Minion

∞

The paper on which this book is printed meets the minimum requirements of American National Standard for Information Sciences-Permanence of Paper for Printed Library Materials, ANSI Z39.48-1984.

Library of Congress Cataloging-in-Publication Data

Beyond the blockade : new currents in Cuban archaeology / edited by Susan Kepecs, L. Antonio Curet, and Gabino La Rosa Corzo ; chapters by Cuban authors translated from Spanish by Susan Kepecs.
   p. cm. — (Caribbean archaeology and ehnohistory)
   Includes bibliographical references and index.
   ISBN 978-0-8173-1720-1 (cloth : alk. paper) — ISBN 978-0-8173-5633-0 (paper : alk. paper) — ISBN 978-0-8173-8492-0 (electronic) 1. Cuba—Antiquities. 2. Archaeology—Research—Cuba. 3. Excavations (Archaeology)—Cuba. 4. Ethnoarchaeology—Cuba. 5. Archaeology and history—Cuba. 6. Archaeology and history—Florida. 7. Cuba—Relations—Florida. 8. Florida—Relations—Cuba. 9. Historic conservation—Cuba. 10. Heritage tourism—Cuba. I. Kepecs, Susan, 1946-II. Curet, L. Antonio, 1960-III. La Rosa Corzo, Gabino.
   F1769.B49   2010
   972.91′01—dc22
                                                                                         2010017775

Contents

List of Illustrations   vii

1. Introduction: New Currents in Cuban Archaeology
   Susan Kepecs and L. Antonio Curet   1

2. Prologue: Homage to Dr. Betty Meggers
   Lourdes Domínguez   13

3. Cuba and Florida: Entwined Histories of Historical Archaeologies
   Kathleen Deagan   16

4. La Loma del Convento: Its Centrality to Current Issues in Cuban Archaeology
   Vernon James Knight Jr.   26

5. New Early Tradition Stone Tool Industries in Cuba
   Lorenzo Morales Santos   47

6. Investigations at Laguna de Limones: Suggestions for a Change in the Theoretical Direction of Cuban Archaeology
   Daniel Torres Etayo   70

7. Recent Archaeological Fieldwork from the Region around Los Buchillones: An Indigenous Site on the North-Central Cuban Coast
   Jago Cooper, Roberto Valcárcel Rojas, and Jorge Calvera   89

8. Turey Treasure in the Caribbean: Brass and Indo-Hispanic Contact at El Chorro de Maíta, Cuba
   Roberto Valcárcel Rojas, Marcos Martinón-Torres, Jago Cooper, and Thilo Rehren   106

9. The Archaeology of Escaped Slaves: Utensils for Resistance
Gabino La Rosa Corzo   126

10. Built Patrimony and Historical Archaeology: Problematic Relations in Working with the Past
Iosvany Hernández Mora   143

References Cited   163

Contributors   189

Index   193

Illustrations

Figures

1.1. The editors present a plaque to Dr. Betty Meggers at the 2006 Annual Meeting of the Society for American Archaeology in San Juan   4

2.1. Dr. Lourdes Domínguez with Dr. Betty Meggers at the Smithsonian Institution   14

3.1. The "Daytona Conference" group in 1948   19

3.2. The University of Florida research team arriving at José Martí Airport, Havana, 1983   22

4.1. Agroalfarero sites in the Jagua Bay area   28

4.2. Map of middens at La Loma del Convento   30

4.3. Ford diagrams of pottery, La Loma del Convento   34

4.4. Bronze navigator's compass, La Loma del Convento   35

4.5. Cuban-Soviet excavation of 1986–87, showing Structures 1 and 2   36

4.6. Location of Las Casas's Canarreo, Loma del Convento   41

5.1. Map of the principal regions in Cuba with evidence of Cuba's early stone tool tradition   49

5.2. Map with principal locations of early tradition sites in northwest Villa Clara   51

5.3. Cluster analysis: dendograms showing early tradition tool groups in northwest Villa Clara   56

5.4. Handaxe comparison   59

5.5. Molar fragment, *Megalocnus* sp., in habitational stratigraphic context at Solapa Alta   63

5.6. Partial biface handaxe, Jibá industry   66

5.7. Techno-typological order of the early stone tool industries of northwest Villa Clara   67

6.1. Regional location of Laguna de Limones, San Lucas, and Pueblo Viejo   72

6.2. Principal structural components of Laguna de Limones, with topographic details   81

6.3. Vectoral map showing the direction of rainwater flow   83

7.1. Map of Cuba showing location of Los Buchillones   91

7.2. Plan of posts excavated at Los Buchillones   93

7.3. Plan of site extent based on archaeological evidence   95

7.4. Map of coastal and island survey showing locations of islands with links to Los Buchillones   97

7.5. Photographs of shell artifacts from Cave 1, Cayo Hijo de Guillermo Este, and Los Buchillones   101

7.6. Map of sites with contemporaneous radiocarbon determinations   103

8.1. Agricultural-ceramicist sites in Cuba, including sites referred to in text, with detail of the Yaguajay area showing the location of El Chorro de Maíta   108

8.2. Plan of El Chorro de Maíta   112

8.3. Burial No. 57 with some of the reported objects   114

8.4. Brass tubes (lacetags)   115

8.5. Ornament from burial No. 25   115

9.1. Map of the Habana-Matanzas uplands, with the general locations of sites mentioned in text   130

9.2. The inaccessibility of the sites is still one of their distinguishing characteristics; Cueva de La Jía   133

9.3. Percentages of artifact and tool types, by category   134

9.4. Bowl from a rustic pipe for smoking tobacco, from Cueva de la Cachimba. The star decoration is a recurrent motif in Bantu artifacts.   136

9.5. Presence of faunal species, by number of sites at which they appear   140

10.1. Section of a recent excavation in the church of San Felipe Neri, Old Havana   147

Illustrations / ix

10.2. The façade of the house at No. 602 San Ignacio   154

10.3. Wall on the second level of the house, showing different moments in the life of the building   155

Tables

5.1. Technological and typological values applied in cluster analysis of early tradition stone tools in northwest Villa Clara   55

5.2. Extinct species found in the karst sinkhole at Chuchita 1   64

6.1. Faunal remains identified at Laguna de Limones   85

7.1. Shell species from Cayo Hijo de Guillermo Este; also D2-1 and F-11, Los Buchillones   99

9.1. Characteristics of the fugitive slave sites in the Havana-Matanzas uplands   131

Beyond the Blockade

I
Introduction
New Currents in Cuban Archaeology

Susan Kepecs, University of Wisconsin-Madison
L. Antonio Curet, The Field Museum

This volume is the result of a symposium, "Archaeology Behind the Blockade: New Research in Cuba," which we organized with our friend and colleague Gabino La Rosa (professor emeritus, Center for Anthropology, Ministry of Science, Technology and the Environment, Havana; currently affiliated with the History Section of the Union of Writers and Artists of Cuba [UNEAC]) for the 2006 annual meetings of the Society for American Archaeology in San Juan, Puerto Rico.

The symposium was designed to bring the latest research by emerging Cuban professionals to the SAA's international, Americas-based professional audience. Seven Cuban participants, plus two researchers from the United States and one from England, were included. The Cuban government allots few resources for foreign academic travel, and without support Cuban investigators, whose government salaries are paid in Cuban currency, would be unable to cover the U.S. dollar-based costs of air travel and hotels in Puerto Rico. Thus we wrote proposals and obtained funds from three generous sources—the R. Christopher Reynolds Foundation, Fundación Amistad, and the Social Science Research Council—so that our Cuban colleagues could attend the meetings.

The 2006 symposium was built on previous relations we had established with Cuban archaeologists. Reagan-era visa restrictions on Cubans who work for state-run institutions, including universities, softened in the Clinton years. Both of us took advantage of that situation, traveling to Cuba to meet and work with archaeologists multiple times in the late 1990s and the first few years of the new millennium.

One result of this contact was an earlier SAA symposium, organized by historical archaeologist Shannon Lee Dawdy (University of Chicago) with Curet and La Rosa for the Society's 2002 annual meeting in Denver, Colorado. At that session, four Cuban archaeologists and two Americans presented papers on new research; Curet served as discussant. From that symposium came *Dialogues in Cuban Archaeology*, edited by Curet, Dawdy, and La Rosa and published in 2005 by The University of Alabama Press.

Dialogues in Cuban Archaeology is among a scant handful of recent works by Cuban archaeologists published in the United States since the 1959 Cuban Revolution. Other such publications include the English translation of La Rosa's *Runaway Slave Settlements in Cuba: Resistance and Repression* (2003a), the English translation by Ramón Dacal and Manuel Rivero's *Art and Archaeology of Pre-Columbian Cuba* (1996), an article on Archaic cave burials in Cuba by La Rosa published in *Latin American Antiquity* (2003b), and an article in *Journal of Archaeological Science* on the microanalysis of metal artifacts in "Taíno"[1] burials (Martinón-Torres et al. 2007).

The Cubans who presented papers at the Denver symposium that became the basis for *Dialogues in Cuban Archaeology* also engaged in a forum at that meeting on ways to improve communications between archaeologists in Cuba and the United States. The 2006 symposium in San Juan was a response to the suggestions borne of that event, with the encouragement of University of Alabama Press (then) senior acquisitions editor Judith Knight. But the San Juan session, "Beyond the Blockade: Recent Archaeology in Cuba," did not go as planned.

We knew when we organized the symposium that visa restrictions could be an obstacle. During the 2004 presidential race, George W. Bush, courting the Cuban exile vote in Miami, repeatedly announced plans to topple the Castro government by tightening the United States' hefty plethora of isolation tactics. We hoped reason would prevail, but 2006 turned out to be the year of "baseball sí, academics no," a term coined by *USA Today* writer DeWayne Wickham (2006) when the Latin American Studies Association, which also held its meetings that year in San Juan, reported that 59 Cuban scholars were denied visas and were unable to attend. That same year, Cuban baseball players were first denied visas, then granted them, for the World Baseball Classic. The Cuban team advanced to the finals, but ultimately was beaten by Japan, 10–6, in the final matchup at San Diego's Petco Park.

In July 2005, with our generous funding in hand, we sent official invitations to the Cuban archaeologists, along with the money needed to cover their visa application fees. All seven Cubans began the visa process immediately, and over the next few months we received emails from Cuba letting us know that the proper applications for visas had been filed with the U.S. Special Interests Section in Havana. Various emails followed, their tone increasingly anxious. By January 2006, it became clear that the process of obtaining the Cubans' visas had stalled.

As residents of Illinois and Wisconsin, we immediately solicited and received letters of support for each participant from U.S. Representative Luis Gutierrez (D-IL), U.S. Representative Tammy Baldwin (D-WI), and U.S. Senator Russ Feingold (D-WI). (At the same time, we solicited support from then-U.S. Senator Barack Obama [D-IL], but his office would not consider our request unless we submitted a great deal of additional paperwork, which we had no time to compile.) In addition, we sent letters to officials at the Cuba Interests Section in Washington, the U.S. Interests Section in Havana, the U.S. State Department Cuba Desk, and the deputy assistant secretary of state for Western Hemisphere Affairs. We included the symposium prospectus as clear evidence that this was an academic affair, not a political one. We asked the recipients of these letters to consider the nature of our project and to help facilitate the visa applications made by our Cuban colleagues. Further, Luly Duke, director of Fundación Amistad, took the proactive step of making a personal phone call to the Cuban Interests Section to request that the visas be granted.

To make a long story short, the State Department officials took their time. We received no further notification on the visa process until April 12 (two weeks before the symposium), when we learned that all of the Cubans' visa applications had been denied. On April 14, David Lindsey, government affairs manager for the SAA, sent a letter in the name of SAA President Kenneth Ames to Maura Harty at the State Department, asking for reconsideration. Several days later, at our suggestion, Dr. Ames also sent a letter to U.S. Representative Jeff Flake (R-AZ), who was instrumental in opening trade channels with Cuba during the Bush administration.

Despite these last-minute efforts there was no reconsideration, and the Cubans did not attend the meetings. In San Juan, we asked the SAA Committee on the Americas to recommend that SAA President Kenneth Ames send letters of protest to the State Department, noting the Society's disappointment over the denial of visas to Cuban scholars, and demanding a change in U.S. foreign policy to allow free academic exchange between Cuba and the United States. Our recommendation carried, and President Ames sent the requested letter.

Also in San Juan, we went ahead with the symposium. The Cuban participants had sent us electronic versions of their papers, which were read in the symposium by several Puerto Rican colleagues. In addition, the three non-Cuban participants we invited (who were not covered in any way by the grants we received) presented their papers.

The symposium was dedicated to Betty Meggers, of the Smithsonian Institution, for challenging the blockade through persistent contact with her Cuban colleagues for over three decades. Dr. Meggers attended, and, on behalf of the absent Cuban archaeologists, we presented her with a plaque in recognition of her efforts to keep the door cracked open. We were pleased to report to our funders that the symposium, though lacking the much-anticipated presence of the Cuban scholars, was well attended.

This volume brings the results of the San Juan symposium to a much broader professional audience. We want to stress its importance, because we believe that communication between colleagues and the sharing of ideas and research results are critical to the advancement of all disciplines. The absence of regular avenues for scholarly exchange can slow the processes of discovery, theory-building, testing, and critique that are important to the mature development of any scientific field.

Figure 1.1. The editors (Kepecs, *left*; Curet, *right*) present the plaque to Dr. Betty Meggers at the 2006 Annual Meeting of the Society for American Archaeology in San Juan.

Cuban and U.S. archaeologists have not always been isolated from each other, of course. Throughout the first half of the twentieth century, both communities shared a research paradigm—the minimally scientific pursuit of "culture history" common throughout the Americas—and cited each other's work (see Deagan, this volume). But over the course of our 40-year separation new methods, theories, and findings have developed in both countries. The communication gap has severely limited the great potential benefits of theoretical and methodological discourse. Cuban archaeologists could have profited from the U.S. debate over New Archaeology and the development of cultural resource management archaeology of the 1960s and 1970s (Flannery 1973; Plog et al. 1978; Schiffer 1976). Further, U.S. isolationist policies kept Cuban archaeologists from participating in the raging theoretical debates over poststructuralism in the 1980s and 1990s.

In turn, U.S. archaeologists missed out on the research frameworks developing in Cuba, including the archaeological applications of Marxist theory in postrevolutionary Cuba that supplanted the anemic practice of culture history, and transculturation studies, which examine the two-way processes of prolonged cultural contact (Ortíz 1943; Tabío and Rey 1966). Cuban archaeologists, despite the material hardships of the embargo, also forged brilliant methodological advances in urban historical archaeology (e.g., Domínguez 1995, 1998) and the archaeology of slave resistance (e.g., La Rosa 1988, and this volume). Moreover, U.S. researchers (and many of our counterparts in other areas of Latin America) are largely unaware of major empirical research by Cuban archaeologists. Important case studies on the whole range of Cuban prehispanic archaeology, from Archaic settlement to late-prehispanic "Taíno" sites offer comparative information that is crucial, in the long run, for the interpretation of similar data elsewhere in the Americas.

The intellectual wall that is part and parcel of the United States' ill-conceived, anachronistic Cuba policy has led not only to a near absence of scholarly exchange, but also to misunderstandings about the conditions underlying this silence. For example, in his critique of archaeology in post-1959 Cuba, Dave Davis (1996) implies that the lack of exchange among Cubans and U.S. researchers is *voluntary*. Yet archaeologists who have traveled to Cuba in recent years (ourselves included) have found no support for this assumption. Cuban archaeologists are eager, even hungry, for intellectual exchange and information on the state of the field in the United States. The perception that Cuba's isolation is self-imposed rather than a result of the U.S. blockade is an unfortunate relic of Cold War rhetoric. The chapters in this book are evidence that Cuban archaeologists very much want to share their research with their U.S. counterparts.

Historical Context for This Volume

Most of the chapters in this book provide historical context for the research advances contained therein, so we will not outline the full scope of previous Cuban archaeology here. Nevertheless, the blockade on knowledge produced in Cuba leaves us impoverished. In the vast University of Wisconsin-Madison library system, for example, only seven books on the subject, including *Dialogues in Cuban Archaeology* (Curet et al., eds., 2005) are available. In an effort to contextualize this volume, we offer a very brief look at the historical trajectory of Cuban archaeology.

In this book, both prehispanic and historical archaeology are well represented. Since the two branches of the Cuban archaeological tree have distinct histories, we discuss each in turn.

Prehispanic Archaeology

Early twentieth-century archaeology, entrenched as it was in the particularist, culture-historical paradigm of the times, was carried out in Cuba by a number of investigators on both sides of the Florida Straits, including U.S. investigators Mark Harrington of the Museum of the American Indian (1921), Irving Rouse of Yale University (1942, 1992), and a host of Cuban pioneers (i.e., Herrera 1946, 1964; Pichardo 1934). The 1959 revolution put a stop to archaeological research in Cuba for several years, and when the field opened up again the U.S. blockade had put an end to communications among scholars from the two nations.

In 1962 the Cuban government founded the Cuban Academy of Sciences, with the goal of building the material, technological, and cultural basis of the new socialist state (Tabío and Rey 1966:7–10). Under academy auspices, archaeology was defined as a fundamentally historical science, "with the primary goal of studying the economic conditions, the social forces of production and the applications of technology in the transformation of the early stages of societies." Inherent in this approach (see Tabío and Rey 1966:9, 42) was the directive to marshal empirical evidence toward Engels's nineteenth-century vision of primitive communism laid out in *The Origin of the Family, Private Property and the State* (1884).

As in Cuba, archaeology throughout both the rest of the "developing world" and much of Europe is framed as a historical science as opposed to a generalizing one (i.e., the "new archaeology" of the United States). By casting archaeology as an arm of history, Latin American and African archaeologists affirm their countries' autonomous, independent identities in the face of U.S. global hegemony (Schmidt and Patterson 1995). Ethnohistory is a crucial component in the historical pursuit of the past, and two decades before postprocessual critical theory was integrated into anthropology in the United States, Tabío and Rey (1966:9) advised Cuban archaeologists to examine critically the feudal economic agenda of the Spanish chroniclers.

Two decades after Tabío and Rey laid out the Academy of Sciences archaeological program, José Guarch (1987) provided updated, more detailed directions for Marxist studies in what Guarch called archaeohistory. The goals reprise Tabío and Rey's—the aims of archaeohistory are to provide material information on the modes and relations of production in Cuba's Archaic and agrarian-ceramic traditions. Guarch (1987:22) called for direct and indirect (inferential) analyses, but most of what he added to archaeological practice falls in the realm of empirical information—expanded, systematic data collection, with the incorporation of relevant chemical, physical, botanical, and statistical analyses, mostly learned from Soviet archaeologists in the interim between the publication of his book and Tabío and Rey's.

Yet as Dave Davis (1996:177–179) points out in his synopsis of archaeology in revolutionary Cuba, at least until the fall of the Soviet Union Cuban archaeology was designed not to test and refine dialectical theory, but rather, to exemplify it. Explorations of political and economic complexity were cut short by adherence to Engels's obsolete notion of primitive communism (see Bloch 2004).

Thus U.S. investigators, including Rouse (1992:19), can discuss social complexity—that is, the "complex chiefdoms" of the "Classic Taínos"—but in Cuban archaeology, studies of political or economic complexity have been, until very recently, off limits. Yet in practice, unquestioning adherence to Engels's model was so riddled with contradictions that the theory ended up being more implicit than applied. Thus Cuban archaeology, as Davis (1996) notes, has been largely descriptive, empirical, and culture-historical.

Change since the fall of the Soviet Union has come slowly. In the Canadian peer-reviewed online journal *Kacike,* Cuban archaeologist Jorge Ulloa (2002) offers an assessment very similar to Davis's. After the revolution, according to Ulloa, Cuban archaeology experienced a certain theoretical stagnation, lacking the creative contributions of archaeology in other parts of the Caribbean, Latin America, or North America. In Cuba, archaeology remained a mix of old (particularist, culture-historical) concepts, aided by new methods of analysis and excavation techniques.

Yet the papers in this volume, originally written in 2006, reveal a great deal of change. In addition to an explosion of new data, theoretical horizons are opening up. Notions of primitive communism are crumbling under the evidence of greater late-prehispanic complexity than Engels would allow. Cuba's close contacts with Venezuela bring the literature of South American archaeology into the picture (see Torres, this volume). The renewed ties among colleagues across the Florida Straits that this volume represents also have helped strengthen the libraries of Cuban institutions and individual scholars. Below, we offer a brief synopsis of the chapters contained herein, which reveal how research is advancing, but first we turn to the development of historical archaeology in Cuba.

Historical Archaeology

In Cuba, as elsewhere, historical archaeology has developed independently of prehispanic practices. The leading pioneers in the field of Cuban historical archaeology—both represented in this book—are Lourdes Domínguez and Gabino La Rosa (see Deagan this volume). Domínguez's short contribution, the first chapter in this volume, concerns the history of Cuban archaeology, rather than the method and theory of historical archaeology. But in her concise 1998 summary "La Cuidad," published in *Opus,* a leading cultural magazine published by the Office of the City Historian in Havana, Domínguez writes that urban archaeology began in the 1960s, as a new science based on the simple, particularist strategy of restoring the historic buildings of Old Havana. When the Archaeological Cabinet of the City Historian's Office opened in 1987, the social-scientific goals of archaeology-as-anthropology were incorporated into the ongoing restoration plans for Havana's historical core. In particular, efforts to reconstruct past lifeways in Old Havana now routinely include "traspatio archaeology" (Domínguez 1998:28)—excavations into the back patios of Old Havana's mansions, where the servants were quartered.

Beyond the city, historical archaeology in Cuba encompasses coffee, sugar, and tobacco plantations (e.g., Singleton 2001, 2005); La Rosa's (1988, 1995) groundbreaking studies of runaway slave settlements and contraband sites; and indigenous settlements surviving into the Spanish period (see Domínguez 1995; also Cooper et al. this volume; Knight this volume; and especially Valcárcel this volume).

In Cuba, historical archaeology—in all its variations—is theoretically informed by the contributions of the brilliant multidisciplinary scholar Fernando Ortíz (1881–1969), whose enormous efforts to record and preserve the island's Afro-Cuban heritage transcend the split between prerevolutionary and modern Cuba. Ortíz's 1940 [1995] treatise on what he called transculturation—the multigenerational, multidirectional transition from one cultural condition to another, as experienced by Africans and Europeans in the Caribbean, or by natives and Europeans across the Americas—has undergone a notable revival in recent years. *Cuban Counterpoint: Tobacco and Sugar* was translated into English and reissued in 1995 by Duke University Press, and Ortíz's contributions are the subject of a number of recent books and articles in peer-reviewed journals.

Transculturation—a concept generally underutilized in U.S. and European historical archaeology but key to a great deal of Latin American and Caribbean research—requires a multifaceted approach. As Domínguez (2004) notes, any artifactual assemblage can be read in multiple ways. For example, metal, porcelain, and glass in a single component could indicate a European enclave, a group of hispanicized natives, or runaway slaves who acquire such items either in the market or through robbery or barter. Thus in Cuban practice, assemblages are regularly considered in terms of context, quantity, and the documentary record.

Advances in the hard sciences also hold a key role. Old Havana in particular—a UNESCO World Patrimony zone and a government funding priority—benefits from multidisciplinary collaborations. For example, nuclear physicist Ariadna Mendoza, who trained in Havana and Milan, uses X-ray fluorescence to determine the elemental composition of pigments used in the murals that cover and re-cover the interior walls of the once wealthy eighteenth- and nineteenth-century merchants' mansions of Old Havana. Identifying trace elements in the paints helps track down the geological sources of the colors' raw minerals, allowing restorers to replicate the original colors (Kepecs 2002).

Further, urban archaeologists in Cuba have made great strides by adopting Bermuda-born archaeologist Edward Harris's (1979) revolutionary methods of stratigraphic analysis. The Harris matrix, a stratigraphic concept largely ignored in the United States but used widely in Europe, makes it possible to visualize the temporal as well as spatial dimensions of an excavation. Harris, we should note, graciously offered seminars on his method to Cuban scholars. These sessions occurred in Havana in 2000, under the auspices of the Archaeological Cabinet of the City Historian's Office. Harris's method is useful in any situation, given the various cultural and natural transformations that shape the archaeological record (Binford 1981; Schiffer 1972), but it is particularly useful in urban archaeology (see Hernández, this volume), since the accumulated cultural transformations that affect colonial and postcolonial structures surviving into the twenty-first century are especially complex.

For all of the reasons outlined here, Cuba is becoming a world leader in urban historical archaeology, despite the island's limited economic resources.

Themes and Breakthroughs

The volume begins with three chapters that deal with the history of archaeology in Cuba. The first is Lourdes Domínguez's short contribution, "Homage to Dr. Betty Meggers," since, at the request of the Cuban archaeologists represented here, this book, like the original SAA symposium, is dedicated to Dr. Meggers. In her chapter, Domínguez describes a personal history of contact despite the blockade. Meggers first visited Cuba in 1982, fulfilling an agreement between the Smithsonian Institution and the Cuban Academy of Sciences. Meggers, writes Domínguez, facilitated breakthroughs in the Cuban ceramic sequence by bringing a pan-Latin, pan-Caribbean perspective on archaeological ceramics to Cuba, and by inviting Cuban ceramicists to her lab at the Smithsonian. Moreover, Meggers manages to maintain contact with her Cuban colleagues, providing a constant window on the archaeological literature from beyond the island.

The chapter by U.S. scholar Kathleen Deagan, of the Florida Museum of Natural History, also deals with the history of archaeology in Cuba. Deagan's essay is on the historical and institutional links between Cuba and Florida from the sixteenth century through the early nineteenth, which lead directly to shared anthropological and historical questions today despite the blockade. Deagan lays out a detailed history of prerevolutionary scholarly communications and explains how an earlier generation of Florida scholars forged the links for later exchanges—including Deagan's own adventurous trip to Cuba in 1983, during which she and Domínguez became close colleagues. Other Floridians from Deagan's generation, including Vernon James Knight (this volume) and Theresa Singleton (2005, 2006) keep the connection alive, against all odds.

Knight's contribution to this volume is one of two that take on the nineteenth-century limitations of historical materialism as practiced in Cuba since the 1959 revolution. Knight takes a look at research from the 1970s and 1980s at La Loma del Convento, a late-prehispanic/early-Spanish colonial site on Cuba's south-central coast, identified as the site of Fray Bartolomé de Las Casas' island encomienda. By synthesizing two major projects—one Cuban, one by a Cuba-Soviet team, Knight reveals how La Loma del Convento and its surrounding region fit into the larger scheme of Cuban archaeology; how evidence from this site challenges the prevailing theory that the sole pattern of Arawak ("Taíno") migration in Cuba moved from Hispaniola to the east end of the island, then spread west; and how the regional settlement pattern indicates political hierarchy instead of the nonhierarchical, village-level organization that fits the approved rubric of "primitive communism."

The remaining six chapters all deal with recent, substantive archaeological research on the island. At the early end of the temporal spectrum, Lorenzo Morales offers new insights into the stone tool industries of the island's early inhabitants, collected from over 200 sites in Villa Clara province, central Cuba. Prior to his research only one early stone tool industry was known in Cuba. Morales uses cluster analysis to define three separate industries produced by the pre-Archaic inhabitants of Villa Clara. Further, he considers the possible links between these humans and recovered remains of extinct giant sloths (radiocarbon dates indicate survival into the early Holocene in Cuba)—including bones bearing cutmarks typical of butchery with stone tools. Morales's study indicates greater pre-Archaic complexity on the island than previously suspected, opening new debates on the nature of the island's earliest occupations.

Daniel Torres Etayo's contribution, which follows Morales's, is, like Knight's, a critique of Cuban archaeological theory. Torres approaches questions of political-economic complexity at the "Taíno" site of Laguna de Limones, at the eastern extreme of Cuba, through the open framework of "Latin American Social Archaeology" (Arqueología Social Latinamericano, or ASL) developed and refined by Latin American practitioners outside of Cuba, such as the Peruvian Luis Lumbreras (1974) and Chilean archaeologist Luis F. Bate (1998). ASL—a search for "culture, lifeways and economic organization"—is not a radical break from Marxism, but it overcomes nineteenth-century limitations that have hindered progress in the past.

Torres used regional surveys, horizontal excavations and a variety of mapping techniques to go beyond earlier investigations at Laguna de Limones (e.g., Guarch 1972; Tabío and Rey 1966). With evidence for regional settlement hierarchy and relatively dense population, Torres concludes that Laguna de Limones, which has one of the largest prehispanic ceremonial plazas in the Caribbean, exhibits (like Lomas del Convento) political complexity that clearly surpasses the limits of "primitive communism."

The very empirical chapter on Los Buchillones, on the north-central (Ciego de Avila province) coast, by Jago Cooper, Roberto Valcárcel, and Jorge Calvera—a collaboration among the Institute of Archaeology, University College, London, and the Cuban Ministry of Science, Technology and Environment—is the most complete English-language report on archaeological evidence from a "Taíno" settlement in Cuba to date. Excavations at this well-preserved site provide detailed information on indigenous wooden houses, and surveys reveal the aerial extent of the community and its resource catchment, which includes islands offshore. A series of radiocarbon dates place occupation at Los Buchillones between the thirteenth and seventeenth centuries—solid evidence of the survival of indigenous settlements well into the Spanish period.

Introduction / 11

The next two chapters in this book are outstanding examples of transculturation studies. Roberto Valcárcel, Marcos Martinón-Torres, Jago Cooper, and Thilo Rehren examine indohispanic transculturation at Chorro de Maíta, an agro-ceramic or "Taíno" site on the Banes peninsula of Holguín, east of Ciego de Avila.

Burials at Chorro de Maíta, with radiocarbon dates spanning the prehispanic/Spanish colonial divide, provide two important insights. First, in a departure from the standard Cuban approach to historical materialism, Valcárcel and colleagues identify the presence of elite burials, which, although post-contact, probably reflect social hierarchy in the prehispanic past. Further, the aboriginal inhabitants of Chorro de Maíta obtained from the Spaniards quantities of small brass tubes—lacetags—which fifteenth- and sixteenth-century Europeans used as a sort of button for clothing. In the indigenous burials at Chorro de Maíta, these lacetags were reused as symbolic ornamentation, buried with important individuals. Moreover, Christian elements, such as extended burial position, reflect both intense, prolonged contact and the beginnings of aboriginal/Spanish religious syncretism.

No collection on Cuban archaeology would be complete without a contribution by Gabino La Rosa. In his chapter for this volume, La Rosa examines the natural characteristics and archaeological features of 30 sites—caves and rockshelters—used as refuges by fugitive slaves in western (Havana—Matanzas) Cuba during the first half of the nineteenth century. He then analyzes the artifacts collected from these sites for their functional properties—how were these objects used by escaped slaves? His analysis reveals new insights into resistance, survival, ingenuity, and transculturation that go far beyond the scant extant documentary descriptions, which La Rosa carefully cites.

Finally, Iosvany Hernández tackles the many theoretical and practical contradictions between architectural restoration and scientific urban historical archaeology. Because historic buildings are almost always palimpsests, authentic conservation requires a careful consideration of all of the historic periods and social uses that bear on any given structure. The latest advances in resolving this clash of interests in Europe, Hernández argues, have yet to be adopted in Cuba. After reviewing various cases in Old Havana, he concludes that archaeological concerns too often are overwhelmed by the exigencies of restoration, and calls for better communications between practitioners of the disciplines involved.

Conclusions

This collection, though just a small sample of archaeology in Cuba today, leaves no doubt that the field has advanced dramatically despite the ongoing blockade. This advance is no longer confined to the empirical realm—the new Cuban archaeology reveals important theoretical growth as well. We hope everyone doing research in the Caribbean and Latin America will read the following chapters with care. It is time to incorporate Cuba into the growing panorama of New World archaeology, and the information contained herein will be most useful in that pursuit.

Acknowledgments

The editors of this volume owe a great debt to the funders of the SAA symposium in San Juan—the R. Christopher Reynolds Foundation, Fundación Amistad, and the Social Science Research Council. Further, the Reynolds Foundation helped to underwrite the costs of editing and translating. The Field Museum provided administrative support for the entire process. Other archaeologists in the Caribbean deserve our thanks for their contributions to the cause of bringing Cuban archaeology to a broader audience—among them are Betty Meggers, Dr. Eusebio Leal and the staff at the Office of the City Historian in Havana, Marcio Velóz from the Dominican Republic, and Corinne Hofman of the University of Leiden, the Netherlands. Most important, we cannot end this introduction without expressing our thanks to the contributors, who graciously put up with our slow progress on the manuscript and complied cheerfully with our editorial demands.

Note

1. The reader will notice that we put quotation marks around the word "Taíno." Although the term is widely used to refer to the Arawak-speaking peoples who inhabited most of the Greater Antilles at the time of Spanish contact, its use is hotly debated among the archaeologists, anthropologists, and historians who study these groups. The problem is two pronged. The definitions and criteria for calling a group "Taíno" are confusingly variable, but at the same time the label obfuscates the ethnic, linguistic, and political diversity among the groups it is used to represent (Curet 2009; Torres 2008). The term is valuable as an expedient cultural reference; thus we, like some of the authors of the following chapters, put it in quotation marks; others prefer the more neutral term agro-ceramic *(agroalfarero)*.

2
Prologue
Homage to Dr. Betty Meggers

Lourdes Domínguez, emeritus and senior lecturer, Gabinete de
Arqueología, Oficina del Historiador de la Ciudad de La Habana

I was asked to prepare an homage to Dr. Betty Meggers for the symposium on recent advances in Cuban archaeology organized by Drs. Curet and Kepecs for the 2006 Society for American Archaeology annual meeting in San Juan, Puerto Rico. How strange to find my visa request denied, when I planned to honor a woman whose very presence marks milestones in the history of archaeology in the United States of America. From afar I offered these words, knowing that they expressed the sentiments of many of my colleagues who unfortunately were unable to attend the meeting, from across Latin America and the Caribbean, and especially from Cuba.

Betty Jane Meggers was born in December 1921, in the state of Washington, and in 1952 she received her doctorate with a thesis on Latin American archaeology. Her union with another great North American archaeologist, Clifford Evans, launched the history of two human beings entirely dedicated to the science of archaeology. Together they made hugely significant contributions to the archaeology of the Americas and the world. For this reason—and this is the mark of great scientists—one can arrive at any archaeological gathering in Brazil, Chile, Ecuador, Venezuela, Puerto Rico, or Cuba, and everyone there will know the works of Dr. Meggers; everyone will have read her books.

Her students and her friends remember clearly her presentations; in some cases her colloquia have been ongoing through the years. Her friendship and her teachings are so well appreciated that many times family ties are forged. The most interesting part of all of this is how, especially in Cuba, Dr. Meggers's teachings are passed along in order to keep alive the science of archaeology in spite of so much that stands in its way.

It would take a book to lay out the vast itinerary of Dr. Meggers's life, so for now I limit myself to her links to Cuba. In 1982 she arrived in Havana, fulfilling an agreement between the prestigious Smithsonian Institution and the Cuban Academy of Science. Already, some Cuban investigators had visited her laboratories at the National Museum of Natural History. To carry out her part of this exchange mission Dr. Meggers arrived in Havana alone. She had just lost that which she most loved in this life—her beloved husband Clifford. That in itself was difficult. But to

Figure 2.1. Dr. Domínguez (*left*) and Dr. Meggers, at the Smithsonian's Natural Museum of Natural History.

make matters worse, times were complicated in Cuba; among Cuban archaeologists not all understood her objectives, her message, and the great value of her stay among us. There are always people who love controversy and people of mediocre spirit, and in this case there were those who tried to dim the light Dr. Meggers radiated.

In the end they failed. Dr. Meggers shared her knowledge with everyone. Her books were individual gifts to each of us. And in her classes she offered us not only all that she knew, but also how to develop that knowledge appropriately within our Cuban reality. Whoever works today with aboriginal ceramics, not just in Cuba but in all of the Caribbean, does so on the basis of her teachings and her works. And no one among us has ever set up a ceramics laboratory without following her directions.

As part of this exchange, Dr. Meggers was able to bring Cuban specialists to work in her laboratory at the National Museum of Natural History at the Smithsonian, in Washington, D.C. For me it was an unforgettable experience to participate in her world. I harbor many lovely memories, along with a few sad ones. But mostly I remember feeling hopeful. Dr. Betty is one of those souls who opens pathways, a person who creates and maintains special relationships, and despite the passing of time the ties between her and the archaeologists of Cuba remain special.

I am less familiar with Dr. Meggers's second trip to Cuba, and I have been unable to find anyone who can tell me about it, but what I do know is that her work in eastern Cuba was ample and fruitful. There, she was able to develop a substantial ceramic sequence. And among the gifts she has given Cuban archaeologists is the ability to publish in the excellent scholarly journal *El Caribe Arqueológico,* which she helped establish on that visit to Santiago de Cuba. This effort—open to everyone, without the restrictions common to similar journals—represents a solution to the lack of opportunities for Cuban archaeologists to publish their work.

The archaeologists who boast of being doña Betty's students are many; many are they who owe their success in archaeology to her, to her advice, her attention, and her assistance. Many are the nations that receive her help, as calm and ethereal as she is herself, always solid in her promise and in her support. Cuba, perhaps the most discriminated-against country in recent history, has always had her on its side, breaking barriers of all kinds and extending her hand where it is most needed.

Dr. Meggers is someone who thinks carefully about how to help people; she enters the realities and dreams of every archaeologist who passes by her side, discovers in seconds where that person's material or spiritual problems lie, and understands how she can be of use. We all remember how this godmother made us members of the international community with indispensable texts for our daily work, with her relevant advice, and sometimes, most impressively, with a photocopy of one of her own works. We were unable to make our own copies, given our daily necessities, and we were too embarrassed to tell her about it. But she intuited our needs as if she herself lived in our difficult and heroic world.

For all of these reasons we Cuban archaeologists offer this simple but affectionate homage to someone who has contributed to maintaining communication between us and our North American colleagues despite the existence of shadowy obstacles for over 47 years. Doña Betty attends to this link, making sure it does not break in spite of all that is done to destroy it; she carries this out punctually and accurately without boasting or political maneuvering, in the service of scientific justice rather than with the aim of diminishing history, in this case that of Cuban archaeology. For all of this, and for the respect she has for Cuban archaeologists, we owe her a great debt of gratitude.

How unjust that the Cuban archaeologists were unable to attend the meeting in San Juan, to present this homage to Dr. Meggers in person. When someone helps where in truth there is pain, that help will never be forgotten. Doña Betty, please receive our respect and our affection, and always know that the Cuban archaeological community holds you in the highest esteem.

3
Cuba and Florida
Entwined Histories of Historical Archaeologies

Kathleen Deagan, Florida Museum of Natural History

In this essay I offer observations on the close developmental and intellectual connections in historical archaeology between Cuba and Florida, beginning in the 1940s. Historical archaeology as a field of study became quasi-formalized in both Cuba and North America during the late 1960s, a consequence in both areas to increased governmental interest in defining patrimony and preserving historic sites. Before that, however, some of the earliest North American historical archaeology was carried out in Florida during the 1940s and 1950s by such researchers as Hale Smith, John Goggin, Irving Rouse, and Charles Fairbanks, all of whom maintained professional connections with Cuban historical archaeologists and anthropologists, including Oswaldo Moráles Patiño, René Herrera Fritot, José Prat Puig, and Lourdes Domínguez. I suggest that the early emphasis on transculturation and acculturation between American Indians and European colonizers in North American historical archaeology was directly influenced by the work of these Cuban scholars.

En este capítulo ofrezco observaciones sobre las estrechas conexiones intelectuales que han marcado la arqueología histórica en Cuba y Florida desde los 1940s. Este ramo de estudios se formalizó hasta cierto grado a finales de los 1960s, como consecuencia de un creciente esfuerzo de parte de los gobiernos de ambos paises para definir el patrimonio y conservar los sitios historicos. Sin embargo, en los Estados Unidos la arqueología histórica se practicaba antes, en los 1940s y 1950s, por investigadores como Hale Smith, John Goggin, Irving Rouse y Charles Fairbanks, todos con conexiones profesionales con sus homólogos cubanos, incluyendo a Oswaldo Moráles, René Herrera, José Prat y Lourdes Domínguez. Sugiero que el énfasis temprano en la transculturación entre los indios norteamericanos y los colonizadores europeos fue directamente influenciada por las ideas de estos investigadores cubanos.

I begin this essay with the confession that I am not, in fact, going to discuss any new research in Cuban archaeology, and that I myself have not done any research in Cuba since 1983. I have, however, tried from my vantage point in Florida to follow historical archaeology in Cuba over the past two decades, and from this perspective I will offer some observations on the close developmental and intellectual connections in historical archaeology between our two regions. I use "historical archaeology" to refer broadly to text-aided archaeology, which, in the Americas, is most essentially the study of post-1492 European expansion and its impact. Central to these observations is the assertion that in many ways, Florida and Cuba form a coherent geographic historical and cultural unit of historical archaeological focus and, were it not for twentieth-century global politics, would today comprise a unified region of historical archaeology.

The historical and cultural relationships between Florida and Cuba have always been obvious, close and troubled. For Floridians, that relationship has perhaps never been more complex than it is today in the North American political climate of the twenty-first century. The current national landscape of Cuban-U.S. relations has been significantly shaped by the political demographics of Florida, which have in turn, been largely shaped by the post-1959 migration and highly successful adaptations of Cubans to Florida (see, e.g., Mormino 2005:284–289).

This is not a new phenomenon. Migrations of people between Florida and Cuba—in both directions—have taken place for centuries, and perhaps for millennia. During the period of Spanish colonization, at least, these exchanges created strong historical and cultural ties that have influenced historical and archaeological research in both regions.

Although not a focus of this essay, it is worth noting that the nature of potential culture contact and exchange between Cuba and Florida before the arrival of Europeans in the region is considerably less clear, and remains contested. Caribbeanist archaeologists and anthropologists have posed questions about such contact for more than a century (e.g., Fewkes 1904; Griffin 1943; Rouse 1949; see Knight and Worth 2007 for a recent English-language summary). Comparative studies of pre-Columbian Cuba and south Florida have focused on pottery styles, lithic and shell tools, farming systems, and ritual elements (Bullen 1974; Febles 1991; Herrera 1964; Knight and Worth 2007; Sturtevant 1960); however, no widely accepted archaeological evidence for pre-Columbian exchange has yet been documented in either Cuba or Florida. As chronometric dating schemes, archaeometric analyses of artifacts, and cyber communication opportunities are refined, these questions will undoubtedly be revisited by archaeologists throughout the region.

In contrast, the movements of people between Florida and Cuba after Spanish colonization are richly documented. From the time of Spanish settlement in Florida in 1565 until the end of Spanish domination in 1821, Cuba was Florida's closest neighbor, both socially and geographically. Government and Church in St. Augustine—the capital of Spanish Florida—were administered from Havana. The Florida governors came to the *Palacio de los Capitanes Generales* in Havana (also the site one of the most important urban archaeological programs in Havana) to be debriefed before assuming their posts. Exchanges among the members of the Florida and Cuban military regiments were frequent, and Havana was the primary source of imported goods for St. Augustine. Families in colonial Florida and Havana were interconnected by blood, marriage, and economic partnerships (Bushnell 1981:128–29; Parker 1999; Tepaske 1974:97–102).

At the end of the Seven Years' War in 1763, Spain ceded Florida to England in exchange for Havana (which had been captured by the English). The Spanish, African, and Indian residents of St. Augustine emigrated en masse to Cuba rather than remain in their homes under protestant English rule (Gold 1969; Landers 2004). Twenty years later, Florida was returned to Spain, and many of the original emigrant families came back from Cuba to reclaim property lost in 1763 (Johnson 2001). Florida remained a Spanish colony until 1821, sustaining its close ties with Cuba.

Cuba and Florida clearly shared a historical and administrative context from the sixteenth through the early nineteenth centuries. It would be therefore surprising if Cuban and Floridian historical archaeologists did not also share a number of specific anthropological and historical interests. Historical archaeology as a field of study became quasi-formalized in both Cuba and North America during the late 1960s, a consequence in both areas to increased governmental interest in defining patrimony and preserving historic sites (albeit with considerably less explicit awareness in North America) (see Deagan 1982; Domínguez 2005:66; Schuyler 1978). Well before that time, however, archaeologists in both Florida and Cuba were carrying out some of America's earliest archaeological research on the complex cultural changes set in motion by European arrival. Fernando Ortíz's extraordinary work on multicultural exchange and transculturation (first published in 1940 in Havana, and in English in 1947 [Ortíz 1995]) endures to the present day as a seminal influence on studies of cultural contact, transformation, and ethnogenesis throughout the Americas, and had clearly focused attention to these questions in the Cuban archaeological community by the 1940s (e.g., García 1947; Morales and Pérez 1946; Pichardo 1945).

At nearly the same time, in the late 1940s and early 1950s, Florida archaeologists John Griffin and Hale Smith were addressing the influences of the Spanish mission system on the native people of Florida (Boyd et al. 1951; Griffin 1949; Griffin and Smith 1948), and the comparative impacts of Spanish and English colonialism in the southeastern United States (Smith 1956). Although this work was somewhat more unidirectional in its emphases on Native American cultural responses to European presence than that of Ortíz, these Cuban and Floridian studies were among the earliest archaeological efforts to understand contact-induced culture change in the Americas.

While their respective inspirations undoubtedly lay partly in the correspondence of a shared Spanish colonial past, there is good reason to suggest that Cuban

Figure 3.1. The "Daytona Conference" group, 1948, including several Florida archaeologists who became engaged with Cuban archaeologists and scholars.
Clockwise from lower left (foreground): John Goggin, Charles Brookfield, Albert Manucy, John Griffin, Hale G. Smith, Wesley Hurt, Charles Fairbanks, Antonio Waring, and Gordon Willey. (Courtesy Florida Museum of Natural History)

intellectual influence also was significant in shaping the agenda of early Florida historical archaeology. The Yale University Caribbean program, established in 1934, provided one of the principal means by which connections were established between Cuban and Floridian archeologists. Irving Rouse, who worked in the Maniabon Hills of northeastern Cuba during the late 1930s (Rouse 1942), subsequently introduced his student John Goggin to Cuban archaeologists and collections. Goggin did research in Cuba from 1949 to 1952, gathering data that would help provide a basis for his opus, *Spanish Majolica in the New World* (Goggin 1968:vi–vii). He worked closely with Oswaldo Moráles, René Herrera, and their associates in the Grupo Guamá. This organization of Cuban archaeologists—the first in Cuba—was founded by René Herrera and was actively engaged in research, publications, and the development of museum displays throughout the Caribbean in the 1940s and 1950s.

It was during the same period that the first generation of professional Florida archaeologists—including Hale G. Smith, John W. Griffin, and Charles Fairbanks (Figure 3.1)—came to know many of these Cuban scholars through Rouse and

Goggin. Florida archaeologists made several trips to Cuba to attend conferences, visit colleagues, and study collections during the late 1950s.

An interesting illustration of this connection was the friendship between Ivan Gundrum, the Yugoslavian artist who served as Grupo Guamá art director, and (then) Florida State University archaeologists Hale G. Smith and Charles Fairbanks (Uyemura 1967). Gundrum is well known for his extraordinary reproductions of Taíno vessels, of which he made many hundreds in Cuba. Following the revolution, Gundrum left Cuba and emigrated to Tallahassee, Florida, working with Hale Smith and reproducing Florida Indian pots, until his death in 1969.

John Goggin died in 1964, but Smith, Griffin, and Fairbanks continued their investigations of Florida culture during the Spanish colonial period, remaining mindful of—and communicating to their students—the importance of colonial Cuba for understanding colonial Florida. The primary concerns of these Florida archaeologists included continued attention to contact-induced cultural change; the refinement of methodologies for understanding the organization and meaning of Spanish colonial material culture; the study and reconstruction of historic sites for public interpretation; and, after 1970, the archaeological study of plantation slavery (see Fairbanks 1968, 1972, 1974, 1984; Griffin 1978, 1990, 1996).

These archaeologists, along with their students and "grandstudents" at the University of Florida and Florida State University, dominated historical archaeology in Florida until the mid-1990s (when a major program of research and training was established at the University of West Florida in Pensacola; Bense 1999, 2003). Several former students of this period have been involved in collaborative exchanges and research programs with Cuban scholars, including archeologists Teresa Singleton (2001, 2005), James Knight (this volume), John Worth (2004 a–b), and myself; and historians Jane Landers (1999, 2001), Sherry Johnson (2001), Bruce Chappell, and Eugene Lyon. Chappell and Lyon in particular engaged in cooperative agreements with a number of organizations in Cuba, including the *Academia de Ciencias*, the *Archivo Nacional*, and the *Biblioteca Nacional* in Havana to microfilm document collections pertinent to the shared histories of Cuba and Florida. Copies of these filmed collections are now in Havana and at the University of Florida Smathers Library (see Smathers Library 2001, http://www.uflib.ufl.edu/pio/Summer2001ChapOne).

In contrast, historical archaeology in Cuba during the period between 1970 and 1990 *was*, essentially, Lourdes Domínguez and her colleagues. Having worked with José Prat and Adolfo Payares on some of the earliest explicitly post-Columbian archaeological projects in the Caribbean, Domínguez brought focus to the discipline of historical archaeology in Cuba, developing and emphasizing many of the same concerns of culture change and material analysis methodology that were important to Florida (and many other) historical archaeologists. With colleagues Eusebio Leal and others in the Oficina del Historiador de la Ciudad e la Habana, Domínguez helped forge one of the earliest and most impressive programs of urban archaeology in the Americas, addressing research, rescue archaeology, and heritage management concerns (Domínguez 1978, 1981, 1984, 2004, 2005; Romero 1981). The subsequent establishment of the *Gabinete de Arqueología* and its formal program of urban archaeology in Havana took place in 1987, which was coincidentally the same year that St. Augustine, Florida, adopted an archaeological preservation ordinance and established the first Office of City Archaeologist, held since 1990 by Carl Halbirt.

We must also make note of the pioneering work of Gabino La Rosa, beginning in the 1980s, in the archaeological study of cimarronage and slave resistance (La Rosa 1984, 1991, 1995, 2005). La Rosa's work—deriving from a specifically Caribbean historical and intellectual perspective—has done much to enlarge and redirect the scope of archaeology of the African American experience in North America by his early attention to slave resistance and the creation of maroon communities. African American archaeology in North America before the 1990s had been largely dominated by a historical and social perspective that associated African American history with slavery (see, for example, Fairbanks 1984; Orser 1990; and essays in Singleton 1985). La Rosa's visits to the United States during the early 1980s brought resistance and nonplantation occupations of colonial-era African Americans to the first serious attention of a number of English-speaking historical archaeologists, including myself. Our excavations at Fort Mose, Florida, for example (the colonial and legally sanctioned free black community near St. Augustine comprised by escaped slaves), began just a year after La Rosa's visit to the University of Florida in 1985 (Deagan and McMahon 1995). By the late 1990s, U.S. archaeologists studying the African American past in North America had come to regularly incorporate resistance and freedom as foci of research (see essays in Franklin and McKee 2004; Orser 2001; Singleton 1999).

The influence of Cuban historical archaeologists on my own work was not restricted to studies of St. Augustine's free black community. In the early 1980s I was working in Spanish colonial sites of St. Augustine, Florida, and in the sixteenth-century Spanish townsite of Puerto Real in Haiti. I was well aware of the important work of Lourdes Domínguez on colonial sites in Cuba, both through my mentor Charles Fairbanks, and through colleagues in the Dominican Republic and Puerto Rico. I was therefore delighted to be included in 1983 in a research trip to Cuba intended to develop a *convenio* between the University of Florida and the Acadèmia de Ciéncias de la Habana. We hoped that the program would allow an exchange between Cuba and Florida of both archaeological and archival information that pertained to our shared colonial-era histories.

We arrived in Havana in a privately owned, four-seater Piper Cub piloted by University of Florida historian Michael Gannon and another UF professor, dangerously weighed down with books (Figure 3.2). Archivist Bruce Chappell and I

Figure 3.2. The University of Florida research team arriving at José Martí Airport in Havana, 1983. *Left to right:* Bruce Chappell, Michael Gannon, Kathleen Deagan, and (Pilot) Woody Keistler. (Photo: anonymous, on K. Deagan's camera)

spent a few weeks with our incomparable hosts, Lourdes Domíguez and Fé Iglesias, viewing museum collections and archival collections, visiting archaeological sites, and meeting colleagues. On one memorable excursion, we visited Ceiba Mocha, the town (near Santiago) to which many of Florida's residents emigrated after the English takeover in 1763. There, in a partly ruined eighteenth-century church, our group located the previously undocumented Parish registers for those same immigrant Floridians, begun in 1765 after their arrival in Cuba.

The *convenio* was, in fact, established, and in 1985, Lourdes Domínguez, Fé Iglesias, and Gabino La Rosa came to Florida for a month with a similar research agenda—to visit and document Florida's archaeological collections and pre-Columbian and historic sites. Our joint considerations of the archaeological resources in Cuba and St. Augustine were particularly provocative for us, revealing a shared, Spanish-derived material life in both communities, but at the same time reflecting a markedly more elaborate and diverse expression of that material life in Havana—St. Augustine was indeed a stripped-down backwater. This very pattern of convergence and contrast, however, offered intriguing possibilities for comparative archaeological studies of migration, frontiers, identity formation, and other colonial adjustments. Other important issues that we thought could be usefully explored through archaeological juxtapositions in St. Augustine and Cuba included the agency of native Americans in shaping community life; relative patterns of creole participation in contraband and intercolonial trade, and maintenance and transformation in the material expressions of Hispanic and Afro-Hispanic identity after English material culture gained global ascendancy in the 1760s.

Some of these questions have, in fact, been addressed archaeologically since then (Cusick 1993; Deagan 2006; Domínguez 2004; Rives et al. 1991) but (regrettably) independently rather than as comparative, collaborative efforts between Cuban and Floridian researchers. While intellectual exchange has been sustained between Cuban and Floridian archaeologists, few joint field expeditions have been realized owing to the severely difficult economic realities in Cuba as well as to the United States' and Florida's policies for relations with Cuba (considered below). Exchange of information and ideas has been made possible largely through such international conferences as the International Association for Caribbean Archaeology and those organized by the *Centro Avanzado de Estudios Puertorriqueños y del Caribe* in San Juan. Increasingly, the Internet is providing the primary venue for the free exchange of information and ideas.

The scope of historical archaeology has expanded dramatically in both Florida and Cuba since the 1980s. A great deal of work is now focused on sites and industries of the nineteenth and early twentieth centuries, a period during which Florida became part of the United States, and the social, economic, religious, linguistic, and political ties between Florida and Cuba became considerably weaker. Cultural exchange nevertheless continued, and these later episodes are being increasingly addressed by archaeologists as part of our shared Florida-Cuba heritage. The establishment of fishing communities on the southwest coast of Florida by Cuban fishermen during the early nineteenth century is the subject of University of Florida research (Palov 1999; Worth 2004), and the migrations of Cuban tobacco workers between 1867 and 1900 to Key West and Ybor City (Tampa) have been the focus of history and public archaeology through the University of South Florida at Tampa (Ellis 1977; Haidar 1998; Mormino and Pozetta 1998). Theresa Singleton's work on nineteenth-century Cuban coffee plantations brings together the interests of both North American and Cuban researchers in the study of plantations and slavery (Singleton 2001, 2005).

Historians on both sides of the Florida Straits have been less divided than archaeologists, since extended periods of fieldwork are not required, and many of the documentary sources used by historians in both Cuba and in Florida are held in repositories in Spain. Until now, collaborative efforts among Cuban and Floridian historians have continued relatively unimpeded. Microfilming and exchange of documents in the archives of Cuba and in the University of Florida P. K. Yonge Library of Florida History have been carried out intermittently since the 1980s, and have created enormously improved access both in Florida and in Cuba to document collections, including the *Papeles Procedentes de Cuba, The East Florida Pa-*

pers and several series of ecclesiastical records (both important as well to archaeologists) (http://web.uflib.ufl.edu/spec/pkyonge/papdcuba.html; http://web.uflib.ufl.edu/spec/pkyonge/brdrland.html).

I should note here another similarity in the development of historical archaeology in Cuba and Florida, that of the formal interdisciplinary organization of historical archaeology to include archaeologists, historians, and architectural historians. In Cuba this has been a conscious institutional decision (see Domínguez 2005). In Florida, I often suspect, it is because most archaeologists cannot competently read Spanish documents (Deagan and Scardaville 1978). Whatever the reason, however, Floridian and Cuban historians have been intimately involved in the historical archaeology of both areas since the beginning of the discipline.

Florida-trained historians working in collaboration with archaeologists have tended to concentrate their efforts in Cuba on the Florida migrations to Cuba during the eighteenth century. Historian Eugene Lyon and anthropologist John Worth, following work by Lourdes Domínguez, are studying the Native American Floridian families who settled in Guanabacoa during the eighteenth century (Domínguez 2004; Lyon 2006; Worth 2004). Vanderbilt historian Jane Landers has directed microfilming of Cuban archives related to Afro-Cuban and Afro-Floridian groups since 1991 in collaboration with the staff of the Archivo Provincial de Matanzas. This work includes tracking the descendants of St. Augustine's free black population who settled in Ceiba Mocha and Havana (Landers 1999:61–67; http://lib11.1ibrary.vanderbilt.edu/diglib/esss.pl). Sherry Johnson, historian of Cuba at Florida International University, has concentrated on the Spanish and creole émigré exchanges between Florida and Cuba in the late eighteenth century (Johnson 2003).

All of these projects build upon the geographic proximity of Cuba and Florida, as well as our close historical and cultural connections and more than half a century of academic exchange in history and archaeology. They provide a foundation for what should be exciting collaborative historical archaeology in Cuba and Florida. It is increasingly unlikely, however, that this potential can be realized in the present political climate of the United States. This was revealed with dramatic clarity by the denial of entry visas to the Cuban academics who were to attend the Society for American Archaeology meetings in San Juan in April 2006 to take part in the symposium on which this volume is based.

Academic collaboration between Floridian and Cuban archaeologists is made even more difficult at the state level. Ironically, as Florida's postrevolutionary Cuban population (ferociously opposed to any kind of engagement with Castro-led Cuba) has gained ascendancy in the economic and political life of the state, the public funds on which most large-scale archaeological projects depend have become even more difficult for Florida scholars to access. In May 2006 Governor Jeb Bush signed SB24324 (SJ00968, "Travel to Terrorist States") into law. The bill, introduced by Miami representative David Rivera, prohibits colleges and universities in Florida from using state, private, or nonstate funds "to implement, organize, direct, coordinate, or administer activities related to or involving travel to (Cuba) terrorist state." This effectively shut the door on student and faculty exchanges, research or participation in conferences, as well as upon a cooperatively informed understanding of Cuba's and Florida's entwined history and archaeology.

Conclusions

Florida and Cuba share both a colonial history, and a tradition of archaeology that is focused on enlightening that shared historical past. Some of the first archaeology in the world intended to understand the consequences of post-1500 European expansion and colonization took place in Cuba and Florida, where researchers have been addressing questions of transculturation and acculturation between American Indians and Spaniards since the 1930s. This took place first in Cuba, inspired by the work of Fernando Ortíz, and I suggest here that it was through their early associations with Cuban archaeologists and historians that Florida archaeologists in the 1950s began to address many of the same questions.

These associations and their mutual intellectual currents were severely curtailed by the politics of the Cold War after the Cuban Revolution of 1959. Although scholarly exchange between Cuban and Floridian historical archaeologists resumed in the mid-1980s, joint archaeological field expeditions have not developed, either in Cuba or in Florida. Financial and political constraints in both nations have contributed to this, including the severely difficult economic conditions in Cuba and the political policies of the wealthy United States, which have made it extremely difficult for archaeologists wishing to work in Cuba to access the research funding sources that support American archaeologists throughout the rest of the world.

This is ironic, in that the earliest history of Hispanic-Ladino people in the United States began in Florida, also a place where today people of Hispanic origin have gained political ascendancy. The shared past of Cuba and Florida offers an authentic platform for dialogue and understanding among our citizens, and a path by which to find our way back from the isolation created by political decisions of the past 40 years. If we want to begin building a foundation of mutual understanding and cooperation for the years to come, we must develop policies that allow and encourage academic exchanges between North American and Cuban scholars.

4
La Loma del Convento
Its Centrality to Current Issues in Cuban Archaeology

Vernon James Knight Jr., Department of Anthropology,
University of Alabama, Tuscaloosa

La Loma del Convento is a prominent late-period site on the south-central Cuban coast. Research there during the 1970s and 1980s produced one of the most useful cultural chronologies for the Cuban "agroalfarero" stage. Evidence from the site is central to discussions of the Arawakan expansion and the rise of sociocultural complexity on the island. Moreover, no other site in Cuba is more clearly linked to a documented Spanish encomienda, in this case that of the famous cleric Las Casas. For this reason, the site holds particular relevance to the nascent archaeology of the encomienda period.

> La Loma del Convento es un sitio precolombino prominente en la costa sur-central de Cuba. Las investigaciones durante los 1970s y 1980s produjeron una de las cronologías culturales más útiles para la etapa "agroalfarera" cubana. Las evidencias del sitio son centrales para el tema de la expansión arauaca y el origen de la complejidad sociocultural en la isla. Además, ningún otro sitio en Cuba se identifica tan claramente con una documentada encomienda española, en este caso, la del famoso clérigo Las Casas. Por esta razón, el sitio tiene una importancia singular para la arqueología naciente de la época de las encomiendas.

Since its discovery in the 1970s, the site of La Loma del Convento[1] has become a recognized landmark in Cuban archaeology (Domínguez 1991:21). The site is in Cienfuegos province, near Jagua Bay on the south-central coast, near the present city of Cienfuegos. It has been a subject of repeated investigation and commentary by Cuban and Russian specialists, yet there is no recent synthesis of this research. I take that as an opportunity for the following review. I will suggest how the findings at Loma del Convento articulate with several broad themes of interest in modern Cuban archaeology. These themes are (1) the nature of the inferred Arawakan expansion across the island; (2) the rise and character of sociopolitical complexity among the late-prehistoric agricultural peoples; and (3) the effects of European colonization on indigenous Cubans and their modes of resistance to subjugation.

At the close of the conquest of Cuba, one of several areas the Spaniards found most promising for settlement was the native province of Guamuhaya, centered on Jagua Bay. It was from a base of operations at Jagua that Diego Velázquez, conqueror of Cuba, sent a letter to the king of Spain summarizing his conquest in April 1514 (Marrero 1972:233). Velázquez found Guamuhaya to be a thriving indigenous population center with an exceptionally good port. A Spanish settlement on the lower Arimao River he had founded just a few weeks before his letter to the king had already begun to thrive, with a growing complement of livestock. Moreover, the Spaniards discovered that placer gold could be washed from the sediments of the Arimao River that drained the nearby Sierra de Escambray (Rodríguez 2000:21). But although some Spanish interest continued in the Jagua Bay area, their nucleus of settlement soon shifted coastwise to the east, to the present city of Trinidad.

Archaeological Background

Archaeological evidence of the native towns making up the province of Guamuhaya began turning up in the 1930s, starting with the exploration of Cayo Ocampo in Jagua Bay by the Grupo Guamá, led by Oswaldo Morales and René Herrera in five expeditions between 1930 and 1946. Within a short span of time, two more late-period sites in the vicinity were located and explored by the same group. Morales and others discovered and excavated the extraordinary Cantabria site (González and Avello 1946). This was closely followed, in turn, by the discovery of the site of El Abra de Castellón by González (Sanjurjo 1950), which was, like Cantabria, located in the upper Arimao River drainage. In the 1940s, this small group of sites was believed to be the westernmost expression of the pottery-making agricultural peoples in Cuba.

These early investigators recognized that the pottery from the south-central district was different in many respects from that of late-prehistoric agricultural settlements located farther to the east in Cuba. A subsequent study of pottery from Cayo Ocampo and Cantabria by Herrera (1964:18–19, 28–29) led him to name the phenomenon the "Cantabria phase or style," which, due to its simplicity of decoration, he classified as "early Taíno." That is to say, Herrera believed that the Cantabria style mostly antedated the previously defined Baní style in eastern Cuba. As the Cayo Ocampo and Cantabria material became better known, there was considerable discussion and debate among southeastern U.S. and Cuban archaeologists about possible connections between the Cuban assemblages and those of the Glades culture of south Florida (Bullen and Laxon 1954; Herrera 1964; Rouse 1949, 1958). Most modern Cuban archaeologists acknowledge the general affinities of south-central Cuban ceramics as Meillacan (or Meillacoide), while insisting on their regional distinctiveness, a position with which most scholars today agree.

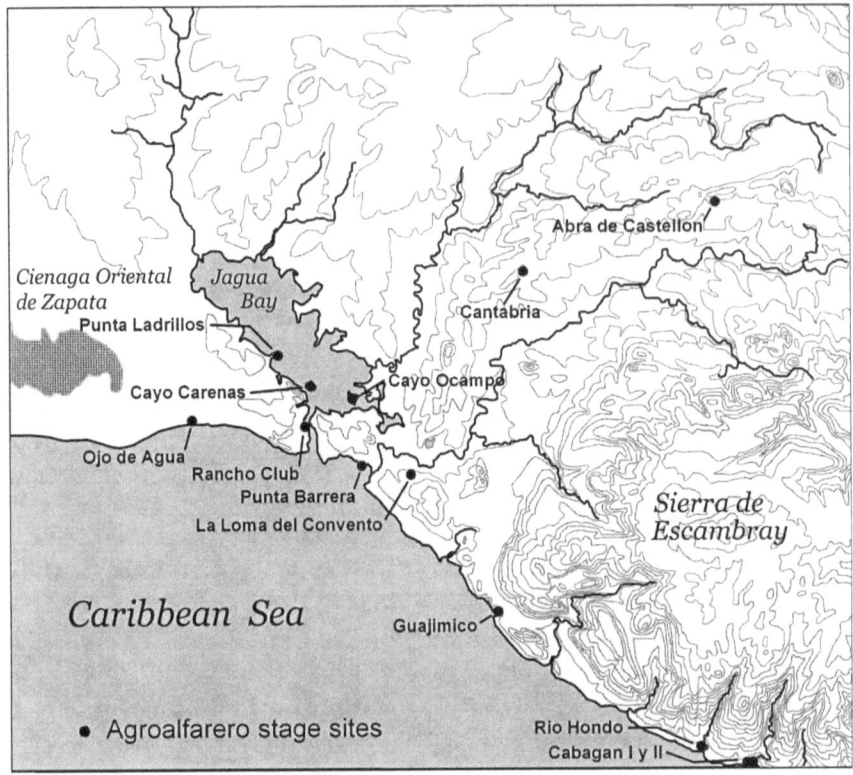

Figure 4.1. Agroalfarero stage sites in the Jagua Bay area.

Guarch (1990:60–63; see also Celaya and Godo 2000) suggested "cultural variant Jagua" as a name for the regional phenomenon. For their part, Bashilov and Golenko (1992), like Herrera before them, suggested "Cantabria culture" as a name, but only for the latest chronological levels. It appears that the name "Cantabria" has priority of usage.

Numerous additional sites with ceramics of this general style group have been reported in the last several decades (Figure 4.1), most of which are included in the Archaeological Census of Cuba (Febles 1995). At the present time, some 30 late-period sites classified as *agroalfarero* are documented within the south-central region (Angelbello and Delgado 2003).[2] Several localities have seen some degree of fieldwork and reporting. Among the more important excavated coastal sites is Ojo de Agua, with fieldwork done in 1978 and 1979 by Martínez (1991).

Turning to the geography, Jagua is a classic Cuban "pocket bay" with a narrow entrance and spacious interior that occupies a relatively flat zone of limestone-bedded coastal plain fronting the Caribbean. Four rivers empty into Jagua Bay, the easternmost being the Arimao, an evident focus of indigenous settlement. Constraints to human settlement lie on both sides of Jagua Bay. Just to the east rises the precipitous Sierra de Escambray, one of the three prominent mountain ranges in Cuba, a massif formed primarily of metamorphic rocks. The most conspicuous natural feature west of the bay is the Cienaga Oriental de Zapata, an expansive mangrove wetland.

Late-period sites in this area are found in several kinds of environments (Domínguez 1987, 1991). Sites front the bay margins or perch on islands within Jagua Bay, including Cayo Ocampo. More sites are situated at intervals along the Caribbean coastline, especially at river mouths. There are, additionally, a few sites in the interior, within the Arimao River basin. It is of much interest that each of the interior sites is located on a high ridge top overlooking the alluvial valley below. In this regard, the settlement pattern recalls that of the more densely settled Banes district on the eastern side of the island where interior settlements also are found in elevated terrain (Rouse 1942; Valcárcel 2002). Interior sites of the Arimao River basin show unusually heavy occupation, with conspicuous midden buildup including midden-mounds; these midden accumulations have produced the majority of skillfully crafted goods so far found in the region, such as stone beads, shell pendants, shell teeth from carved wooden "cemis," and vomitory spatulas of bone. Anthropomorphic pottery vessel rim adornos and pottery talismans in the shape of hands and feet also have been found. The interior sites are not, however, especially large. The site size data that are currently available show horizontal dimensions comparable to sites on the bay margin and nearby Caribbean coast.

Discovery and Fieldwork at Loma del Convento, 1974–88

Loma del Convento is customarily classified as one of the interior sites of the Arimao basin, although the distance to the sea in this case is not great, being only some 4 km. The site was discovered in August 1974 by Alfredo Rankin Santander, in the company of a group of amateur archaeologists who had assigned themselves to do a thorough survey of the east bank of the lower Arimao in the vicinity of a colonial-era hacienda called Las Auras. Rankin's survey was motivated by a search for the remains of the encomienda of Bartolomé de Las Casas, said to be in this vicinity. They located an Amerindian site atop a steep limestone ridge spur, traditionally called La Loma del Convento or the Hill of the Monastery, a provocative toponym with an obvious clerical connotation although no known monastery ever occupied the locality. The hill bearing this name rises about 50 m above a broad expanse of valley floor currently farmed by an agricultural cooperative. Rankin returned in November 1974 and again in January 1975 to undertake several test excavations in the southern half of the largest midden-mound, Mound 1. Rankin's report of this work was submitted in manuscript to the Institute of Social Sci-

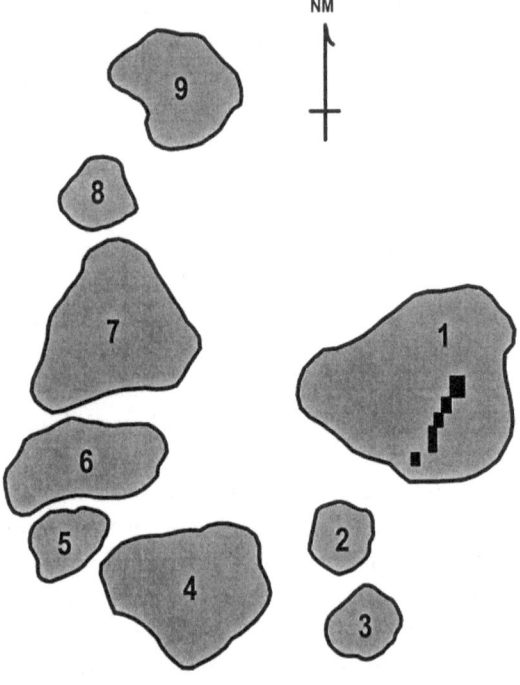

Figure 4.2. Map of mounded middens at Loma del Convento. After Rankin 1980.

ences of the Academy of Sciences of Cuba. His write-up of the ceramics was subsequently revised by José Guarch and was published (Rankin 1980). Rankin's article provides a sketch map (Figure 4.2) showing nine midden mounds arranged in an irregular loop, a pattern reminiscent of site plans documented for agroalfarero sites in eastern Cuba (cf. Castellanos 1991:Figure 3; Guarch 1991:Figures 1, 3; Tabío and Rey 1985:Figure 18).

Rankin's ceramic study provided a detailed description of the assemblage, illustrated with characteristic vessel shapes, rim profiles, and decorations. His main purpose was to provide descriptive and quantitative grounds for comparison with better-known assemblages from eastern Cuba. Based on the fact that no European-derived artifacts were found in the test excavations, Rankin concluded that the site was entirely pre-Columbian. He obtained the first radiocarbon date for Loma del Convento, and tentatively hypothesized that the earliest levels dated to the twelfth century A.D. Rankin noted the presence of several postholes in his test pits, suggestive of structures. As to the hilltop location, he noted that the frequent inundation of the Arimao River floodplain made the elevated situation ideal.

The next excavations at Loma del Convento, realized by Lourdes Domínguez in 1985, were of a different character. Domínguez's work was in the context of a regional survey, designed to test specific hypotheses concerning sociopolitical development among the late-period sites. For this purpose, some 16 documented agroalfarero sites for which collections were available were classified by environmental zone. Five of these sites underwent new test excavations, including representatives from each environmental category. Loma del Convento was selected to represent the interior sites. Domínguez excavated five new test pits. Much of the work focused on an area adjacent to Rankin's earlier test pits in the south and central portions of Mound 1; additionally one 2-x-2-m test was placed within Rankin's Mound 2, just to the south of Mound 1. She encountered rich, stratified midden deposits during this episode of fieldwork. As with Rankin's work, Domínguez's excavations yielded no evidence of European contact.

Among the most important conclusions Domínguez reached on the basis of this study was that the interior hilltop sites, including Loma del Convento, assumed, over time, the character of regional centers. In her model, as the population of the area developed a greater reliance on food production, the focus of production shifted from the coast to fertile interior valleys, in which root crop production could be intensified. More complex, more highly differentiated social relations among kin groups emerged in connection with this economic development. Domínguez interpreted the degree of hierarchization as incipient, not reaching the level seen among Taíno of Hispaniola and Puerto Rico. In her view, the now regionally integrated society was still kin organized, but with centralized, "hegemonic" roles (Domínguez 1987, 1991:79-87).

Domínguez's developmental model is embedded within a hypothetical population history for the agroalfarero communities of the region. According to this hypothesis, the first agroalfarero communities in the region were Arawakan migrants who brought the cultivation of bitter manioc, and who settled at various points along the south-central coast at river mouths, lagoons, and keys in approximately the tenth century A.D. Later, through a process of local environmental adaptation, these communities expanded into the fertile interior valleys, not abandoning, however, the coastal settlements as the region became economically and socially interdependent. These changes imply a population increase within an ethnically homogeneous Arawakan population. Based on limited evidence, Domínguez saw some of the communities as lasting well into the Spanish colonial era (Domínguez 1991:46, 83-91).

Data brought to bear in support of Domínguez's model of economic and social centralization included several highly noteworthy within-site and between-site differences. At the intra-site scale, at Loma del Convento, suggestive differences in pottery designs were noted between Mounds 1 and 2, while differences in the distribution of polished versus flaked stone were noted between Mounds 1 and 9. Insofar as the separate midden mounds might correspond to different domestic units organized in reference to a central plaza, such variation could be interpreted as indicating a division of labor among kin groups—with the caveat that the middens at the site had not been broadly sampled (Domínguez 1987, 1991:79).

At a larger scale, differences were found between coastal and interior sites. Just as objects of personal adornment and skillfully crafted goods were more prevalent at interior sites, so were fragments of *burenes* or griddles, presumably reflecting greater agricultural activity in the riverine settings. In contrast, burenes were scarce at coastal sites, suggesting to Domínguez (1991:38, 62, 81) that economically specialized coast-dwellers may have obtained some proportion of the cassava bread they consumed from the surpluses of interior settlements. A similar economic interdependence was suggested by the distribution of terrestrial and marine fauna and marine shell. Somewhat paradoxically, Domínguez reported that hunted terrestrial fauna such as hutia were less prevalent at Loma del Convento than at coastal sites; in contrast fish bone and marine shell was actually more prevalent in the interior than on the coast. Domínguez (1987, 1991:68–69) suggested that this extraordinary finding, assuming that it was not an artifact of sampling, was evidence of a strong economic interdependence between coast and interior in which the organization of production was perhaps dictated by the interior centers.

Ceramic differences between coastal and interior sites were largely technological. One emphatic difference that may reflect differences in foodways lies in the differing distribution of vessel sizes based on rim orifice measurements. At coastal sites the size distribution was unimodal and the vessels were small. At interior sites the distribution was bimodal, with a large size mode in addition to the smaller vessels (Domínguez 1991:37). One implication of this finding is that larger groups were being served at apparent civic centers such as Cantabria and Loma del Convento.

Moving ahead, the most extensive excavations to date at Loma del Convento began a year after Domínguez's fieldwork, with two seasons carried out in 1986–87 and 1987–88 by a joint Cuban-Soviet project. On the Soviet side, the work was supervised by the late Vladimir Bashilov, an Americanist archaeologist with prior experience in highland South America, assisted by Viktor Golenko. Supervision from the Cuban side was by Jorge Calvera. Unlike the two previous episodes, the Cuban-Soviet project focused on large-scale horizontal exposure, the objective being to investigate the spatial organization of the settlement including the location of houses, workshops, areas of funerary activity, and areas of food preparation. Most artifacts were piece plotted horizontally within each stratigraphic zone. During the initial season, the Cuban and Russian team exposed a contiguous area of some 120 m^2 on Mound 1, excavating much of the northern side of the site's primary midden mound. During the second season they expanded this block excavation by adding a long, narrow trench downslope to the west, bringing the total area excavated to 168.75 square meters. It is of interest that the second season's western trench convinced Bashilov that Rankin's map was inaccurate; there were no deposits due west of Mound 1 (V. Bashilov, personal communication, May 2005).

After three years of laboratory research, conducted in Russia as well as in Cuba, the collaborative project was prematurely brought to a close by the collapse of the Soviet Bloc and the abrupt withdrawal of the Russians from most of their Cuban interests. Because of this withdrawal, there is no report for the second season.[3] However, Bashilov and Golenko compiled a comprehensive manuscript report on the first season, filed with the Institute of Archaeology of the Academy of Sciences of Cuba. Moreover, this first season of work was the basis for three articles in Russian journals.

After publishing a short summary of the first season's work (Bashilov 1988), Bashilov and Golenko (1992) produced a much more thorough paper entitled "The Problem of the Periodization of Subtaíno Culture in South-Central Cuba." In this paper, they criticized Cuban archaeologists' approaches to the culture history of late-period agroalfarero sites. They claimed that the Cubans had neglected to come up with classifications that would properly differentiate some six centuries of agroalfarero development over an enormous expanse of territory. Consequently the focus of their study was the construction of a ceramic sequence for Loma del Convento based on three superimposed strata, labeled from earliest to latest Horizons I through III. Contrary to Cuban practice, they developed a typological approach to pottery chronology, defining 15 pottery types based on a combination of attributes including vessel shape and rim form. They also defined some 30 modes of vessel ornamentation and five basic forms of external lugs. Ornamentation and lug forms were treated as independent modes, crosscutting the pottery types. The stratigraphically derived pottery chronology resulting from this analysis is one of the most useful so far published for late-prehistoric Cuba.

The classification resulted in chronotypes whose relative percentages increase or decrease monotonically through time in a highly useful way. By re-casting Bashilov and Golenko's data in a Ford diagram (Figure 4.3) one can see that the early, Horizon I assemblage is dominated by modeled arcades arranged in panels above the vessel shoulder, whereas the late, Horizon III assemblage is dominated by incised zigzags. These trends can be broken down further. When decorative techniques are plotted independently from motifs, it becomes evident that the early assemblage is dominated by modeled decoration, while the latest assemblage is almost entirely incised rather than modeled. By ignoring the technique of decoration, we see that the earlier pottery is dominated by arcades and several more infrequent designs lumped as "other." The later pottery is dominated by zigzags. These chronological trends can form the basis for a valid regional seriation. For example, in this light the pottery assemblage published for the Cantabria site as well as those of several coastal sites closely resemble Horizon III, the latest assemblage, whereas that published for Abra de Castellón, the farthest inland of the Arimao River basin sites, more closely resembles the early Horizon I assemblage at Loma del Convento. Bashilov and Golenko, recognizing the probable regional validity of this sequence,

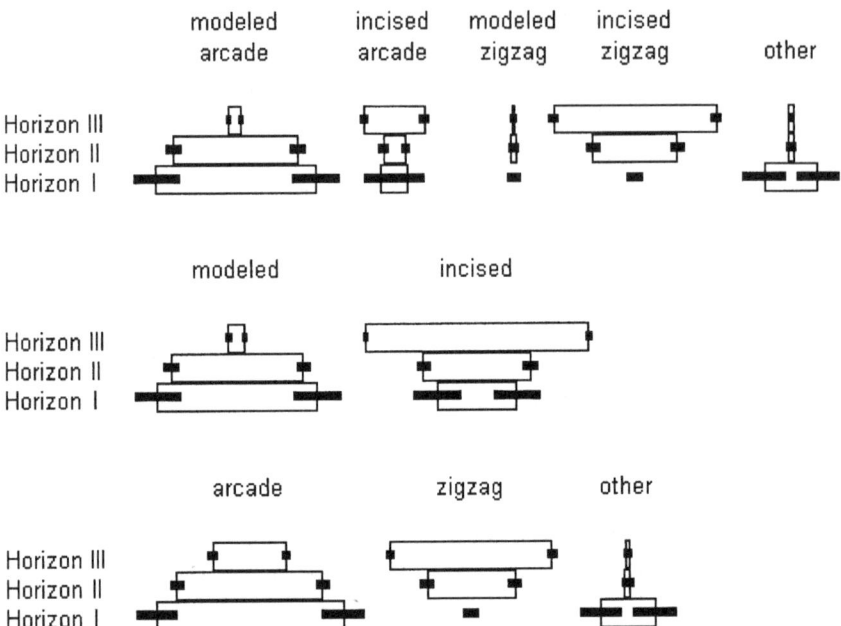

Figure 4.3. Ford diagrams of (a) modes of pottery decoration by horizon; (b) modeled versus incised decoration by horizon; and (c) decorative motifs by horizon.

recommended (1992) that the term "Cantabria culture" be reserved for the latest assemblages, in which incising and zigzag decoration are dominant over modeled and arcaded decoration.

Horizon III is a period of intensified use of the Mound 1 locality, as seen by greatly increased midden density. In terms of dating, it is now clear that Horizon III correlates with early sixteenth-century European contact. During the Cuban-Soviet project, unambiguous Spanish-derived artifacts began to appear for the first time in one part of the site. These included a small rectangular piece of ferrous sheet metal and several small sherds of Spanish majolica (Columbia Plain), including one piece that had been shaped and notched. The most striking of the European-derived artifacts is one-half of a bronze navigator's compass that had been turned into a pendant (Figure 4.4). It is Rodríguez's opinion (2002, 2004:70) that the grooving on the upper part of the piece has been added by an indigenous artisan to emulate stylized anthropomorphic pendants of tabular shell.

Relevant laboratory dates include one radiocarbon assay, tree-ring corrected to A.D. 1279–1388 at one sigma.[4] According to Bashilov and Golenko, this sample, collected by Rankin, is associated with materials of Horizons I or II. This ^{14}C date is complemented by two dates on faunal bone using the so-called collagen

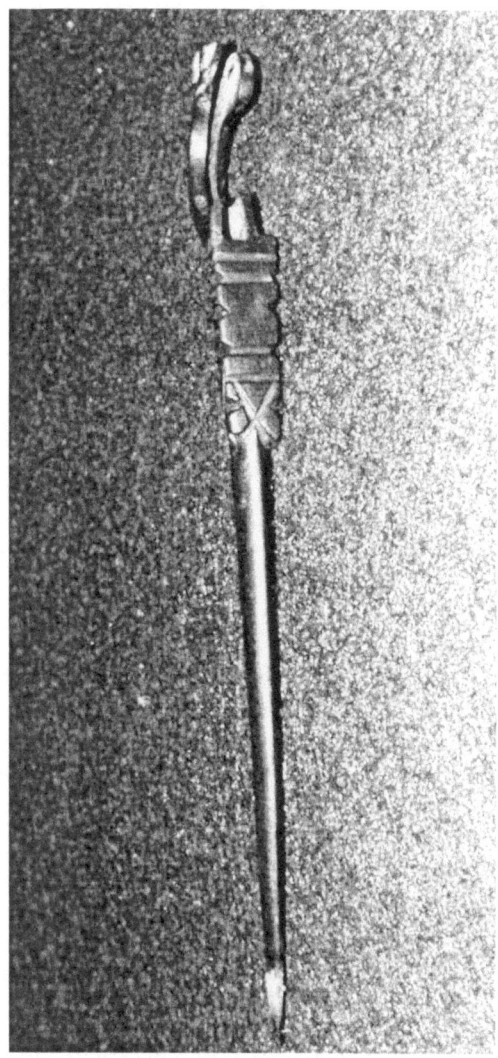

Figure 4.4. Bronze navigator's compass from Loma del Convento. Length: 15 cm (Courtesy of Marcos Rodríguez Matamoros)

method.[5] These collagen dates are 650 ± 20 B.P. (M 150, ca. A.D. 1340) and 400 ± 20 B.P. (M 178, ca. A.D. 1590) (Pino Rodríguez 1994). The first of these, from the basal level (0.60–0.80 m), generally supports the earlier radiocarbon date while the latter, falling in the sixteenth century, is from an upper level probably corresponding to Bashilov and Golenko's Horizon III. Rodríguez (2004:47) interprets the combined evidence as indicating that Loma del Convento was initially occupied around the beginning of the fourteenth century A.D. He dismisses as questionable another collagen-method date of 1080 ± 20 (M 179, ca. A.D. 900) from the related Rancho Club site at the mouth of Jagua Bay, as this date is far earlier

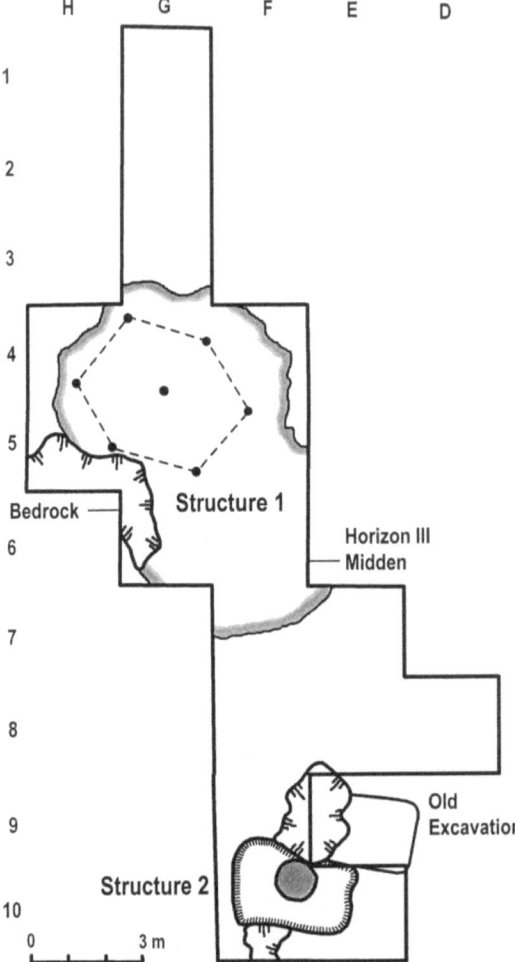

Figure 4.5. Cuban-Soviet excavation of 1986–87, showing Structures 1 and 2, after Bashilov and Golenko.

and out of line with the accepted age of initial agroalfarero sites in eastern Cuba such as Damajayabo in Granma province (Martínez 1968). A total occupational duration of Loma del Convento of about two centuries, as Rodríguez's interpretation would have it, seems reasonable in view of the amount of stylistic change seen in the pottery.

To amplify their picture of the site, the Cuban-Soviet exploration of 1986–1987 found and mapped two complete structures within the northern section of Mound 1 (Figure 4.5). The first, Structure 1, coincided with the horizontal limits of a mounded midden dating to Horizon III, and thus the structure probably dates to the late period at Loma del Convento. Structure 1 was of modest size, about 5 m by 3 m in diameter, outlined by six widely spaced postholes, hexagonally arranged around the wall margin, with a small center post. There was no evident internal hearth. Because Structure 1 was built directly over uneven, sloping limestone bedrock, an extraordinary preparation included artificially leveling the floor by chipping away the soft bedrock to an even grade. All of the postholes were also dug directly into the bedrock, just as were the postholes previously found by Rankin within his test pits at the base of the southern section of Mound 1.

The Horizon III deposit overlying this floor was rich in potsherds and burén fragments, with a special concentration of ceramics and dietary remains mapped within an area corresponding to the western half of the structure floor. Rarely in Greater Antilles archaeology have the contents of a mounded midden of a specific period been correlated with a specific structure in this manner. (For comparable structures in Puerto Rico, see Oliver 2003; currently structure patterns are being linked to domestic refuse at the site of El Cabo in the Dominican Republic [Samson and Hoogland 2007].)

Structure 2 was located closer to the central portion of the mound. It was mapped within Horizon II, just south of the limits of a midden concentration of that period. Structure 2 was quite small, only 3 m by 2 m in diameter, and showed construction features considerably different from those of the first structure. The defined floor area was roughly oval, lacking post holes either delimiting the wall or internal to it. Central to this floor area was a circular ash deposit about one meter in diameter, containing a small rock cluster and four sherd clusters. Within the structure floor and external to the hearth, the excavators mapped several items including a second rock cluster, five additional sherd clusters, two burén fragments, and a concentration of dietary remains. Just outside the defined limits of Structure 2 there were three more sherd clusters and two additional concentrations of dietary remains. Given its size and characteristics, it is doubtful that Structure 2 represents the remains of a domestic structure. Rather, it seems to represent a small specialized facility of some sort, provided with a hearth and used in food preparation involving pottery containers and possibly burens.

In sum, a series of excavations of Loma del Convento in the 1970s and 80s by Rankin, Domínguez, and the Cuban-Soviet team are, in each case, documented in publications presenting us with an increasingly well-defined agroalfarero assemblage from the south-central Cuban region, an increasingly well-developed internal chronology based on stratigraphy, laboratory dating, and European artifact associations, documentation of two forms of architecture, and regional survey data suggestive of a process of sociopolitical consolidation. Other contemporaneous sites in the region also have seen varying degrees of published investigation. In this combination of particulars, only the Banes district of eastern Cuba offers a comparably rich dataset for Cuba's agroalfarero stage (for a summary, see Valcárcel

2002). Moreover, a number of secondary and complementary studies addressing ceramic and ethnohistoric data have enhanced this baseline considerably.

Collections Research

One attempt to seriate the south-central Cuban sites was by Castellanos and Rives (1991), using assemblages from the sites of Cayo Ocampo, El Masío, Cabagán, Abra de Castellón, and Cantabria curated in the Department of Archaeology of the Institute of Social Sciences in Havana. This effort was made prior to the availability of a stratigraphically based chronology by the Russians, Bashilov and Golenko (1992). Castellanos and Rives ordered the sites primarily by the relative frequencies of coarse versus fine pottery temper, reproducing an observation also made by Domínguez (1991:35) that the coastal sites tend to have greater amounts of fine-tempered pottery than the interior sites. Unfortunately, this ordering by technological traits does not result in a chronology, as is shown by the relative confusion introduced by accepting this order as a guide to understanding change in pottery decoration.[6] Castellanos and Rives obtained more convincing results in grouping the same sites by means of cluster analysis. In their analysis they essentially confirmed the homogeneity of the south-central group in contrast to agroalfarero sites in eastern Cuba. The pottery of the south-central group is distinctive in its simplicity of decoration, in the dominance of arcade and zigzag motifs in both incising and appliqué work, and in the relative lack of anthropomorphic and zoomorphic design elements.

Independently of the work done by Domínguez on the pottery technology of the agroalfarero sites in the south-central group, Bobrinski and Loman (1992) of the Russian Institute of Archaeology made a detailed technological study of a sample of 104 specimens from all three stratigraphic horizons at Loma del Convento. They recorded some 23 macroscopic and microscopic variables on these potsherds. Among the more important observations were the following: First, sooting and other characteristics show that the ordinary bowl shapes at Loma del Convento were commonly used over fire, as cooking vessels. Second, sherds from all three horizons frequently have interior surfaces saturated by carbonized, fatty food residues. Third, the pottery tempers are intentional additives rather than fortuitous inclusions in the clay. These tempers come from several geological sources, not to mention the use of organic tempers seen as carbonized vegetal material in the clay body. Fourth, vessels made of marine-deposited clays were found in each horizon, together with more common vessels made of iron-rich alluvial clays. Fifth, all three horizons of Mound 1 contain direct evidence of on-site pottery-making in the form of incompletely fired, thermally fractured pieces, or "wasters," from the firing process.

These technological observations by the Russian scientists complement those of a more recent study of pottery clay composition at agroalfarero sites in the south-central region. Using neutron activation analysis, Padilla and Celaya (2003) characterized the pottery clays used at 11 agroalfarero sites in the south-central region, including Loma del Convento where some 30 sherds were analyzed.[7] Principal component analysis of the results yielded three aggregates of elemental variables that the authors propose are correlated with the geology of the Jagua Bay area in a definite manner.

One group, they suggest, derives from clay sources in the upriver sections of the Caunao and Arimao River drainages. A second group correlates with clays from beds closer to the mouths of the Caunao and Arimao. A third group was assigned a provenance near the mouth of the Damuji River, on the northwest side of Jagua Bay. Padilla and Celaya (2003:132) make the important observation that sherds of pots made from all three of the inferred clay source areas are found at Loma del Convento, confirming the site's function as a regional center of interaction. They also observe that sherds characterized as coming from the upriver source area increase through time at Loma del Convento, indicating "some displacement of the pottery activities to territories located inland" in the latest period (Padilla and Celaya 2003:129).

In recent years increasing attention also has been paid to the stylistic study of pottery decoration among agroalfarero sites throughout Cuba, including those of the south-central region. Celaya and Godo (1998, 2000), in particular, have worked toward refining the picture of stylistic variation in central Cuba. They see the "schematized" arc and zigzag designs within continuous panels characteristic of Jagua Bay region pottery as derived ultimately from earlier representational motifs found farther to the east. This derivative relationship is, in turn, thought to reflect a migration history in which the Jagua-area peoples came most immediately from communities in the Guacanayabo region of Granma province in eastern Cuba.[8] One intriguing suggestion is that the Jagua Bay region's tendency toward simplified geometric forms in panels is a result of these peoples' intimate contact with nonagricultural, Archaic peoples (Padilla and Celaya 2003:121).

Historical Research

Turning to recent documentary history, it is Rodríguez Matamoros's (2000–2002) conclusion that the site of Loma del Convento is precisely that of the encomienda presided over by Bartolomé de Las Casas and Pedro de Rentería during 1514 and 1515. It is well known that Diego Velázquez granted an encomienda on the Arimao River to these two Spaniards in recognition of their service during the Cuban conquest. In his *Historia de las Indias,* Las Casas (1875) remembers the name of the native village commended to him as Canarreo, a name that also appears in other documents and maps of the sixteenth century. It is this encomienda that the cleric Las Casas renounced in 1515, in protest of the maltreatment of Amerindians under Spanish rule.

As early as 1952, Pedro Cancela laid out criteria for physically identifying the site of the encomienda. Cancela suggested that the Amerindian town of Canarreo would be recognized as a late-period archaeological site on the banks of the lower Arimao River between Jagua Bay and Trinidad. Moreover, the site should yield artifactual evidence of Indo-Hispanic transculturation (Cancela 1952). As we have seen, the site of Loma del Convento meets these criteria. It is the only site on record along the lower Arimao that does so.

Rodríguez (2000–2002) makes the identification more specific, primarily by a kind of triangulation (Figure 4.6). In his *Historia,* Las Casas says, and Velázquez appears to independently confirm, that the haciendas of the cleric were on the Arimao River one league from the port of Jagua (Las Casas 1875; Marrero 1972). It appears to be well established that "port of Jagua" in that era specifically meant Cayo Ocampo, the island in Jagua Bay that served as a Spanish anchorage and operational base. Historians Rousseau and Díaz (1919) say, without citing their source, that the encomienda was one-half league from the mouth of the Arimao. Cosculluela (1918) further specifies, again without revealing his source, that the town of Canarreo was on the left margin of the Arimao River near the hacienda Auras.

Rodríguez (2002, part V), assuming that the itinerant league of 7.4 km is the measure used in the *Historia,* concludes that these combined specifications bring us to within 221 meters of La Loma del Convento, where we have a large archaeological site of the correct period that has yielded direct evidence of early Indo-Hispanic contact. Rodríguez adds that sixteenth-century cartography consistently shows the place-name Canarreo on the east side of Jagua Bay, that the site is close to the old Spanish road between Jagua and Trinidad, that the place-name Loma del Convento preserves the memory of a clerical connection, and that several other previously suggested locations for the encomienda in this vicinity have been systematically ruled out. He notes that Rankin's 1974 survey of the lower Arimao with this question in mind was "exhaustive." All of this leads Rodríguez (2002, part V:61) to suggest that his identification is conclusive.

With this background, I now want to examine how the record at Loma del Convento and related sites bears on three issues of broader importance in Cuban archaeology.

The Arawakan Expansion

The dominant model governing Cuba's late-period or "agroalfarero" populations is one of migration and colonization of the island by Arawakan agriculturalists,

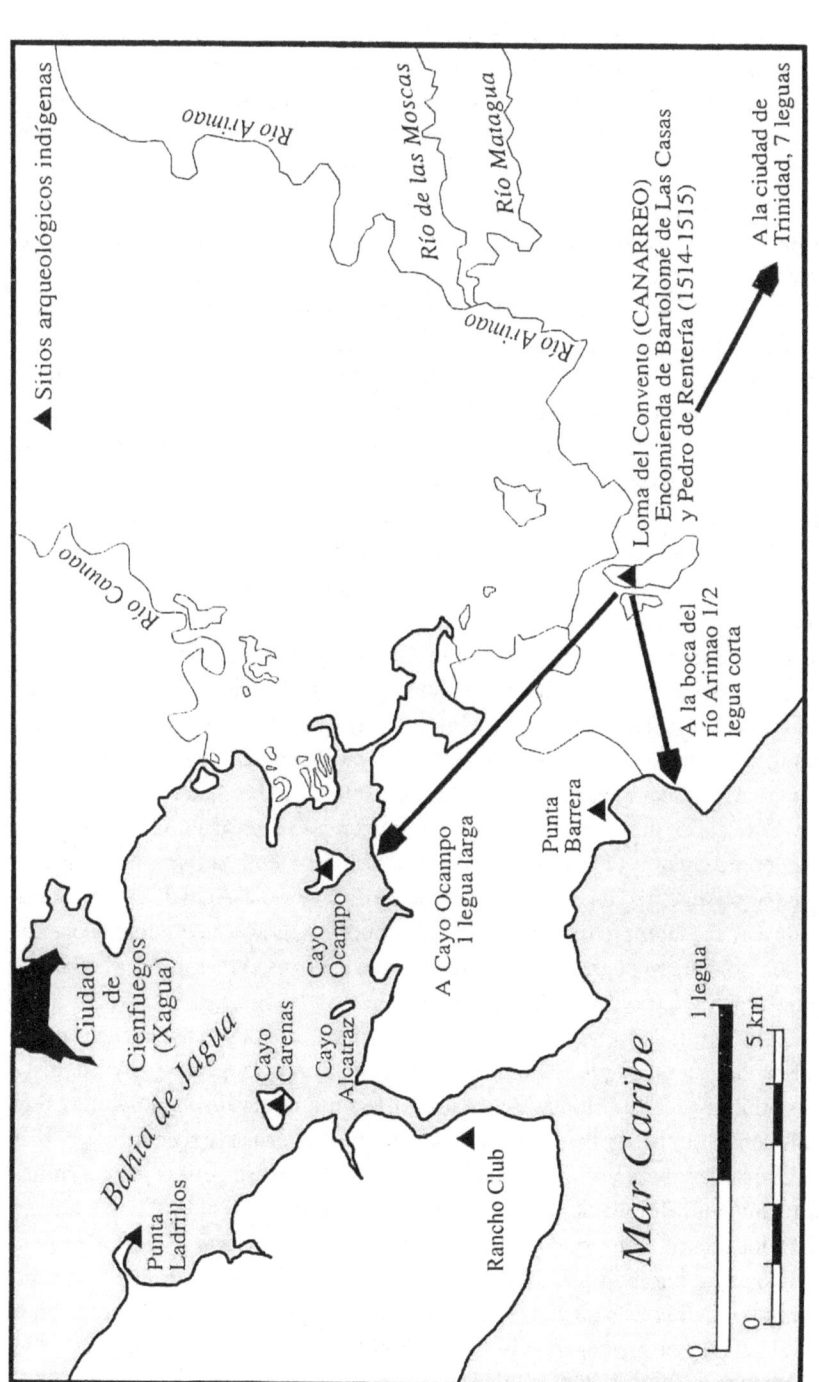

Figure 4.6. Location of Las Casas's Canarreo at the site of Loma del Convento. (Courtesy of Marcos Rodríguez Matamoros)

proceeding from east to west. This model has its antecedents in the early work of Harrington (1921), Loven (1935), and Ortíz (1935), among others. Modern proponents envision Cuban territory, previously inhabited by hunter-gatherer-fishermen, as encroached upon in about the ninth century A.D. by peoples emigrating from neighboring Hispaniola. These Arawakan colonists established multiple settlements in eastern Cuba, and from there gradually expanded westward as far as modern Havana province. Along the way they displaced local groups; eventually a frontier formed in western Cuba between emigrant Arawakan agriculturalists and a remnant population of Archaic peoples in Pinar del Rio province. In this persistent model the emigrant population is framed as uniform in ethnicity, language (Arawakan), physical type (with artificially flattened crania), and cultural characteristics (manioc horticulture, pottery of Meillacoid and Chicoid stylistic traditions, burenes, and generically Taíno ritual gear). It is noteworthy that this migrationist scenario for the sweeping introduction of agroalfarero traits in later prehistory clashes with orthodox dialectical materialism in Cuban archaeological theory, in which prehistory is seen as driven by gradual evolutionary processes of environmental adaptation and technological change (e.g., Domínguez et al. 1994; Guarch 1990; Tabío 1984).

It is my guess that the near future of Cuban archaeology will include an increasingly critical interrogation of the homogeneous Arawakan expansion model in its simple form. That is to say, the view of early agroalfarero settlements in Cuba as resulting from a westward wave of one biological people/one language/one culture that arrived completely intact and that displaced the original population will give way to more subtle models based on the complexities of local sequences. To some degree Guarch (1990) anticipates this trend by emphasizing internal evolutionary change, regional differentiation, and Arawakan-Archaic transculturation during the later prehistory of Cuba. Beyond this, however, it remains open to question how many migrations were involved, what caused them, and whether the emigrating populations were large or small.

Moreover, it is conceivable that the westward expansion was as much an incorporation of preexisting locals into new sociopolitical arrangements by linguistic and economic acculturation as it was a relentless migratory displacement. As such details come into better focus, it is possible to posit alternative scenarios in which the cultural landscape of Cuba during the agroalfarero stage was always multiethnic and multilinguistic, united by a trade language (western Taíno), and by rapid adoption of elite ritual gear in the Taíno mold, as outward signs of new integrative social and political roles. In such scenarios, the role of preexisting complex hunter–gatherers who already used pottery and perhaps practiced some plant cultivation may be greater than is usually envisioned (e.g., Domínguez et al. 1994; Rodríguez et al. 2008; Ulloa and Valcárcel 2002).

La Loma del Convento and related sites in south-central Cuba, being in geographic proximity to a posited Archaic frontier of long standing, are highly pertinent to any reconceptualization of the Arawakan expansion. Cuban archaeologists (Padilla and Celaya 2003) are already contemplating a possible contemporaneous relationship between these sites and other communities in the region that are classified as *Protoagrícola* or late mesolithic, meaning in this case, Archaic-with-ceramics. Cuban researchers (Celaya and Godo 2000) also have speculated that the regional shift from representational to purely decorative motifs on pottery may be due to Archaic influence. Other points of reference for a reconceptualization are potentially distinctive economic traits and settlement patterns.

With regards to the latter point, it is worth suggesting that the elevated location of large inland communities in settings of rugged topography may reflect considerations of defense. At any rate, the viability of the Arawakan expansion model in its present form will increasingly rest on the comparison of developed micro-chronologies in different regions. What is most needed at this juncture are stylistic-technological sequencing and comparison of artifact forms at several scales including the pan-regional, together with a greater emphasis on the dating of assemblages. In this respect Loma del Convento currently stands as a key point of reference.

The Rise of Sociopolitical Complexity

Las Casas (1875) wrote that at the time of the Spanish conquest, the largest political entities in Cuba were only at the level of the village and village chief, unlike neighboring Hispaniola with its powerful regional *cacicazgos*. Loven (1935:81–83) took this observation literally to mean that when the Spaniards used the term "province" in Cuba they were usually referring only to "the village with its surrounding conucos," or in the case of more spatially expansive "provinces," named districts that were not organized as true chiefdoms. Some more recent archaeologists (e.g., Tabío and Rey 1985:169) have been in basic agreement with these statements.

However, it seems more than plausible that simple chiefdoms did develop in Cuba and were pervasive at the time of first contact (Moreira 2003). These simple chiefdoms would not have compared in scale or complexity to the chiefdoms of Hispaniola, the latter with their compound levels of political hierarchy. However, the Cuban chiefdoms would have measured up to Carniero's (1981) criterion, in consisting of more than one community joined under the same political authority. Spanish colonial archives pertaining to Cuba have not been researched with this specific question in mind. This needs to be done, together with more systematic archaeological surveys to document settlement distributions and densities.

In recent years Cuban archaeologists have begun to document the emergence of political complexity that is clearly beyond the scope of the village. For example, in the Banes district of eastern Cuba, Valcárcel (1999, 2002) shows that skillfully crafted objects of personal adornment and ceremonial use concentrate in only five sites distributed among a much larger number of communities. Moreover, within important communities, such objects are spatially restricted to areas in or near the largest mounded middens. Since objects of this nature tended to be associated with spiritual aspects of chiefship, Valcárcel concludes that their possessors lived in regional civic-ceremonial centers to which many other communities were subordinated. The process of centralization was a late development, culminating in the fifteenth century.

Domínguez (1987, 1991) reached a similar conclusion based on her research in south-central Cuba. Domínguez views regional centralization in the Jagua area as a process of local development that reached its highest level in late-prehistoric times. Here, the case for regional integration includes contrasts in dietary remains among regional communities that suggest economic interdependence. Loma del Convento is posited as one of several central places of interaction that developed superordinate roles in the region. The excavations at Loma del Convento have provided key evidence of this development, including economic specialization, differences in vessel sizes, exchange of foodstuffs and pottery, clustering of ritually important goods, and hints of intrasite spatial differentiation in pottery and stone industries. Domínguez's work shows the promise of such studies as the question of regional integration and political dominance in Cuba continues to be debated.

Effects of European Colonization

Despite the historical significance of the Spanish system of *repartimiento* and *encomienda* in the subjugation of Amerindian peoples in the Greater Antilles, the archaeology of this institution remains undeveloped. To date, Deagan's (2004) study of the post-contact component of the En Bas Saline site in Haiti is the only such study to examine this topic archaeologically.[9] In Cuba, there is a long history of reportage of post-contact sites and materials showing evidence of Indo-Hispanic "transculturation," to use the term coined by Fernando Ortíz (e.g., Domínguez 1978, 1984; García 1949; Morales and Pérez 1945; Rouse 1942). There is a remarkable concentration of such sites in Holguín province in eastern Cuba. These contexts in Holguín are variable in character, suggesting a prolonged period of Indo-Hispanic interaction during the sixteenth century (Valcárcel 1997).

Deagan's work at En Bas Saline emphasizes Taíno reactions to Spanish domination that varied by social class and by gender within a large community. Her conclusions hint at the unrealized potential of an archaeology of the encomienda system, which surely varied in its implementation under specific circumstances. Some differences may have depended on whether labor drafts were primarily used in agricultural work and ranching within previously settled districts, or alternatively were used to work mines in remote uplands far from established settlements. We know that in some areas of Cuba, but not all, indigenous peoples were gathered and removed to new artificial communities called *reducciones* in order to concentrate their labor near Spanish commercial enterprises (Wright 1916). Forms of indigenous resistance to the encomienda system no doubt also varied according to local circumstances. In certain times and places, according to written sources, resistance took the form of open rebellion against the Spanish overlords. At other times and places, there were reactions ranging from flight to attempts at political negotiation through indigenous caciques. Perhaps the most dramatic form of resistance on record was mass suicide, either by hanging or by self-inflicted starvation through consumption of dirt. The latter response, which smacks of a nativistic movement, was prevalent in south-central Cuba (Pérez 1972).

At the present time there is no archaeological site more clearly connected to a documented encomienda than La Loma del Convento in the south-central region. This fact comes to our attention only because the *encomendero* was none other than the famous Las Casas, Protector of the Indians, who happened to write profusely about his experiences in a form that has come down to us intact. The precise localities at Loma del Convento that date to the encomienda period are not yet known, so it is premature to say how the site contributes to the discussion of the encomienda system generally. It is safe to say, however, that additional progress on the topic will depend in large measure upon new, directed archival research, especially in the Archivo General de Indias in Seville. With this research, it should be possible to identify other encomienda settlements on the ground, and to refine the questions that the archaeology of these settlements might elucidate.

Acknowledgments

For their generosity in conversations about the archaeology and early history of south-central Cuba and their indispensable help in acquainting me with its literature, I wish to acknowledge the late Vladimir Bashilov, Lourdes Domínguez, Alfredo Rankin Santander, and Marcos E. Rodríguez Matamoros.

Notes

1. La Loma del Convento is also known in the literature simply as "El Convento."
2. Although Tabío's (1984) *agroalfarero* (agriculture/pottery-using) stage still enjoys currency in Cuba in reference to sedentary Arawakan manioc horticulturalists, the connotations of the name are increasingly objectionable. Pottery was made well prior to the appearance of sedentary communities (e.g., Rodríguez Ramos et al. 2008; Ulloa and Valcárcel 2002), and it is strongly suspected that plant domestication was underway earlier as well. Domínguez, Febles, and Rives (1994) have substituted a stage

nomenclature in which their "neolithic stage" would be a rough synonym, although the latter is more inclusive, referring to post-A.D. 500. "developed" horticulturalists. The concept of a Cuban neolithic sidesteps any dependence on a migration scenario, while recognizing that early pottery and initial plant cultivation were characteristic of their earlier "late mesolithic" stage.

3. According to Bashilov (personal communication, 2005), the graphic and photographic documentation for both seasons are in the Russian Institute of Archaeology, while the field materials were deposited with the Institute of Archaeology in Havana.

4. Cited as GD 1053 666 ± 50 B.P.

5. The collagen method is based on the rate of protein decomposition in bone as measured by the amount of nitrogen present. Like similar chemical methods, it is influenced by any number of local environmental factors and should be considered a relative dating technique at best.

6. The decorative trends suggested by Castellanos and Rives are either erratic or are basically inverted (e.g., 1991:Figure 3). Domínguez (1987-88, 1992:Figures 39, 40) independently seriated some 15 south-central agroalfarero site assemblages based on pottery temper and evidence of the firing conditions, producing orderings that demonstrate the cultural uniformity of the region but once again do not appear to be chronologies, when compared to the stratigraphic results of the Russians at Loma del Convento.

7. Altogether, Padilla and Celaya (2004:126) analyzed 142 sherds from 11 south-central agroalfarero sites.

8. In particular, Godo (2000:75-76) derives the Jagua Bay-area appliqué arcaded designs from representational elements associated in the eastern regions with the supernatural figure known as "llora-lluvia," or "cries-rain." This motif is most strongly associated with Guarch Delmonte's (1990:65) "Cultural Variant Bayamo."

9. While this is true for the Antilles, the editors have kindly pointed out to me that archaeological patterns of early Spanish governance are being actively addressed in Mexico (e.g., Kepecs and Alexander, eds. 2005).

5
New Early Tradition Stone Tool Industries in Cuba

Lorenzo Morales Santos, Villa Clara Center for Environmental Studies and Services, Cuban Ministry of Science, Technology and Environment (CITMA)

Until 1988, only the lithic industries of the Seboruco-Mordán complex were recognized as belonging to the earliest (proto-Archaic or early pretribal) tradition in Cuba. In 1989 my colleagues and I initiated extensive surveys in the northwest region of Villa Clara, which resulted in the discovery of over 200 stone tool sites. Techno-typological and statistical analyses recently applied to the artifacts from seven of these sites indicate that the assemblages from these early occupations in northwest Villa Clara are variations of the universal Paleolithic norm.

Hasta 1988 sólo las industrias líticas del complejo Seboruco-Mordán formaban parte de la tradición más temprana de Cuba. En 1989 mis colegas y yo iniciamos la prospección extensiva de la región Noroeste de Villa Clara, teniendo por resultado el descubrimiento de más de 200 sitios con predominio de herramientas líticas. Los análisis tecnotipológicos y estadísticos recientemente aplicados a siete de estos sitios regionales indican que los conjuntos de estas ocupaciones tempranas del Noroeste de Villa Clara son variaciones singulares de la norma paleolítica universal, que dichas variaciones se agrupan en tres industrias, y que su compleja articulación conforma una misma tradición regional temprana.

Previous Studies

During the first half of the last century the archaeologist Irving Rouse (1941), working at the preceramic site of Courí in the Dominican Republic, made clear the importance of archaeological deposits with abundant macrolithic artifacts in considering the oldest human occupations in the area. Later reports of similar sites in the Dominican Republic (Cruxent and Rouse 1969; Roumain 1943) as well as at Farallones de Seboruco in Cuba (Jiménez 1948) formed the basis of the Seboruco-Mordán tradition (Kozlowski 1975). These discoveries had a crucial impact on the field since they confirmed the presence of early hunting groups in the Caribbean by at least 8000 B.P.

The discovery of surface deposits with numerous quartzite macroliths at Farallones de Seboruco and other nearby points along the Mayarí and Levisa river basins in eastern Holguín province led to new in-depth techno-typological studies led by Polish archaeologist Janus Kozlowski, who published the first stone tool typology in Cuba (Kozlowski 1975). Various Cuban archaeologists followed up on Kozlowski's work with the goal of ordering and interpreting the multiple technical and typological variations evident in the Cuban stone tool record.

Most of the resulting reports, which focused on the significance of the accumulations, normative descriptions of the tools, and recommended methodologies for analysis, appeared some years later in the first handbook on the stone tools of Cuba's aboriginal communities (Febles 1988). This volume contributed significantly to the later development of classification and analysis, adapting for the Cuban case the general techno-typologies commonly used in the Old World. Until the publication of Febles's manual, few tool industries had been clearly defined, and among these, only one belonged to the early pretribal[1] tradition: Seboruco.

Other early lithic industries that appear in Febles's manual are hybrids, the results of complex processes of adaptation and exchange among the carriers of the Seboruco tradition originating in South America. Additional stone tool groups appeared technically adapted as a solution for economic tasks indigenous to the island environment (Dacal and Pino 1968; Guarch 1970; Martínez 1963; Villavicencio et al. 2003). Most of these indigenous tool complexes, linked to the early pretribal/Archaic transition or to later times, appear related or similar to the numerous early stone tool industries of the Caribbean and the early-pretribal-era Mississippi River basin (Febles 1982).

In this study I deal with three lithic industries determined via techno-typological and statistical analyses, all based on cores and atypical, retouched, or reused fragments, macroliths, and a variety of moderate blade-flakes that precede the microlith industries. In order to better understand the temporal and social nature of these lithic industries I consider them within their spatial and energetic frameworks. In the following section I present the Northwest Villa Clara Project that I began in 2001 with my colleagues Raúl Villavicencio, author of numerous studies on the lithic industries of northwest Villa Clara; Néstor Gómez, curator of paleontology and archaeology at the Center for Environmental Studies and Services (CESAM) in Villa Clara; and Carlos Arredondo, distinguished extinct vertebrates specialist in the Anthropology Department at the University of Havana.

The Northwest Villa Clara Project

My colleagues and I began surveying the northwest zone of Villa Clara province (Figure 5.1) in 1989. From the start, we were surprised by the area's rich archaeological record, represented by over 300 sites, most of them linked to hunter-gatherer groups at distinct levels of development. The prevalence of this affiliation is one of

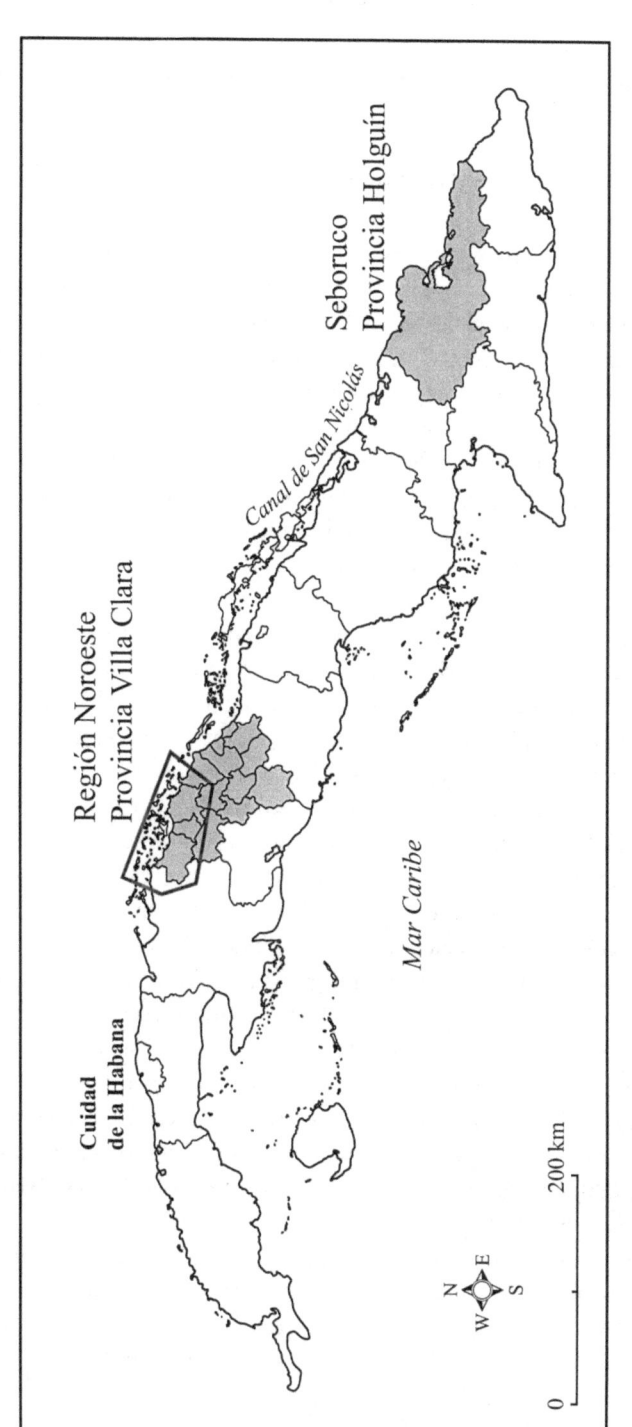

Figure 5.1. Map of the principal regions with evidence of Cuba's early stone tool tradition.

the distinct features of the region, which, compared to other parts of the country, contains scant evidence of protoagricultural or agricultural-ceramic occupation (Venegas 1980).

The Spatial Energetic Framework

The use of contiguous space is partly determined by natural conditions that form the relative borders of the region. In this way, regions—or energetic frameworks—directly influence the subsistence strategy of any hunter-gatherer group, and, ultimately, the archaeological record and its change through time (Gamble 1983). In northwest Villa Clara, the activity of early groups in the pursuit of indispensable resources coincides with a zone of woods and small arroyos fed from an old hilly range that reaches its maximum height at 180 m above sea level.

The spatial energetic framework of our study (Figures 5.1, 5.2) includes the modern municipalities of Sagua la Grande, Quemado de Güines, and Corralillo. The region's northern limit is the Canal San Nicolás; to the west is Matanzas province; to the east and south are other precincts in Villa Clara province. Our study region measures roughly 2,000 km^2, including the geosystems of the coast, the karst plains, and the mountain range (Trujillo 2008). Within its limits is an extensive river network composed of tributaries that feed mighty rivers (the Sagua Grande) and streams that flow all year. The region also contains numerous exposed nodule deposits (including the Veloz deposit, mentioned later) consisting of chalcedonies, opals, flints, and other varieties of fine-grained silica. Also available are lesser-quality varieties like crystaline quartz, quartzites, and argillites.

The central part of the region has undergone transformations since the Plio-Pleistocene boundary, with the emergence of relatively low-lying lands (Iturralde-Vinent and MacPhee 1999). Later, during the Middle Pleistocene, the region consisted of periodically inundated lowland patches linking the north and south coasts. These wetlands endangered several terrestrial species that eventually were extinguished. At the end of the Late Pleistocene new land formations emerged, heightening the contrast between the mountainous zones and the lowlands. During the Pleistocene/Holocene transition, two events of great importance occurred. There was a surge in the speciation and migration of the surviving land biota (Arredondo 2000); in addition, this era witnessed the arrival of the island's first human groups (Febles 1993).

Recently my colleagues and I extracted sedimentary columns in karst sinkholes, called "casimbas" in Cuba, as part of a project aimed at determining the degree of association between the remnant megafauna of the Pleistocene and the first human hunters in our study region. At the bottom levels (up to 1.7 m deep) these columns contain the skeletal remains of extinct fossil vertebrates, along with unquestionably human-modified flint. Most frequent among these extinct

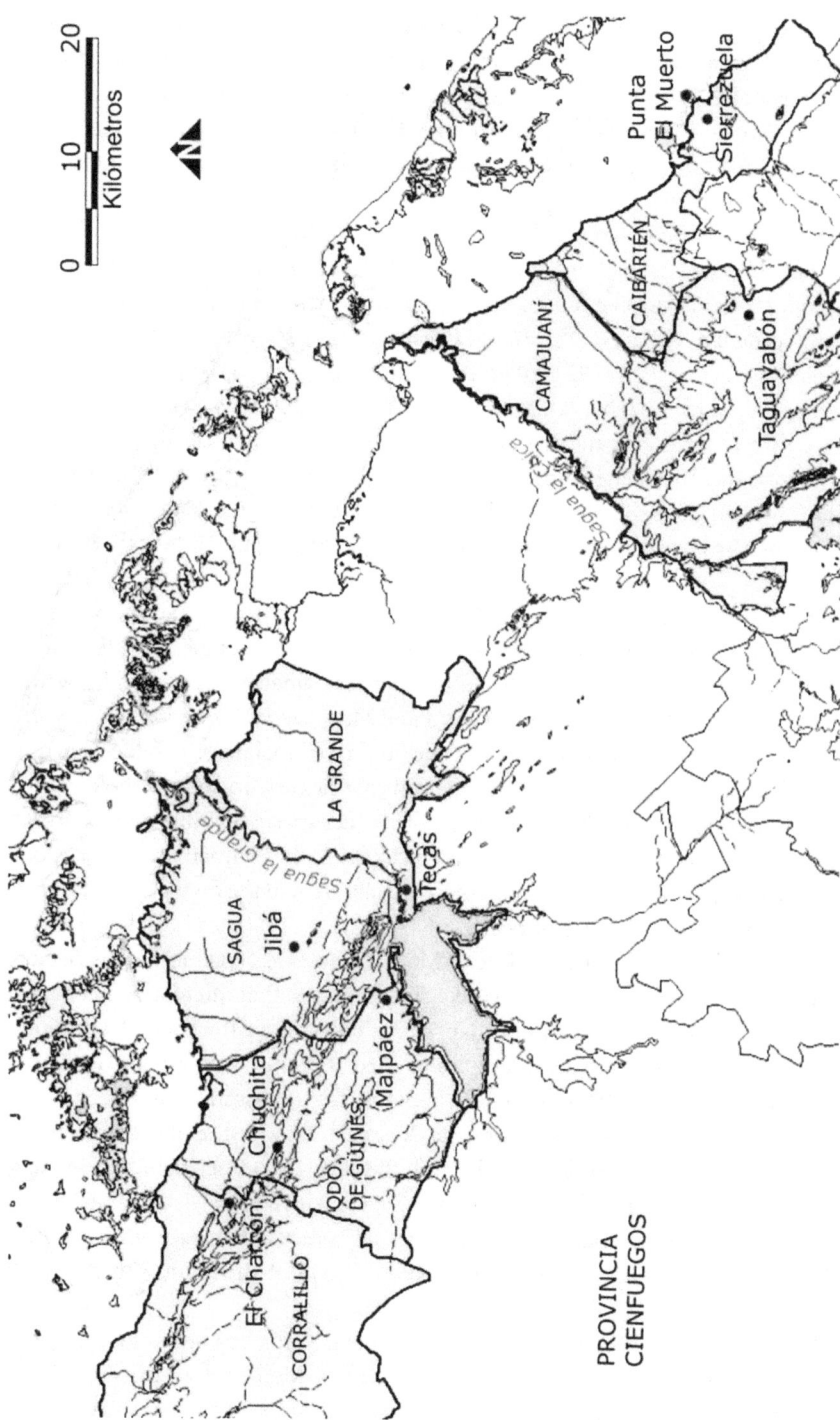

Figure 5.2. Map showing the principal locations of early tradition sites in northwest Villa Clara.

mammals are various species of the Megalonychiadae (sloth) family *(Megalocnus rodens, Parocnus browni, Parocnus torrei, Miocnus antillensis, Neocnus gliriformis,* and *Neocnus major).* Remains of large birds, including the Cuban condor *(Gymnogyps varonai)* and reptiles of great size like the Pleistocene crocodile *(Crocodilus rhombifer)* and the giant tortoise *(Geochelone cubensis)* also have been reported (Arredondo 2002).

These studies show that northwest Villa Clara is a region with great potential for clarifying questions about the relationships among Cuba's early human inhabitants, Late Pleistocene fauna, and remnant Pleistocene fauna at the start of the Holocene. The debate on this theme began early, when the North American archaeologist Harrington (1925) collected *Megalocnus* (great sloth) bones in an archaeological midden in Cueva Caleta in eastern Cuba; nevertheless, no conclusive links between the bones and the aboriginal refuse were established. There were later reports of Pleistocene fauna and archaeological debris in central and western Cuba, but in all cases these lack solid proof of association; post-depositional processes and/or insufficient precision in excavation practices contribute to the lack of certainty.

Although archaeologists believe they are very close to demonstrating the links between the paleontological and archaeological records in northeast Villa Clara, paleontologists generally discount the notion that aboriginal hunters coincided with extinct Pleistocene fauna (Iturralde-Vinent and MacPhee 1999), and in particular, that humans were responsible for the deposits in Villa Clara (Iturralde-Vinent, personal communication). Nevertheless, multiple factors, including the coincidence of stone tools with skeletal remains of extinct species exhibiting V-shaped cutmarks (described in detail below) lead us to think that human action was not only present but more important than mechanical forces in the final production of the sediments in the casimbas of northeast Villa Clara.

Moreover, the most recent absolute (AMS 14C) dates assigned to the fossilized remains of Pleistocene megafauna on the island indicate that interaction between humans and these animals is more than a possibility, since the zone of chronological overlap between the last examples of extinct fauna (from Solapa de Sílex, La Habana: 4190 ± 40 B.P.) and the first humans (from Levisa I, Holguín: 5140 ± 170 B.P.) is approximately 1,000 years (MacPhee et al. 2007). Other dated examples situate the disappearance of extinct sloths in the early Holocene, including *Megalocnus rodens* bones from the limestone cave Cueva Berovides in Matanzas, 6330 ± 50 años B.P. (MacPhee et al. 1999) and bones of *Parocnus browni* from Breas de San Felipe, a tar pit in Matanzas Province, 4960 ± 280 B.P. (Iturralde-Vinent et al. 2000).

Thus, the notion that the first waves of humans in Cuba had access to remnant Pleistocene fauna is a reasonable working hypothesis. Moreover, we consider that the sediment cores containing both bones of extinct species and artifacts constitute a chronologically diagnostic indicator of the early presence of humans in the region. We believe this debate will prosper as more systematic data are rigorously examined by joint teams of archaeologists and paleontologists.

While we lack both absolute dates for our samples and sufficient stratigraphic sequences to create a chronology for the earliest aboriginal groups in our region, our study deepens our understanding of the lithic industries in the area and their variation with respect to the spatial energetic framework. In the following section we add to the conventional techno-typological stone tool classifications a multivariate statistical analysis, to diminish the sensory errors and interpretive biases of the investigator.

Cluster Analysis

Although typological and statistical analyses alone are not capable of generating an absolute chronological order, their results permit better comprehension of the assimilation, transfer, and change of technical norms; that is, the evolutionary complexity of typologies in space and time. Specifically, using cluster analysis we were able to determine with some precision the existence of three industrial groups within the early tradition of northwest Villa Clara, and, in certain measure, the degree of exchange of diagnostic types among these industries.

Cluster analysis has been used for similar purposes by various archaeologists. The first studies referenced automated biometric models such as those by Gower (1971) and Wood (1974), designed to simultaneously group a limited number of examples on the basis of quantitative, qualitative, and binary variables. John O'Shea (1984) carried out similar analyses on artifacts from North American Indian burials. Christopher Peebles's dendograms (in Renfrew and Bahn 1993), based on materials from 719 burials at Moundville, revealed 15 conglomerates or attribute clusters related to burial types.

In Cuba, the first cluster analyses applied to archaeological cases were published at the start of the 1990s. The most relevant of these, with respect to flint tools, was applied to a sample of 120 projectile points from the Seboruco type site Melones 10, to determine the relationships between certain types of points with coastal or interior woods ecosystems (Febles and Rives 1991). At this time available computerized statistical programs in Cuba restricted analysis to samples of under 100 artifacts; for larger samples we created separate dendograms (each representing 40–50 artifacts), so that ultimately we could bring all of the information together to produce unified results. Our cluster analyses determined what we consider to be stone tool industries, based on Gamble's (1990) concept that an industry is a complex of characteristics or variables that reappear repeatedly in two or more assemblages. We distinguish this concept from "tradition"—an overarching category containing multiple industries with artifacts sufficiently similar to suggest their origins in the same large culture-historical block of ideas and technological norms (Laville et al. 1980).

To determine the existence of general industrial groups and their connections within the early tradition of northwest Villa Clara we created four dendograms (clusters) based on a list of variables (Table 5.1), Euclidian distance measures and unweighted pair-group averages. We selected Euclidian distance measures since this index is designed to process quantitative values; additionally, this index does not affect distances obtained on previously processed objects when new values are added (Abraira and Pérez 1996).

The first dendogram (Figure 5.3) is based on a random sample of 302 artifacts from the localities of Punta El Muerto, Cayo Conuco, Las Tecas, Malpáez, Jibá, Chuchita, and El Charcón, all within our study region. After we applied the general dendogram to evaluate behavior at the traditional scale we processed the examples in each group separately to discover their behavior at the industrial scale, as well as the links between key types within these industries. The result of the analysis was the discrimination of three fundamental industrial groups.

Group I (Tecas) is characterized by low formal diversity and poor technical resolution; this is the most precariously identified group among the three regional industries. Group II (Seboruco) is more diversified, represented by flakes and regular blades, some of great size, produced with various coarse-grained silicates. Seboruco is recognized as the oldest lithic tradition in Cuba and the Caribbean, and was presumed to be the precursor of the stone tool tradition in northwest Villa Clara, although we believe it is the second industry to develop in our region, given the degree of techno-typological complexity within the group. Group III (Jibá) is characterized by its excellently crafted flakes and moderately sized blades made of local fine-grained chalcedonies. The artifacts present well-defined sections and regular edges. Most exhibit significant use; some have minor retouching. In what follows we provide more substantial descriptions of the early stone tool industries of northwest Villa Clara.

The Regional Tecas Industry

The name Tecas comes from the type site, located near the town of Sitiecito in the municipality of Sagua la Grande. Although the first human groups in Cuba were clearly fully modern *Homo sapien sapiens*, the tool groups in this industry have atypical characteristics very similar to the stone tools made by premodern hominids in Africa over two million years ago (Brezillion 1968; Engerrand 1905). The scant indicators of modification led early hominid specialists to doubt the authenticity of these artifacts, a problem that persists today since conventional typologies are useless for their classification.

To assume that Tecas is indeed a stone tool industry is perhaps the most po-

Table 5.1. Technological and Typological Values Applied in Cluster Analysis of Artifacts Belonging to the Early Tradition of Northwest Villa Clara

Type of Variable	Variable	Condition
Technological	raw material	cobble; quartzite; fine-grained flint
	length*	(in millimeters)
	width	(in millimeters)
	weight	(in grams)
	striking platform (talon) angle	between platform and ventral surface, in degrees
	plane angle	between platform and principal striking surface, in degrees
	base of production (typical)	prepared core; flake; blade; flake or blade fragment; chip
	base of production (atypical)	natural fragment; artificial fragment; triangular; artificial spheriform; artificial fragment, parallel edges; artificial fragment, amorphous; spherical PTE; spherical/tabular PTE; nucleoid base
	profile**	absolutely straight; absolutely curved; relatively straight; relatively curved
	section**	absolute trapezoid; absolute triangle; relative trapezoid; relative triangle; semispherical; amorphous
	thermal fraction	very affected; little affected; without affect
	cortex (surface coverage)	over 50%; under 50%; none
	patina	tertiary patina; secondary patina; primary patina; no patina
Typological	retouch type	abrupt; semiabrupt; smoothed; semi-smoothed; fine
	shape / location of secondary flaking	end scrapers, side scrapers, denticulates, perforators, notched, massive retouch, other retouch, others with use, combinations
	maximum length of attack	extension of retouch or use, in millimeters
	angle of attack	edges retouched or used, in degrees
	reutilization	restoration; substitution; not reutilized

*In the case of artifacts that could not be oriented, maximum specified values were used.

**Relative values refer to artifacts produced on atypical bases.

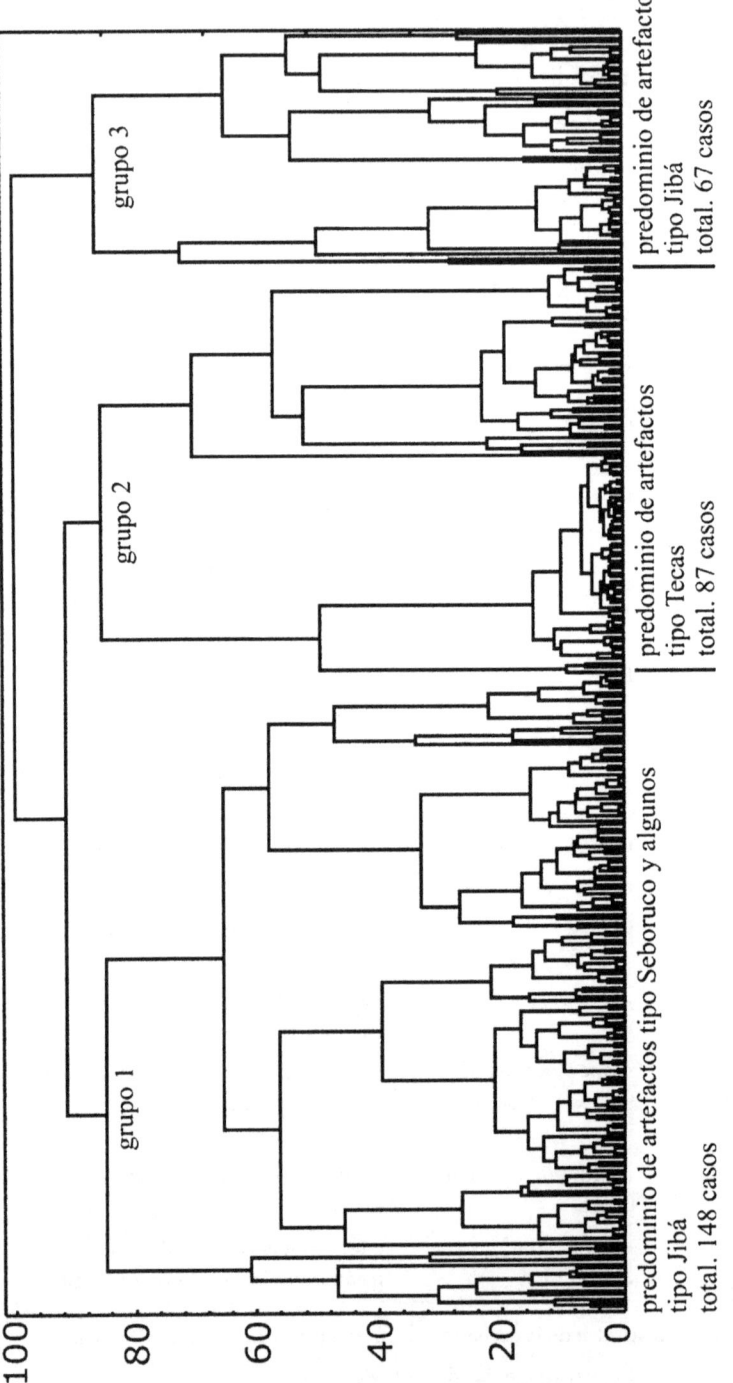

Figure 5.3. Cluster analysis: Dendograms showing early tradition tool groups in northwest Villa Clara.

lemical issue in our study. Let us clarify that the low level of energetic investment in these tools should not be understood as an indicator of maximim antiquity in the relative chronological framework for the early tool tradition in our study region. As we discuss later, monotonous, simple tool types are time transgressive, extending from the first human-made implements through the latest phases of stone tool development.

Recent studies demonstrate that the stone tool industries of the Caribbean are characterized by a clear tendency toward opportunism and not, as in the Old World, by symmetric, exhaustive standards (Müller-Beck et al. 2008). In the case of Tecas, steps in the process of production were skipped, resulting in artifacts of very simple appearance. Tecas tools, made directly from cores, natural or artificial fragments, or formally diverse, atypical flakes, may be associated with the phenomenon that processual archaeologists call expedient solution (Gamble 1990). Theoretically the size of such artifacts is circumstantial, dependent on the economic task the tool is to be used for, the distance between the mineral source and the location of the task, and the dimensions of the nodule or core from which the tool is created.

The resemblance between the Tecas artifacts and the Lower Paleolithic tools of the Old World reveals something about the essential nature of progress across the spatial and chronological abyss. The distinctive patination we see in our samples indicates prolonged exposure to the environment, as well as the effects of cultural reuse and natural disturbances. Since we have no absolute dates directly associated with Tecas strata, the identity of this lithic complex as the earliest in Cuba is uncertain; Tecas tools may represent a pre-projectile point horizon introduced by the first humans on the island, or they may instead have been produced through time under conditions of stress (Bate 1969; Binford 1962).

Raw Materials

Most primitive stone tool industries run the gamut of available silicates (Brézillon 1968; Febles 1988; Hamilton et al. 1989; Piel-Desruisseaux 1989). Tecas artifacts are often found in proximity to the best exposed chalcedonies of the karst plain; nevertheless, Tecas toolmakers used pebbles or cobbles of low quality, usually covered completely with cortex. The few exceptional specimens made from optimal minerals show evidence of inexpert fabrication.

Toolmaking Techniques

The dimensions of Tecas tools are variable. The presence of cortex in over 70 percent of the complete artifacts reflects a tendency toward immediate use of cores and fragments, practically without reduction to their natural volume and lacking evidence of the skill to create independent preforms. About 50 percent of the sample tends toward medium values (5–10 cm); 20 percent of the artifacts are over 10 cm long; the remaining 30 percent are microliths produced by violent percussion or heat fracture, or adapted from small natural formations, though not through reduction techniques or controlled fracture. When we refer to violent percussion we mean hitting together blocks of stone of similar hardness and composition, which results in fragments of variable size, texture, and thickness. Usually the flakes and fragments lack indicators—striking platforms, bulbs of percussion, bulbular scars, flake scars—of typical flintknapping. In the case of heat fracture we refer to cores or natural formations submitted to high temperatures, cracking the core from which multiple fragments detach.

Among the tool types in the Tecas industry, the so-called Roughly Spherical Stones (Piedras Toscamente Esféricas or PTE), 80 percent show evidence of high temperatures and pressure used to obtain convex surfaces on the cores and concave ventral faces on the flakes. We took this pattern into account, carrying out an experiment to simulate the creation of PTE using thermal fracture alone. The experiment consisted in exposing a block of silicate (7 x 7 cm long by 5 x 6.2 cm wide) to fire in an open hearth. Within 20 minutes the block cracked, with the consequent detachment of eight fragments showing concave ventral surfaces equal to those found in archaeological context.

The use of alternative techniques using open or underground hearths partially explains the repeated presence of PTE, not only in Tecas but also in the remaining tool groups of the early tradition in our study region. Thermal fracture produced decortication flakes, natural fragments, fragments modified on one or two axes with over 50 percent of the cortex removed, and irregular flakes with over 50 percent of the cortex remaining on the surface.

In these tools evidence of retouching is practically absent. However, there is clear evidence of immediate use on the atypical flakes, cores, and artificial fragments. The estimated functions by type for this industry are limited to scraping and cutting. In numerous cases these uses are evident in combination. Another characteristic of these tools is the reiteration of specific functions according to the form of the core or fragment. The most notable use-form coincidences are scrapers with abrupt retouch on the concave ventral surfaces, with parallel or triangular edges. Convex scrapers occur on both natural fragments of tabular profile and amorphous fragments with evidence of use. The median angle of attack is 90 degrees in the case of end scrapers, 75 degrees for side scrapers, and 60 degrees on generic knives.

Tecas Artifact Types

Roughly Spherical Stones (PTE): These artifacts present evidence of intentional conservation of portions of the cortex related to the envisioned final form. The tools are classed as Spherical or Spherical-tabular. Their dimensions fall into small (2–4 cm), medium (4–10 cm) and, more rarely, large (over 10 cm). PTE may have been used as thrown projectiles, reported worldwide as artifacts used for hunting

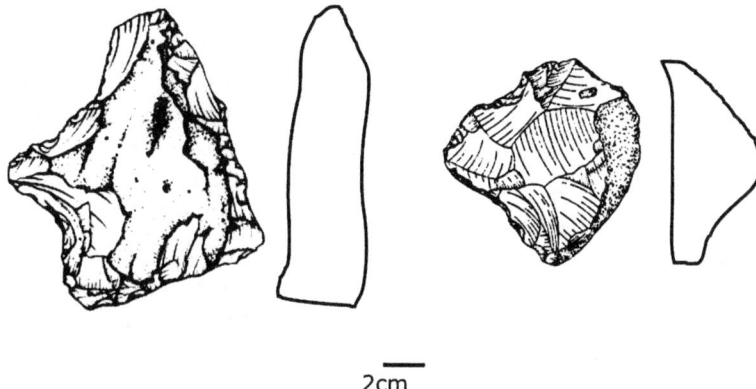

Figure 5.4. Handaxe comparison: (a) Malpáez (Tecas) beaked axe made on limestone bedrock, Malpáez 3, northwest Villa Clara; (b) Seboruco beaked axe on thick flint macroblade, Seboruco 5, Holguín (from Febles 1988).

or defense during early development stages (Engerrand 1905; Le Paige 1971). Certainly PTE were not reduced with the same intensity as other core tools. Some investigators working in northwest Villa Clara (Arredondo 2000; Ramírez and Morales 2001; San Pedro et al. 2001; Villavicencio 1995) believe that simple thrown projectiles may have been used to bring down slow-moving members of the Pleistocene sloth family, especially the tree dwellers.

Malpáez Beaked Axes: Discovered in Malpáez, a rich archaeological and palentological locality, these axes constitute another class of massive Tecas artifacts (Morales 1989). In contrast to the beaked axes reported in the Seboruco complex reported in Holguín, which are fabricated on massive flakes or subdiscoidal cores (Febles 1988), those found locally in northwest Villa Clara are made of natural flat limestone. The axes in our sample retain over 80 percent of the cortex. The beaks, defined by large, nonalternating notches, profusely retouched on their interior, are much more pronounced in the Malpáez specimens than in those of the Seboruco industry from Holguín (Figure 5.4).

Atypical flakes with usewear: Made of optimim-quality silex, these tools cannot be classified as typical preforms since they lack defined striking platforms and bulbs of percussion. A considerable portion of the surface is covered with cortex. The orientation of the conchoidal fractures is aberrant. Clear indications of use appear on the tools' prominent axes.

The Seboruco Industry in Northwest Villa Clara

The name Seboruco comes from Dr. Antonio Núñez's (1948) mid-twentieth-century discovery of the type site at the locality of that name in the Mayarí municipality of Holguín province. At the site were great surface concentrations of massive lithic artifacts made from coarse-grained silicates. In contrast to Tecas, which generally manifests as small concentrations of artifacts, the Seboruco deposits in northwest Villa Clara are characterized by high concentrations of raw material in its natural state and artifacts in various phases of elaboration. In addition there are habitational sites with complete artifacts of worked stone, hearth structures, and the remains of associated fauna.

Although the archaeological remains at Seboruco sites are not limited to stone tools, these are the predominant element in the archaeological record. The lithic artifacts of this industry include blade cores, flakes, and flake-blades manufactured from large quartzite blocks. The preforms are usually macroflakes and macroblades, some of the latter measuring over 30 cm in length. Also included are massive core tools, various types of blade and flake tools, basic punctiforms, and abundant debitage.

Although the earliest available date for human occupation in Cuba, from a human bone at the site of Levisa I in Holguín province, is 5140 ± 170 B.P. (calibrated 5590–6280 B.P.) (Kozlowski 1974), various authors (Domínguez et al. 2003; Febles 1990; Rey and García 1988) now believe the presence of the Seboruco industry in Cuba is owed to continental migrations arriving on the island at the end of the fourth glacial period, circa 10,000 B.P. This is possible since, during the Wisconsin Age, cold temperatures pushed waves of animals, and behind them, humans, toward the tropics, south of the periglacial boundary. On the continent, the Western Lithic Co-Tradition macroblade industry is quite similar to the Seboruco complex in Cuba and the Mordán industry in the Dominican Republic (Febles 1990; Irving 1971; MacNeish 1976; Rey and García 1988).

Although the exact origins of this industrial influence are unknown, most specialists believe that Seboruco-Mordán is not only the oldest reported stone tool technology in the Antilles, but also the only lithic industry recognized as belonging to the early pretribal tradition (Bate 1998; Febles 1990; Sampedro and Izquierdo 2001; Tabío and Rey 1979). Specifically in the Cuban case, it is assumed that the locality of Seboruco, in east-central Cuba, is the first space occupied by the makers of these tools. Upon this notion rests the premise that the appearance of Seboruco tools in other parts of the country depended on westward migration from Holguín.

Nevertheless, the distribution of Seboruco sites in northwest Villa Clara suggests the existence of additional migration routes, including direct entry via the north coast to the modern municipalities of Sagua la Grande and Caibarién in Villa Clara, as well as farther west in the province of Matanzas (Febles 1990). From the keys closest to the coast (Conuco and La Punta del Muerto) the route turned south-southwest toward the mountain range that terminates on the coastal plain, as if some of the first waves of Seborucoid population arrived directly from the continental area rather than exclusively along the route from eastern Cuba.

Once the migrants arrived in the northwest mountains and their terraces, with the available sources of high-quality silicates, the macroblade industry underwent certain changes. At Casimbas 2, right in the center of Villa Clara province, numerous Seborucoid artifacts were reported in a test pit at a depth of 30 cm. This discovery is significant for two reasons: first, for the existence of tool concentrations in preserved strata, unusual at early sites in Cuba; and second, for their interior location, since the majority of Seboruco sites are found near the coast.

The advance into the interior, to sites where high-quality materials are exposed, breaks the pattern of original or pure Seboruco, and may be explained by the existence of a southern migratory route. Recent work has determined the presence of a Seboruco corridor running along the Damují River basin from central-south Cuba, near Cienfuegos Bay, to Casimbas in Villa Clara. The Damují geological formation that coincides with this route is composed principally of biogenic calcites. Thus the advance toward the north from areas predominantly characterized by poor-quality stone might have delayed the adoption of the tool types belonging to the recognized macroindustry made with optimal varieties of chalcedony, available farther north at the Veloz formation.

Based on the archaeological surveys in the northwest Villa Clara portion of this corridor, we can infer that Seborucoid groups were few, and the lapse of time during which the techno-typological characteristics of their lithic industries remained intact was short. The relation between the technology of these primitive populations and their spatial frameworks was dynamic (Bradley 1985). Technologies and tool types were constantly modified in response to the changing nature of the economic processes required for sustenance and the degree of accessibility of the necessary resources.

In northwest Villa Clara, specifically in the zone north of Caibarién, researchers have located two Seboruco habitational sites. The first, Cueva del Puerco, was excavated by members of the Department of Archaeology of the Cuban Academy of Sciences in the 1990s (Godo et al. 1987). The second, Punta del Muerto, was excavated as part of a regional project by members of the Center for Environmental Studies and Services of Villa Clara in 2003 (Morales et al. 2004). Like other important Seboruco sites in Holguín, Matanzas, or Cienfuegos, Cueva del Puerco is a karst depression of medium proportion that contained considerable amounts of archaeological trash (Godo et al. 1987). Punta del Muerto is located on a clear area some 100,000 m^2, on the south coast of an offshore key. Surface collections contained evidence of in situ preparation of large quartzite blocks and primary preforms for cores. In addition we found numerous related artifacts—large blades with parallel borders, massive flakes similar to Clactonian tools in Europe, massive discoidal forms, and preforms for points, scrapers, and choppers. In smaller amounts we found PTE and other Tecas types. In this vicinity we dug three test pits and an equal number of transects into the trash middens; the stratigraphic richness of the occupation terminated at a depth of 45 cm.

Raw Materials

Although stone tool industries commonly substitute one material for another, in Seboruco the use of quartzites follows a rigid scheme. The selected color is soft white or beige. Chemical composition is mostly silicified carbonate with small traces of other minerals including silicon dioxide. The stone varies in hardness and texture, from very porous to quite soft. The exposure of the artifacts to the ocean atmosphere accelerated the process of patination. In no case could the quartzite be considered optimum for the confection of lithic artifacts.

Toolmaking Techniques and Tool Types

Some Seboruco cores were used to extract both blades and flakes; others were used only to obtain a few preforms. The tools were struck from bipolar and discoidal cores, similar to those of the Mousterian industry of the Middle Paleolithic in the Old World. The striking surfaces of blade cores have consecutive flake scars at least twice as long as they are wide; the controlled production of blades is the most notable characteristic of Seboruco technology.

In the Seboruco assemblages from northwest Villa Clara we noted the repeated presence of a Clactonian-like technical variation used to produce massive flakes. These were based on the preparation of striking platforms with angles ranging from 110–140 degrees. The basic forms that resulted were used to make beaked axes, choppers, and other massive artifacts. In most cases the basic blade-flake forms lack secondary modification or retouch; tool edges are sharp and demonstrate a high potential for direct attack. The edges generally present traces of immediate use.

The range of functions in Seboruco tools is ample in comparison with the small, monotonous Tecas repertory. To cutting tools, end scrapers, and side scrapers we can add perforators, burins, rabots, beaks, wedges, and others linked to the preparation of foods and the elaboration of raw materials. In addition, Tecas-type tools and debitage, made from quartzites, appear in the Seboruco assemblages.

The Regional Jibá Industry

The name Jibá comes from the 1999 discovery, during our surveys in northwest Villa Clara, of a concentration of flake-blades in the locality of that name in the municipality of Sagua la Grande. This third industry of early pretribal tradition is amply represented in the region. The most notable sites, including the type site, are all located in the northern strip of our study area, which includes the municipalities of Sagua la Grande, Quemado de Güines, and Corralillo.

In general, the industry is characterized by blades and flakes of medium dimensions, made from high-quality silicates. Most of the technological norms con-

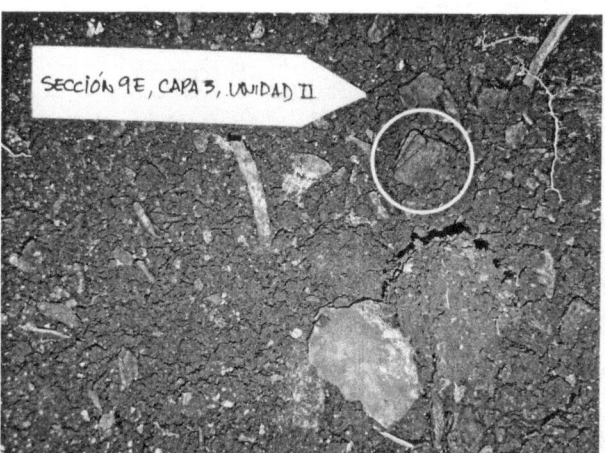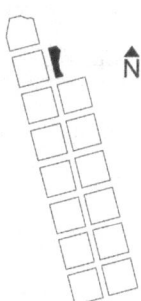

Excavación 2008
Solapa Alta, localidad El Charcón
Seccion, 9E
Capa 3 (20-30cm)
Unidad II

Figure 5.5. Molar fragment, *Megalocnus* sp., in habitational stratigraphic context at Solapa Alta.

nect to the Seboruco industry, probably as a result of evolution. Jibá tools show clear qualitative changes in terms of the selection of raw materials and the production of flakes and blades of regular, medium dimensions. The quantity of tools also stands out, since Jibá sites often have thousands of artifacts on the surface, among which over 20 percent show clear traces of immediate use.

The Jibá sites, like other early pretribal sites in northwest Villa Clara, demonstrate a spatial correlation with the wooded zone at the base of the mountain range and are most frequently located along the basins of the Manacas and Sagua la Grande rivers. Habitational sites provide important details on early pretribal lifeways. A representative case is the site called Solapa Alta, on the boundary between the municipios of Quemado de Güines and Corralillo. Solapa Alta, a rock shelter just over 50 m above sea level, is only a few meters from the Majá arroyo and the archaeological/paleontological site of Solapa de Megalocnus.

At Solapa de Alta, which we excavated in 2006 in collaboration with a team of German archaeologists from the University of Tübingen (Morales et al. 2008), we encountered numerous silex artifacts of the Jibá industry and faunal remains around hearth structures at a depth of 40 cm. In one of the excavation units (Figure 5.5) we found a molar fragment identified as *Megalocnus* sp. (giant Caribbean ground sloth). At Solapa Alta we also noted the spatial patterning of determined activities. Cores in diverse phases of exploitation and basic forms without modification were localized around the exterior edge of the excavation, while complete artifacts, faunal remains in context, and ash lenses—the remains of cooking—were situated in the northern sector, which coincides with the structural wall of the shelter.

Table 5.2 Extinct Species Found in the Karst Sinkhole at Chuchita 1

No.	Class	Order	Family	Species
1	—	Anura	Bufonidae	*Bufo cf peltacephalus*
2	Reptilia	Crocodilia	Crocodilidae	*Crocodilus rhombifer*
3	—	Rodentia	Capromyidae	*Capromys pilorides*
4	—	Pilosa	Megalonychidae	*Megalocnus rodens*
5	—	Pilosa	Megalonychidae	*Parocnus browni*
6	—	Pilosa	Megalonychidae	*Miocnus antillensis*
7	—	Pilosa	Megalonychidae	*Neocnus minor*

The flat, open site of Chuchita 1 in the municipality of Quemado de Güines, which includes a casimba with a rich deposit of Jibá tools and the skeletal remains of extinct vertebrates (Table 5.2), raises complex questions. How did these sinkholes, formed in the processes of karst dissolution, come to contain the remains of dozens of individuals belonging to Pleistocene megaspecies? And, even more interestingly, how did complete flint tools, neither broken nor rolled like natural sediment and especially made to cut and scrape, end up in the same place?

Some of the bones from these extinct animals have V-shaped cutmarks, especially on parts of the skull and the distal portions of various long bones of neonatal and juvenile specimens. We also encountered whole coprolites of various species from animals in different phases of development. These deposits probably have mixed origins; some contents probably were deposited mechanically, via flooding, from higher grounds. But many items, undamaged and evidently *in situ*, must have been deposited directly by humans (Arredondo 2005).

The explanation for this pattern is ecological. The casimbas, aligned along the mountain axis of the Alturas del Noroeste, accumulated rainwater; in the dry season they must have become sources of drinking water, heavily disputed by both human and animal groups dependent on woodland resources for subsistence. In circumstances of environmental stress humans had a clear advantage over slow-moving megafauna that were easily ambushed, especially in open, unprotected areas where they were easily spotted.

Chuchita 1, with its viable environment, was reutilized over time. To obtain stratigraphic information we dug a test pit 60 cm deep by 50 cm^2 at the center of the area with the highest concentration of archaeological materials. At the bottom of the excavation we encountered numerous Tecas artifacts. Above the Tecas stratum we extracted artifacts of hybrid appearance, with varying traits of Seboruco and Jibá. The artifacts from these well-preserved strata, along with a surface concentration spread over 200,000 m^2, make Chuchita 1 one of the most complete and complex sites of the early tradition in all of Cuba. Within its limits all of the early pretribal artifact types reported to date in northwest Villa Clara are present.

Preliminary study of the artifacts from Chuchita 1 reveals the complete cycle of stone tool production. We recorded cores, hard silex hammerstones that become cores when they break, and thick stone blocks that function as anvils or passive hammers. Preforms, debitage, and spent cores are common. On the striking platforms of some thin blades we noted traces of punctiform impact, probably evidence of some kind of indirect percussion (Piel-Desruisseaux 1989).

Raw Materials

We recorded a total of 43 Jibá sites, the most important of which are aligned with the Veloz deposit, mentioned earlier. A select range of chalcedonies from this source was used in the manufacture of Jibá tools. On certain terraces we found clear evidence of exploitation; in some cases thousands of cores and basic forms were left behind as the result of this activity. The systematic selection of certain varieties of stone over others minimized the risk of breakage.

Toolmaking Techniques

At Jibá sites we observed satisfactory preparation and moderate dimensions (5–10 cm) on 75 percent of the cores. These generally have a simple striking platform and a slightly convex striking surface with consecutive flake scars, though some cores have two opposite or independent striking planes. In both cases the striking platforms present steep angles. The backs of the cores maintain their natural cortex until they are almost used up, facilitating the toolmaker's grip. As in all of Cuba's early stone tool traditions, in Jibá the percentage of retouching is low; tool use generally is indicated by edges prepared for specific functions.

Tool Types

The use repertory of Jibá exceeds that of Tecas and Seboruco. Flake-blade cores prevail in the Jibá collections. As in Seboruco, cores similar to those of the European Levallois and Mousterian traditions also are present. In their terminal state these centripitally reduced cores resemble discs. Although polyfunctional core tools are rare, massive partial bifaces (Figure 5.6) stand out, including coup de point and lageniform types (Bordes 1965) previously unreported in Cuba and the Caribbean (Villavicencio 1995).

Among typical blade tools are regular and overshot (outrepassé) blades (Tixier 1961), sharp blades with curved backs, scrapers (some on cores), burins both simple and multiple, on blades and flakes; perforators, and retouched truncated blades. Some of the blade tools are noteworthy for excellent craftsmanship. Common flake tools include side scrapers and denticulates as well as notched and re-

Figure 5.6. Partial biface handaxe of the Jibá industry.

touched flakes. Tools with hafts or peduncles are represented by projectile points with deep flake scars on the base. The percentage of secondary modification is low; more commonly use is identified by edges designed for specific functions.

Summary and Conclusions

To reiterate, we lack absolute dates for the early stone tool industries of northwest Villa Clara; thus we are unable to determine precisely when the tools were in use or which industry came first. All we can do is indicate the presence of more or less technological complexity (Figure 5.7) among the three groups as determined via cluster analysis, conventional techno-typological analysis, and, in smaller measure, by stratigraphic association. Yet, while we cannot discount other possibilities—simpler tools may be related to alternative sources of raw materials or to circumstantial expediencies—the characteristics that determine each group coincide, in general, with concrete stages of evolution in stone tool industries across the globe.

Our identification of the Tecas industry remains controversial, in comparison with better-defined lithic industries. It consists of cobbles, atypical flakes, and amorphous fragments barely modified for use. Seboruco, long recognized in Cuba (Jiménez 1948), consists of typical massive flake-blade artifacts made on large-grained varieties of stone, principally silicified calcites. Jibá, which my colleagues

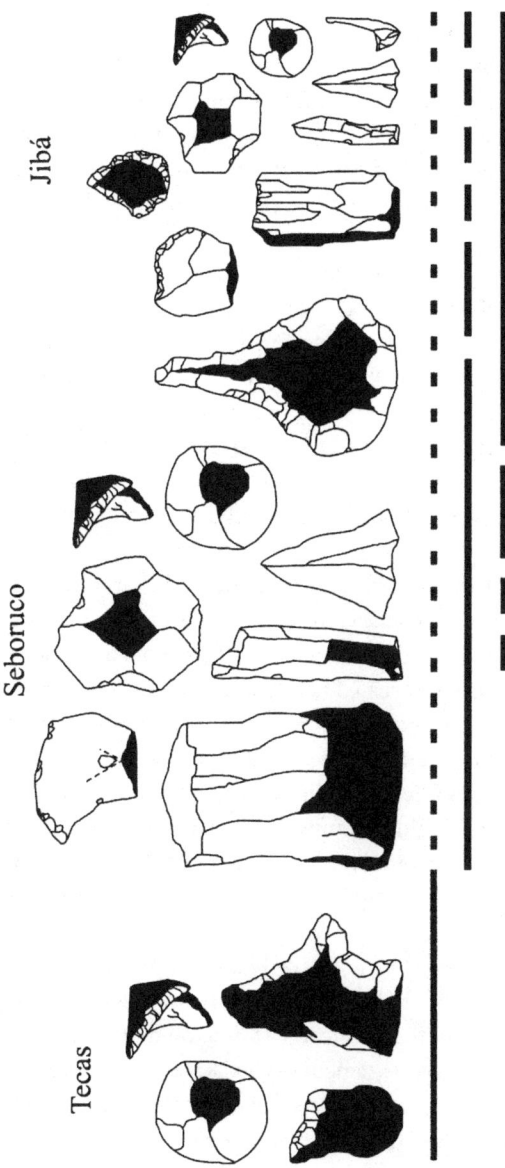

Figure 5.7. Techno-typological order of the early stone tool industries of northwest Villa Clara, based on the results of cluster analysis.

and I identify as a regional industry in northwest Villa Clara, coincides to some degree with the technological and typological norms of Seboruco, though the inventory is greater and the tools are executed on better-quality stone, an adaptation that positively affected the toolmaking cycle.

In the Tecas industry, prepared cores barely exist; instead, natural forms (cobbles or geofacts) or artificial, atypical forms were used as tools. Tecas is the most limited and least efficient of the three industries. Still, Tecas does not appear to be a variant of other early stone tool industries in Cuba, such as Seboruco. If that were the case, Tecas tools would represent a marked devolution in human strategy, since compared to Seboruco, Tecas toolmakers were far less expert and favored poorer-quality stone.

The notion that Tecas is the earliest of the industries is supported by its stratigraphic position at Chuchita 1, below levels with hybrid Seboruco-Jibá materials (Villavicencio 2000). My colleagues and I discount the idea that Tecas represents simple circumstantial expediency, since, if Tecas artifacts were not an independent industry, they should be found in contexts that include other tool types. To date, that has not occurred. In northwest Villa Clara we have registered 82 exclusively Tecas sites, although Tecas-type tools—PTE, atypical triangular flakes, and other atypical fragments—are occasionally included in Seboruco or Jibá assemblages (Morales et al. 2008).

To all indications, the arrival of the Seboruco macroblade tradition to central-north Cuba, whether from the island's northeast or directly via migrations from the continent, established a base of typical toolmaking in the region. Since some of the principal Seboruco settlements are located near the sea rather than in areas better endowed with good stone, we suspect that these locations mark the original entries of migrating groups and that Seboruco types changed drastically in a relatively short time. The scant presence of Seboruco in the region's interior biotopes leads us to think that the spatial pattern of technological change reflects (1) the stagnation of the industry due to the incompatibility of functional potential and functional requirements, and (2) the necessity to adapt existing technology and typology to new contexts.

The principal artifact type of Seboruco—the flake-blade core with a cortical back and a simple striking platform—is present without essential modifications in the third industry, Jibá. Nevertheless, for the most part Jibá toolmakers selected fine-grained chalcedonies rather than coarse-grained silicified limestone. This adaptation allowed Jibá toolmakers to diminish the violence of percussion and, accordingly, moderate the size and regularity of the basic flake-blade forms.

In Jibá we can see the synthesis of the traditional experience; my colleagues and I consider Seboruco to be this industry's direct predecessor. Among the items that link these traditions, in addition to the above-described cores, are massive flake and blade cores, blades with triangular or trapezoidal cross-sections showing evidence of use and, in some cases even retouch, knives made on flakes or blades with curved backs, notched flakes, and basic punctiforms.

Jibá is an authentic industrial product of the regional early tradition. Its typological inventory is the result of complex processes of dynamic exchange that took place among overlapping human groups and reflects the ways in which they used the spatial energetic framework in pursuit of subsistence. The three industries determined by our study, and the interaction we see among key artifact types, whether in terms of continual evolution or assimilation, are contained within a common tradition—the Early Tradition of northwest Villa Clara.

While we lack absolute dates, this common tradition evidently is associated temporally with Late Pleistocene/early Holocene conditions in which some Pleistocene megafauna were not yet extinct. The variations within the early tool tradition of northwest Villa Clara are components of an extremely complex process, extending to the early tradition across all of Cuba, in which techno-typological influences introduced via continental migrations were intermixed with internal population movements as well as autochthanous technological progress. The island's relative insularity also functioned as a determining element in these tool groups, which, although they are related to the universal experience of stone toolmaking, present significant variations from their non-Cuban counterparts along their trajectory toward efficiency.

Acknowledgments

The editors would like to thank Dr. Jeffery A. Behm of the Department of Religious Studies and Anthropology, University of Wisconsin-Oshkosh, for his careful reading of the English translation of this chapter. We deeply appreciate his help with early stone tool terminology.

Note

1. In Cuba, Paleolithic-type traditions are variously called proto-Archaic, pre-agroceramic, or Paleolithic. Most recently, Luis F. Bate (1998) has used the term *apropiadores pretribales,* which translates roughly as human groups with pretribal adaptations. The notion of "pretribal" overcomes some of the limitations of terms like "Paleolithic" or "Paleoindian," but is somewhat too broad to succinctly describe the makers of the early stone tools analyzed in this chapter, since it also can include proto-agricultural groups. Thus I follow Bate's current Cuban terminology, modifying the designation to "early pretribal" so that it clearly refers to the makers of the Paleolithic-like tools.

6
Investigations at Laguna de Limones
Suggestions for a Change in the Theoretical Direction of Cuban Archaeology

Daniel Torres Etayo, National Center for Conservation,
Restoration and Museology (CENCREM), La Habana, Cuba

The site of Laguna de Limones, at the far eastern end of Cuba, is located among a group of Cuba's most important archaeological sites. The presence of a ceremonial plaza of great dimensions and various adjacent settlements makes this site an ideal location for testing a new theoretical focus related to hierarchical organization within the tribal socioeconomic model. In this article I offer a critical evaluation of the theoretical and methodological approaches employed in Cuban archaeology to explain the phenomenon of social complexity, based on empirical evidence from fieldwork I carried out at Laguna de Limones beginning in the year 2000.

> El sitio arqueológico de Laguna de Limones, en el extremo oriental de Cuba, se ubica dentro de un conglomerado de sitios arqueológicos de los más importantes del país. La presencia de una plaza ceremonial de grandes dimensiones y de varios sitios adyacentes hace de este lugar un lugar adecuado para proponer nuevos enfoques teóricos relacionados con la aparición de formas jerárquicas dentro de la Formación Económico Social Tribal. En el artículo hago un análisis crítico de las perspectivas teóricas y metodológicas empleadas en la arqueología cubana al respecto de los fenómenos de la complejización social basado en los estudios de campo llevados a cabo en Laguna de Limones a partir del año 2000.

Without doubt, one of the great anthropological debates of recent decades has concerned the development and identification of nonegalitarian societies, in which inequality is instituted by various means and elites become separated from the communities. Such societies go by various names. In the Antilles they are "cacicazgos" (Curet and Oliver 1998; Drennan and Uribe 1987; Veloz 1991); in English they often are classed as "chiefdoms," and sometimes as "middle range societies." Studies on the development of social complexity and the origins of inequality, however, have been largely overlooked in Cuban archaeology. With rare exceptions (Cabrera 1978; Moreira 2003; Valcárcel 2002), the theme has barely been touched; thus it has not been incorporated into institutional programs of investigation. In general, Cuban archaeologists have stayed on the edges of the great theoretical discussions generated around this theme in the Caribbean region. In this article I address the theoretical limitations of Cuban investigations concerning the debate over "middle-range societies." I then discuss my investigations at Laguna de Limones, Maisí, in the eastern extreme of Cuba (Figure 6.1), as a point of departure for including this case in the ample international dialogue.

Although clear indicators of societies at the cacicazgo or chiefly level exist in Cuba, the debate over how these are organized has yet to be recognized on the island. My analysis of this problem starts with the concept of historical materialism that supposedly has framed the works of Cuban archaeologists since the triumph of the Revolution in 1959. Nevertheless I establish an important separation, since within the context of historical materialism my analysis takes into consideration the theoretical formulas of Latin American Social Archaeology (Arqueología Social Latinoamericana or ASL), which are not shared by the majority of my colleagues in Cuba.[1]

In Marxist epistemology, the metaphysical priority is logic (Bate 1998; Gándara 1992). In other words, scientific knowledge demands that we must first have an idea of what we want to know in order to develop valid procedures for observation, discovery, or recognition. This view of the general process of archaeological investigation involves three levels, which constitute the solution to three fundamental problems: (1) historical materialism, or the theory of sociohistorical processes; (2) the history of the archaeological contexts under consideration; and (3) the history of the production of the relevant information (Bate 1998:49).

It would be impossible to carry out a full analysis of the performance of these three levels of knowledge in Cuban archaeology in a brief article, and that is not my objective. Instead I limit myself to demonstrating some of the fundamental theoretical propositions and methodological problems over which I have stumbled in the process of studying the development of inequality in eastern Cuba, on the basis of my investigation at Laguna de Limones.

The Theoretical and Methodological Framework

Since historical materialism has been the fundamental theoretical basis for archaeological investigations in Cuba since 1959, it is worth considering how this framework has been used, and what its consequences are. What the literature reveals is that our investigators, until now, have not been very dedicated to theoretically substantive questions; instead they have been consumers of a packaged theory—Marxism, in its least flexible version (Torres 2004). Even so, the great explanatory power of Marxism served as an alternative path to understanding the social processes that occurred in pre-Columbian Cuba.

In the 1960s, the number of archaeological investigations on the island began

Figure 6.1. Regional location of Laguna de Limones (#1), San Lucas (#2), and Pueblo Viejo (#3).

to increase as never before. The science accrued resources and specialized personnel. But an obstacle much greater than the material limitations common in Cuba put brakes on the scientific development of archaeology. The Marxist theory researchers employed was considered harmonic, unshakeable, and complete.[2] Thus Marxism was deprived of its essential dialectical character, and as such, its path was truncated. Theoretical advance in Cuban archaeology was notable, but insufficient.

In addition, the Marxist social theory of the 1960s failed to pay sufficient attention to the empirical objectives of archaeologists; thus the character of the framework they employed was too general to get at specific explanations of the material record.[3] Cuban archaeologists were limited to identifying "mode of production," "socioeconomic formation," "productive forces," "relations of production," and other traditionally Marxist categories. This meant that theory was almost unnecessary, since from this particular point of view all pre-Columbian societies were framed in a single mode of production, the "primitive community."[4]

In consequence, archaeologists had scant interest in developing theoretically based investigations, instead concentrating on aspects of practice and methodology. This brought Cuban archaeology very close to the culture history paradigm that was fundamentally designed to establish chronologies and particular histories, with the understanding that Cuba constituted an isolated case. In general, the results of this practice were investigations with little coherence, translated into the general Marxist idiom. These works fit very well into the empirical-historicist framework, in which, after a very general theoretical introduction, the recovered artifacts were extensively described without going beyond the empirical realm.

This problem is clearly visible in the studies dedicated to explaining the development of social complexity in Cuba. In terms of the so-called cacicazgos, since investigators were unfamiliar with adequate theoretical frameworks, they preferred to turn to other disciplines, especially historical ethnography. The ethnographic record in Cuba effectively negates the existence of social complexity in aboriginal communities. Thus the archaeological path to accurate explanations of past societies is closed. Nevertheless, for over two decades the theoretical developments of ASL have allowed researchers outside of Cuba to move knowledge of middle-range societies forward. The three-dimensional relationship among culture, lifeways, and economic formation at the root of this approach (Bate 1998; Sarmiento 1992; Vargas 1990) is a very effective analytical instrument for confronting the processes of developing social complexity.

From the perspective of Marxist explanation, societies belonging to the tribal socioeconomic formation had attained rational control over the natural means of production by dominating the reproductive cycles of vegetable and animal species. This advance required a change in the structure of social production, since to guarantee the continuation of the society it was necessary to secure ownership of the fundamental means of production—the earth. In this sense the tribal revolution caused the idea of property, although maintained collectively, to emerge. The collective community exercised ownership of the land as a means of distinction and defense against other communities. The appropriation of nature is, then, not only a consequence of production but also a condition in and of itself (Bate 1998:86).

Another characteristic of the establishment of collective property is that it requires demographic growth as a means to guarantee an increase in the average productivity of work. At the same time, increase in population necessitates the creation of intercommunal parentage links that take the form of familial relations, which often span extensive territories. These tribal relations then are a mechanism that regulates the productive forces at the regional level, transforming the social relations of production. The maintenance of these parental relations at the level of social consciousness constitutes one of the essential features of the superstructure that maintains social cohesion through symbolism in cultural manifestations such as mythology, religious cults, and artistic expression.

Tribal societies also acquire forms in accord with the magnitude of development in their productive forces and the particularities of their lifeways. In general, these societies have two developmental phases—the communal or nonhierarchical phase and the chiefly hierarchical phase. The aboriginal tribal communities of Cuba mostly fall into the first phase, but some of them underwent intense processes of differentiation under the social formations we call cacicazgos (or chiefdoms).

Archaeologists in the Antilles have accepted the identification of the first levels of hierarchical tribal communities in the Ostionoid societies of Hispaniola dating to A.D. 1200 (Veloz 1991). Nevertheless, traditional understanding in Cuba is that indigenous society did not develop sufficient complexity to attain the kind of cacicazgos reported by the European conquistadors in Hispaniola or Puerto Rico. Perhaps the reason is that the concept of social complexity that we have been using, formalized as the category of cacicazgo or chiefdom, is rooted in a mix of different social theories that often are not compatible[5] (Domínguez 1991; Moreira 2003; Valcárcel 2002).

For me the transitional nature of the cacicazgo makes its definition much more complicated than the way it is traditionally understood. In the cacicazgo the contradictions implicit in tribal organization—that is, the collective participation in decision-making about the regulation of the fundamental elements of the productive process, given the collective ownership of the natural objects of production and the existence of increasingly complex hierarchical structures that administrate the distribution of those resources and the labor force—are sharpened. Further, outside the tribe, the equilibrium of intercommunal relations in the territory is maintained through an adequate system of exchange and a collective capacity for defense; yet that capacity can be surpassed by stronger communities with better internal organization (Bate 1998:88).

Venezuelan archaeologist Iraida Vargas describes the process as it applies to the Caribbean:

> [I]inter-village relations become truly political. The specialization of social labor, in several or in one of the settlements, dissolves intra-village parental links (except in the domestic units) and replaces them with political ties and with rank among the distinct lineages of the settlement, which leads to the appearance of a locality dominant in the political, the religious, and the economic. The relations of inter- and intra-village reciprocity, within the tribal territory, become relations of subordination, which are expressed via tribute rendered to the principal location and to the principal cacique or chief, who may also be the military chief, or priest, or political boss within a "class" of subordinate chiefs who carry out similar functions in their respective localities. (Vargas 1990:113)

An important consequence of this process is the appearance of specialized producers, not only in the manufacture of symbolic goods for elites, but also in the management of time for production and other classes of services. Exchange networks for exotic raw materials destined for artisanal products that legitimate the status of certain lineages are fortified. And as a reflection of these processes of social differentiation, an ideological superstructure develops, with rituals and traditions that legitimize or justify the perpetuation of elite power. It is in this phase that the first mechanisms of social exploitation emerge, facilitating the development of social classes.

In sum, from a theoretical perspective we can say that evidence of the chiefdom phenomenon includes regions of relatively high population density in which inhabitants share a series of cultural traits, with a spatial political structure experienced socially among the inhabitants of one or several villages, among which the political structure breaks the traditional tribal rules of reciprocity and establishes political ties instead. In these settlements there should be concentrations of sumptuary goods, and together with public works not present in the rest of the region these serve as archaeological indicators of the process of social complexity.

Some Methodological Problems

As noted above, the methods of study for the aboriginal archaeological sites of Cuba, especially since the 1990s, with rare exceptions, have been governed by a concept much like that of culture history. Although this statement may seem too grandiose to my colleagues, an analysis of the literature and of the protocols of investigation (when available) reveals this reality (Torres 2004). The traditional procedure has been the selection of middens, followed by the excavation of units of varying size, and then the processing and analysis of the evidence, to arrive at least at a description of the society under study. In this methodology, test pits constitute windows through which we enter a past reality of much greater dimensions. In this scheme we are looking at the society at hand exclusively through its trash; therefore, we understand that the refuse, independently of the excavation units, and whether the excavated contexts are primary or secondary, is our direct window on the past.

Yet many serious ethnoarchaeological studies provide evidence indicating that we should consider archaeological refuse with great caution. Above all, these studies make it clear that the refuse itself is not a direct reserve of information about the society; instead the data are skewed by processes of site formation and transformation (Hayden and Cannon 1983). Trash middens do not contain the whole of society; the act of disposing of refuse is conditioned by diverse criteria including reuse and varying conceptions of hygiene among domestic units. We cannot produce secure knowledge from such a unit of observation without understanding its problematic and limited nature. The practice of excavating trash middens can offer information on chronology, subsistence economy, imported materials, and sometimes social interactions, but it cannot provide data on fundamental aspects of social conditions or social structure (Curet 2004).

Further, we must understand trash middens as just one part of a site; the central question is how to arrive at a correlation between them and the other elements of the site, which involves different concepts, based on the investigation of elements or features via careful, extensive methods that provide data on (1) the organization of space; (2) the configuration and layout of the houses and other structures; (3) population density; (4) technological level; (5) social organization and symbolism, and (6) the determination of activity areas (Versteeg and Schinkel 1992).

This set of problems leads us, finally, to an epistemological issue—the distinction between units of analysis and units of observation. As Curet (2004) points out, these two concepts are not always considered in research designs, or at least, our units of analysis are usually much larger (for example, communities or societies) than our units of observation, which comprise much more limited spatiotemporal dimensions (i.e., the test pit, trench, or artifact). The proper correspondence between both dimensions should be indispensable in the social science of archaeology.

One final issue can be attributed to factors external to the discipline, and that is the lack of available tools and resources for investigations. Many projects suffer from a shortage of instruments for registering and analyzing archaeological remains, both in the field and in the laboratory. This problem diminishes the potential amount of information we can recover from archaeological materials. A dramatic example is the chronological definition of an entire cultural region[6]—the "Taíno" area of the island—which is based exclusively on a single radiocarbon date (1300 B.P. ± 120) from the site of Laguna de Limones (Tabío and Rey 1979:211), despite the fact that in total, over 300 sites have been classified as belonging to this group.

My colleagues and I believe that the biggest problem underlying most of the issues laid out above is theoretical, and that what is needed is a new, more theoretically informed approach to research designs. Toward this end we have proposed that the multidimensional perspectives of ASL be introduced in the framework for the "Study of the Aboriginal Ceremonial Plazas of the Eastern Extreme of Cuba," under the auspices of the Investigative Project of the National Center for Conservation, Restoration and Museology and the Provincial Center for the Patrimony of Guantánamo. Unfortunately, to date the state of our investigation, which I discuss below, does not allow us to reach strong conclusions; nevertheless we have tried to make the work we have carried out to date serve as food for thought.

The Site of Laguna de Limones in Regional Perspective

The extreme eastern end of Cuba constitutes one of the most important archaeological zones in the country. The exceptional geographic characteristics that come together in this area, as well as the different aboriginal communities that occupied it, make it crucial for understanding the pre-Columbian Cuban world in particular, and the Antilles in general. The curving chain of islands in the "arc of the Antilles" is abruptly interrupted by the tilt of western Cuba, but the extreme eastern tip of the island maintains visual contact with the northwestern end of the Republic of Haiti. The implications of this geographic position for aboriginal migrations are evident, and they are corroborated by the *Cronistas de Indias* (Las Casas 1951:II:507), as well as by numerous archaeological investigations (Guarch 1978:127-131).

Thus it is not surprising that Maisí was a zone of substantial population density at the time of European arrival in American lands. In a preliminary study (Torres et al. 2001) carried out to evaluate the archaeological patrimony of the municipality, we registered the existence of more than 90 sites. Among them, 29 (32 percent) were habitation sites; 22 (24 percent) were funerary sites.

To this evidence of relative population density we can add the existence of public works of large dimensions, including ceremonial plazas. Only three ceremonial plazas have been recognized in Cuba to date, at the sites of Pueblo Viejo, Monte Cristo, and Laguna de Limones (Pichardo 1990; Tabío and Rey 1979). Pueblo Viejo was reported in 1847 by the Spaniard Miguel Rodríguez (1876); the other two were recognized in 1919 by the North American archaeologist Mark R. Harrington (1935). Another site, baptized by Harrington as the "Great Wall of San Lucas," is not considered to be a plaza, but has similar characteristics. Among all four, the best preserved is Laguna de Limones.

All of these sites are located in Cuba's "Taíno zone" (Guarch 1978), within the present municipality of Maisí, in the province of Guantánamo. This exclusive location is an excellent indicator of a regional structure of political relations, since the sites with ceremonial plazas probably were centers for the others that are smaller and do not possess such features. We tentatively assume synchronocity among these sites on the basis of recovered artifacts, although we lack radiocarbon dates.

Previous Work at Laguna de Limones

This important archaeological site is located on a second level of emerged marine terraces, about 3 km southwest of the lighthouse at Punta de Maisí and 600 m south of the road that links the seat of municipal government (La Máquina) with the village of Maisí. North of the site at approximately 800 m is the gulch of the River Maya. The site is named for a lagoon located 100 m east of the plaza, which, until the 1960s, was blessed with permanent water flow. After this date, an attempt to enlarge the basin broke through its sealed bottom, channeling the flow underground.

When Harrington visited the site in 1919, guided by campesinos from the area, he explored, dug a few pits, and made a topographic map of the site, this last with evident errors of location but very good graphic representation. The existence of middens was not what he found most interesting—instead, he wrote:

> This place is especially notable for its roughly rectangular earthwork, an enclosure whose embankment, although rarely more than 2 or 3 ft. high and 14 ft. wide, can still be traced plainly in all its parts, and whose age is suggested by large trees growing upon its crest, such as the mahogany *(cayoban)* . . . This structure measures 502 ft. long and approximately 260 ft. wide, the longest axis NNW and SSE, and the entrance at the southeastern corner . . . The wall is usually higher on the outside than on the inside, showing that the earth for its erection came largely from without. It was probably a ceremonial dance ground and ball court, like those of Haiti and Puerto Rico . . . Test holes within the enclosure revealed a small quantity of village refuse, such as potsherds, shells, etc. (Harrington 1935:216–217)

After Harrington's visit the site was abandoned by science and at the mercy of waves of furtive looters who practically destroyed the middens, but luckily barely touched the plaza. Researchers did not return until 1964, when personnel from the Department of Archaeology of the old Cuban Academy of Sciences, directed by

Ernesto Tabío, began the first systematic excavations at the site. They made a new map that corrected the deficiencies in Harrington's work, especially in reference to the location of the lagoon.

Tabío and his crew defined an area of habitation composed of nine mounds—three more than Harrington reported. These were excavated almost entirely, despite the enormous problems presented by the surface that had been extremely damaged by looters. The investigation of the ceremonial plaza returned the following results:

> One search . . . was archaeologically sterile, the scarce fragments we were able to collect were dispersed, very close to the surface. The rectangular test pit measuring 1 m x .5 m x .4 m deep produced no archaeological evidence; we were able to appreciate that the material of the enclosure is a gravelly earth, very similar to the yellow clay that constitutes the sterile soil at the bottom of the excavated trenches in the eastern sector of the site. We also observed that the external part of the earthen enclosure in general is lower and less inclined than the internal part, as if the construction had been affected accumulating fill, from the interior to the exterior. (Guarch 1972:34)

Because of an observation offered by the campesino Abigail Lores, who lived there, Guarch advanced a hypothesis that linked the ceremonial plaza to the lagoon:

> If the observation made by Abigail Lores over the years has been correct and the impression in the earth that he showed us was made by the torrent that forms in the rainy season, it is undoubtable that the lagoon receives a good supply of water, in little time, at the expense of the earthen enclosure. . . . Even though this may be simple speculation that goes too far . . . we believe it opportune to indicate, by way of hypothesis, the possibility that one of the functions of the earthen enclosure was to supply water to the lagoon, and, therefore, it had to be constructed in a convenient and pertinent place for this to happen. From this a primitive hydraulic works would result, the first of which we have knowledge in the Antilles. (Guarch 1972:36)

The projects carried out by the Department of Archaeology of the Cuban Academy of Sciences during the 1960s and 1970s were the largest of the epoch; nevertheless, also in the 1960s, the University of Oriente and the Montané Museum of the School of Biology at the University of Havana also sponsored work at the site. Small excavations in the mound zone turned up the burial of an adult female whose deformed skull was covered with a clay pot (Dacal, personal communication 1998).

One of the principal fruits of these works was a preliminary plan for the restoration of the site, designed by the archaeologist Ramón Dacal, whose objective (1971) was "the restoration of the archaeological site of Laguna de Limones, converting it into a place of study for the universities of Havana and Oriente." This ambitious project was never executed; on the contrary, the site was subjected to strong anthropic impact, which is made clear in a report presented by Dacal to the then-president of the National Commission of Monuments, Dr. Antonio Núnez, on April 8, 1980: "In the preparation of lands for pasture in 1979, a machine passed over the mounds to level the earth, causing the destruction of the archaeological remains. At the end of the leveled zone they mounded the removed archaeological rubble, along with the brush that covered it.... The enclosure was saved by the negotiations of the campesino Abigail Lores.... Nevertheless, they passed the equipment all along the exterior edge of the walls, in this manner all of the terrain from this point on was cleared of brush. The internal area of the enclosure was not touched; its vegetation remains" (Dacal 1980).

The above-cited document was accompanied by a sketch of the site made by Dacal, which contributes new data. A total of 13 mounds appears on this map, 4 more than reported by Tabío and Guarch. Also indicated are the areas damaged by machines when the soil was cleared. After 1980, the only information we have comes from the expedition of the Department Central-East of the Center for Archaeology of the Ministry of Sciences, Technology and Environment (CITMA) in 1989, during which a new topographic map was made.

New Investigations at Laguna de Limones

Methodology

In the year 2000 I proposed a new investigation at the site. The project was designed in two principal phases. The first consisted of creating high-quality, high-resolution topographic maps using techniques of microtopography that combine field measurements with cartographic computer programs. The end results included various types of maps that allowed the visualization of the different structures that make up the total site. Thus the three component areas of the site—the plaza, the habitation area, and the laguna—were delineated with precision (Figure 6.2).

The second phase of the project was aimed at resolving more specific problems, with an eye toward preparing for future, more ample excavations. I set out to better understand the stratigraphy of the habitation area; to identify possible house remains in the area between the mounds; to recover paleoenvironmental information; and to locate any related sites within a 2-km radius.

The fieldwork for this project was carried out in January 2005. The first step was

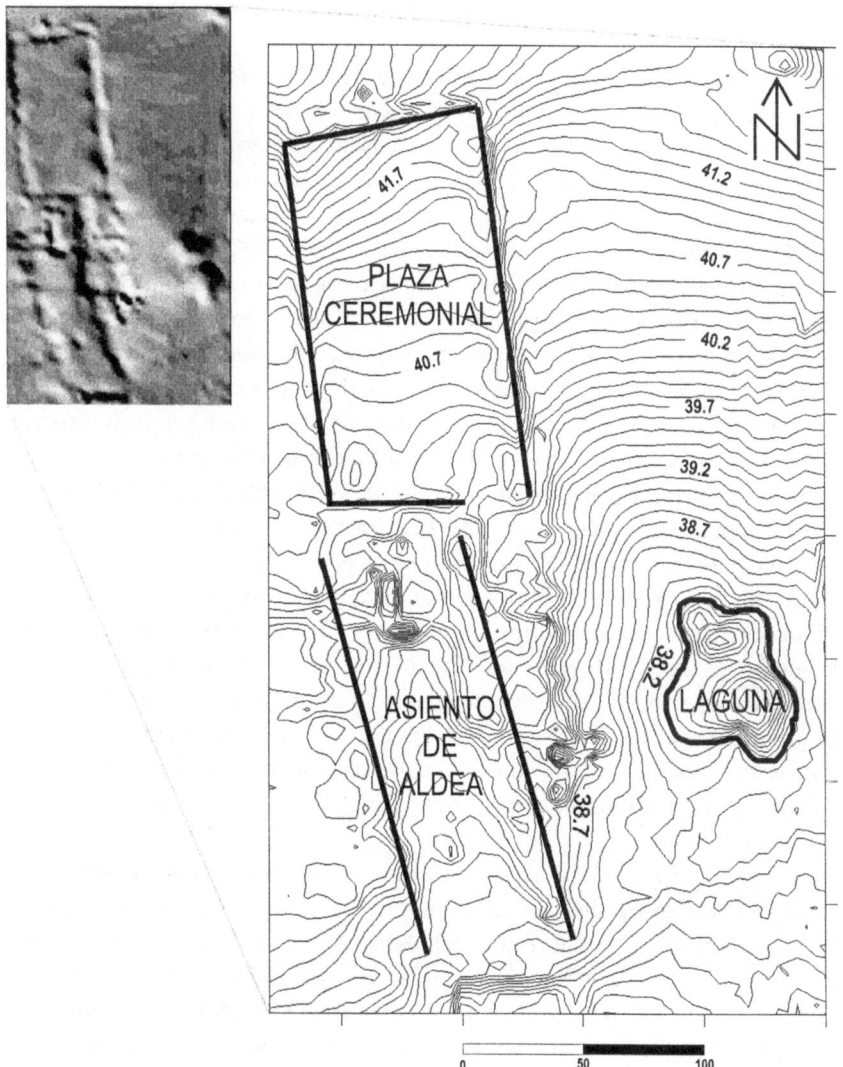

Figure 6.2. Principal structural components of Laguna de Limones, with topographic details. In the upper left, the site in shadow relief. Cartography by the author.

a geochemical prospecting survey for phosphate contamination, following the Eidt procedure (1973), which guided the identification of excavation areas. Next, in an effort to identify any structures or features hidden beneath the topsoil, I shovel-scraped an extensive area divided into 5-x-5-m units, removing the soil in successive 5-cm levels. The total tested surface measured 119.5 m^2; the volume of soil removed was 15.31 m^3.

Preliminary Results

The ceremonial plaza. The new map reveals that the plaza is trapezoidal rather than rectangular. Its longest axis on the median plane is visibly oriented NNW (353 degrees). Its longest side along this axis measures 169 m; the shorter side measures 156 m. On the short axis the longer side is 87 m; the shorter side only 69 m. If we compare these dimensions with those reported by Guarch (142 m x 76 m), we see that the enclosure is larger than previously reported. The total area enclosed, measured from the base of the interior walls, measures 13,834.3 m^2. The walls, although their median height (on the exterior) is .45 m, are not uniform; instead, some parts are so low—especially in the northwest and southwest segments—that they almost disappear. In the southeast corner, the wall is missing entirely.

A test of Guarch's (1972) hypothesis that the plaza was a primitive hydraulic works proved especially interesting. In addition to the topographic map I made vectorial maps of the plaza and of the entire area (Figure 6.3). These vectorial maps provide a model of surface water flow that conclusively points to the lagoon as a catchment for rain runoff in large adjacent areas.

The surface of the enclosure is insignificant as far as the volume of water it could contribute. Further, within the enclosure the terrain slopes from northwest to southeast, exactly where the aperture in the wall is located and directly in line with the lagoon. In my opinion the opening was made in pre-Columbian times to prevent the stagnation of rainwater on the surface of this public space. Since the enclosed space is not a hydraulic feature after all, I conclude, at least preliminarily, that its identification as a ceremonial plaza, originally made by Harrington, is correct.

The habitation area. This area is located in the southern portion of the site and is defined by two parallel midden accumulations, oriented along approximately the same NNW axis as the ceremonial plaza. On my topographic maps the middens did not appear as individual forms, as reported by Harrington (1935), Tabío and Rey (1979), Guarch (1978), and Dacal (1980); instead, they are continuous. This presentation is more realistic than the descriptions in earlier reports; similar configurations are reported (Guarch 1978) for pre-Columbian occupations elsewhere in the "Taíno" region of Cuba.

The western line of middens is approximately 182 m long by 22 m wide, beginning at the extreme southwest corner of the ceremonial plaza. The other line, situated 40 m east, measures 200 m in length by 20 m in width. The space between the lines appears to have been leveled. In total, the known habitation area covers an area about 200 m x 100 m (20,000 m^2). Future explorations may reveal that it originally was larger, since parts of the terrain are still covered in brush. Additional areas of habitation probably exist; geochemical prospecting in a small area southeast of the ceremonial center provided evidence of phosphate contamination.

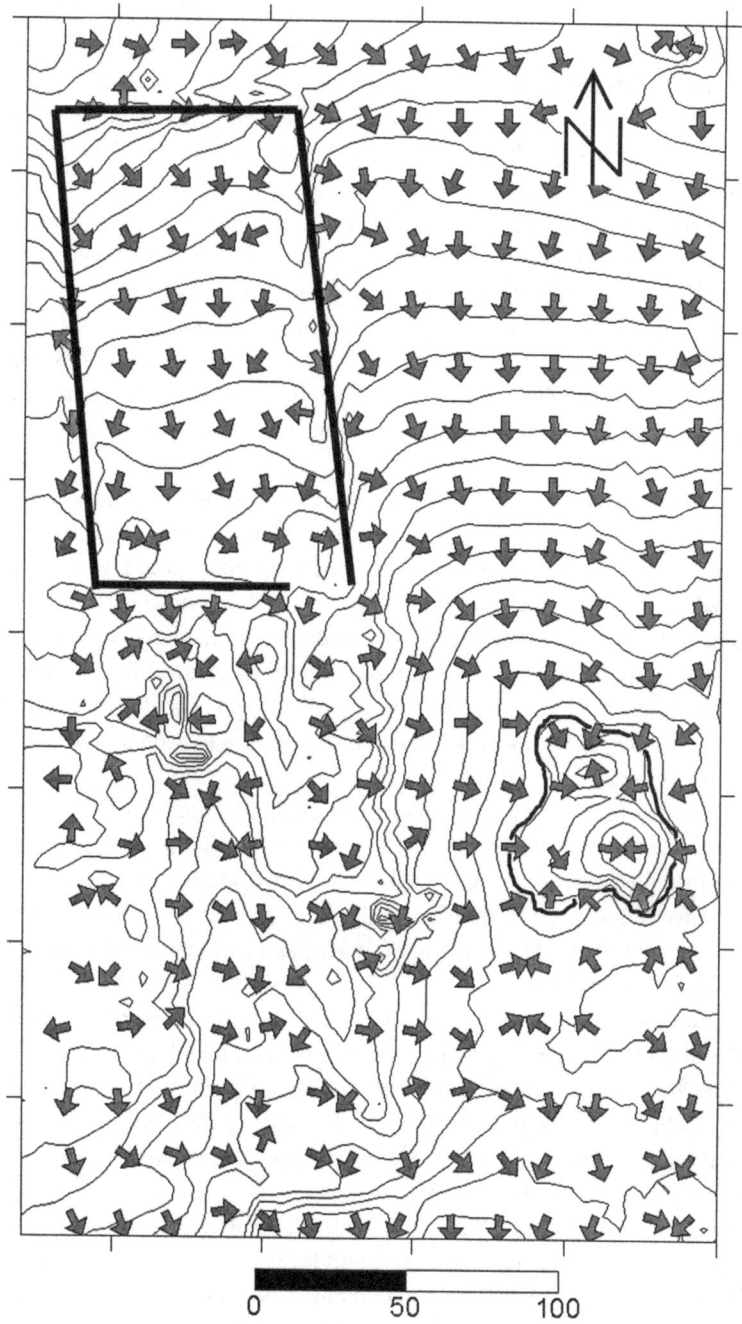

Figure 6.3. Vectoral map showing the direction of rainwater flow. Cartography by the author.

Excavations in the zone between the middens revealed the existence of a cream-colored strata at a depth of .35 m, which would be easily distinguishable from the darker post molds left from houses, if these were present. In one of the excavation units I found the remains of a possible post; the wood was identified as jaragua (*Acrosynanthus trachyphyllus*), notable for its great resistance.[7] Ten undecorated ceramic sherds, a fragment of a petaloid axe, and two discoidal hammerstones are the only additional evidence recovered. Otherwise, the area between the middens was marked by the absence of dietary remains, worked stone, and other artifacts.

The absence of artifacts supports the hypothesis that this zone of the site contained communal houses, since early documentary references (e.g., Las Casas 1951: I:214, 222) mention that aboriginal houses were swept constantly. Thus high concentrations of archaeological materials probably would not be associated with dwellings, although future vertical excavations will provide more concrete information.

Excavation in Mound No. 3. This intervention was aimed at collecting information about the stratigraphy of the mound itself and its relationship to the general stratigraphy at the site, as well as at recovering information on the resources exploited by this aboriginal community. The excavation unit consisted of a trench composed of two 1-x-1-m squares; its long side was oriented east/west, cut into the side of the mound. Since the site was violently altered by machinery at the end of the 1970s, I decided to excavate in .10-m levels. Despite the destruction, this excavation produced both information on stratigraphic variation and an exhaustive collection of data.

From the surface came a great quantity of ceramic sherds of the Chican Ostionoid subseries (Rouse 1992:107) characteristic of the Taíno phase in Cuba. Remains of mollusks and very weathered bones were dispersed in no apparent functional order. These dietary remains (Table 6.1) provide evidence that the site's inhabitants exploited a diverse range of marine and land resources, although crustaceans were predominant.

Explorations in perimetral zones. Within a 1-km radius of the site I located six additional middens, some of which may be the remains of production areas for working shell, lithics, or other materials. In one of these middens I found artifacts including a double microbead of shell and an unfinished idol of the same material—apparently of the sea snail species *Terebra taurinum*,[8] although it was too deteriorated to identify with certainty.

Two more agro-ceramic phase sites, evidently habitational in nature, were not excavated. One, Limones II, is extensive and located 750 m northwest of Laguna de Limones. The other, Limones III, 800 m north, is composed of low middens impossible to determine clearly due to heavy destruction during clearing for agricultural purposes.

Table 6.1 Faunal Remains Identified at Laguna de Limones

Taxon	Species	Common Name
Land crustaceans	*Gecarcinus ruricola* Linn.	Red crab
	Cardisoma guanhumi Latreille	Blue crab
Marine crustaceans	*Callinectes sapidus* Rathbun	Blue crab
Univalve marine mollusks	*Strombus gigas* Linn.	Sea snail
	Cittarium pica (Linn.)	Sea snail
	Tectarius muricatus (Linn.)	
	Nerita peloronta Linn.	
	Nerita versicolor (Gmelin)	
	Astraea caelata (Gmelin)	
	Terebra taurinum (Sol.)	Flame auger
	[partially finished artifact]	
Bivalve marine mollusks	*Codakia orbicularis* (Linn.)	
	Tellina radiata Linn.	
Amphineura	*Chiton marmoratus* Gmelin	Scaled-girdle chiton
Univalve land mollusks	*Caracolus sagemon* Beck	
	Polymita picta	
	Polydontes imperator Montfort	
	Emoda sp.	
	Cerion sp.	
Marine fish	*Balistes vetula* Linn.	Pig fish
	Epinephelus striatus (Bloch)	Bass
	Lutianus cyanopterus (Cuvier)	Cubera snapper
	Lutianus analis (Cuvier)	Red snapper
Rodents	*Capromys pilorides* (Say)	Conga rat (jutía)
	Capromys melanurus Poey	Andaráz rat (jutía)
	Eteropsomys offella (Miller)	(extinct species)
Reptiles	*Cyclura nubila nubila* (Gray)	Iguana

Conclusions

The application of new theoretical and methodological approaches in the investigation of Laguna de Limones yields very interesting conclusions. From the regional perspective I observe that in this corner of Cuba, the substantial aboriginal population represented in the concentration of archaeological sites was organized in a way that corresponds perfectly to the hierarchical phase of tribal socioeconomic formation (Bate 1998), in which some sites stand out because they have large-scale public works that the other sites lack. Although I do not have radiocarbon dates with which to examine the process of hierarchal formation through a diachronic lens, the unity of cultural material at the sites in my study seems to confirm a synchronic occupation prior to the arrival of the Europeans.

By conceptualizing in this way the archaeological remains of the Maisí region, my investigation moves the debate forward in a way that previous research in Cuba could not, even in cases of heroic efforts such as those of Guarch (1978). Laguna de Limones, one of various large sites in the "Taíno zone" of the Maisí district (see Figure 6.1), provides a small-scale panorama of a broader regional phenomenon.

The presence of a hydraulic feature at the site also would have been evidence of increasing social complexity, in terms of growth in the average productivity of work or of the development of a storage system for the vital liquid. Nevertheless, the study I carried out demonstrated that there is no solid basis for attributing hydraulic characteristics to the large public feature at Laguna de Limones. The topographic models demonstrate that a hydraulic system of this type would not have been necessary for the capture of rainwater, since the entire area constitutes a catchment of greater dimensions. The opening at the southeast corner of the plaza coincides with the downslope of the terrain and must have served as an aboriginal solution for channeling rainwater out of the ceremonial area.

Social complexity at Laguna de Limones is visible through this act of engineering and also through other kinds of evidence. First, I want to highlight the dimensions of the ceremonial plaza, within the context of the archaeological patrimony of the Antilles. In agreement with Alegría (1983:151), the ceremonial plazas of Pueblo Viejo and Laguna de Limones have been recognized as the largest rectangular constructions in the Caribbean islands, if considered individually (though some sites present more than one plaza, and thus have more space devoted to such features).

By way of comparison with the rest of the ceremonial plazas known in the Greater Antilles, it is important to note a distinctive characteristic of Cuban ceremonial plazas—the construction material, since they are made of tamped earth, while in the rest of the Antilles they generally were built of vertically laid stone slabs.[9] The two largest examples in the Dominican Republic, at the sites of Padre Las Casas and Palero, measure 110 m x 40 m and 92 m x 35 m, respectively (Alegría 1983). In Puerto Rico, the largest plazas are at Sabana and Palo Hincado, measuring 90 m x 45 m and 72 m x 57 m, respectively (Alegría 1983). The dimensions of the plaza at Laguna de Limones are approximately 169 m x 87 m. Thus among the ceremonial plazas of the Antilles, only the one at Pueblo Viejo, measuring 250 m x 135 m, is larger (Alegría 1983).

It is no longer possible to deny the magnitude of the plaza at Laguna de Limones, the way Tabío and Rey (1979:202) did when the wrote "the Cuban examples are limited to simple earthen enclosures that can barely compare with the stone structures typical of the other Major Antilles." The evidence is conclusive in that respect and we must begin to consider the considerable quantities of time and labor invested in works of this sort—another characteristic of the hierarchical phases of tribal socioeconomic formation (Bate 1998; Sarmiento 1992) I employed as a theoretical model.

In addition, the general placement of the middens, in the form of two large parallel lines, seem to corroborate Guarch's (1978) observation that the houses of these villages followed a lineal orientation. Nevertheless, this detail may be one of several that differentiate Laguna de Limones from the smaller habitational sites in its immediate periphery, since at Limones II and III, the distribution of the middens is circular. Further, if we can assume that the smaller sites are contemporaneous, we clearly have direct evidence of a territorial configuration that fits the model of the initial stage of a cacicazgo, since the presence of the ceremonial plaza confers local preeminence on Laguna de Limones. If Pueblo Viejo and San Lucas also are shown to be contemporary, the pre-Columbian sociopolitical organization of the far eastern extreme of Cuba may even have reached a higher stage of cacicazgo formation.

Future investigations will amplify this picture. Further, more work at Laguna de Limones proper will help determine the significance of the elevated concentrations of phosphates around the ceremonial plaza. These may turn out to be remains of habitations that preceded the construction of the enclosure or residues of fiestas or offerings left during its use.

Finally, the excellent conditions of conservation at the ceremonial plaza of Laguna de Limones make this site a true archaeological jewel in the national patrimony. The most diverse influences, from random chance to the altruistic labor of a campesino, have made it possible for this monument to survive. Unfortunately, the habitation area of the site is largely destroyed. Nevertheless, I am convinced that by taking the theoretical and methodological proposals of ASL as a starting point, creative project designs and modern methods of excavation will be able to make up for the obstacles of destruction in the search for archaeological and historical explanation.

Acknowledgments

I would like to thank the following people, who participated in different phases of the project and who contributed their efforts and knowledge: the CENCREM investigative team, consisting of Darwin Arduengo, Seegrit Labirí, and Alejandro Cruz, as well as our counterparts in Guantanamo, Ana Luisa Gazón and Jesús Otero; the members of the Juan Federico Esper Speleological Group of the Speleological Society of Cuba; Milton Pino, Ulises González, and Oscar Pereira, specialists at the Cuban Institute of Anthropology; my tireless colleagues at *Granma*, Zacarías

Mayo and Roberto Ortíz; and Jesús Santos, curator of the Museum of La Punta, Office of the Historian of the City, Havana. On the academic plane I am indebted to Luis Felipe Bate and Antonio Curet, for their wise orientations, and to Ray Petty and Sandra Rodríguez, for all the support they have offered for this project.

Notes

1. I understand that substantive Marxist theory is not simply historical materialism, but instead, as Luis F. Bate (1978:11) insists, "what defines the specifics of the method of historical materialism in archaeology is not the notion itself nor the theory nor the application of specific techniques, but rather the congruence between the techniques, the logistics of the methodology, and the theory, in an indivisible dynamic unity."

2. To better understand this fact, consider the sociological circumstances in which Cuba's national science developed. Without doubt, political and ideological factors exercised great influence. Cuba's practices developed in a revolutionary framework hostile to North American imperialism after 1960.

3. Since the 1980s this limitation has slowly been overcome. Through a series of meetings in Oaxtepec, Mexico, new analytic categories were generated that enriched Marxism's utility for archaeology, though these are still largely unknown in Cuba.

4. The paradigmatic case is Ernesto Tabío and Estrella Rey's (1979) *Prehistory of Cuba*, in which it is impossible to determine differences between early and late pre-Columbian groups on the basis of the analytical categories employed in the section on paleoethnography. Thus the door was left open for Tabío's "archaeological cultural empiricism" as a means to understanding the material record.

5. The concept of cacicazgo or chiefdom is plagued by different definitions, leading it to be rejected by some authors, including Drennan and Uribe (1987:xviii), who find that "the concept of chiefdoms is useful only for a rough description and the organization of information. It is not, nevertheless, a penetrating analytical tool for understanding the societies that are described as such."

6. It is doubtful that this region was ever a unified social entity.

7. The identification of this sample was made by Dr. Raquel Carreras, who believes it might be the remains of a post. Dr. Carreras also identified the wood remains from the important site of Los Buchillones, in Ciego de Avila.

8. This is evidently the first reported find in Cuba of an artifact made with this type of shell (Milton Pino, personal communication).

9. In a literature search I found a single report describing a plaza with a tamped earth enclosure in the Dominican Republic, at the site of Casa de la Reina, in the Dominican Republic (Peguero 2001). This plaza, measuring 80 m x 60 m, was first reported in 1851, although it is now completely destroyed.

7
Recent Archaeological Fieldwork from the Region around Los Buchillones: An Indigenous Site on the North-Central Cuban Coast

Jago Cooper, Institute of Archaeology (IoA), University College London

Roberto Valcárcel Rojas, Departamento Centro Oriental de Arqueología, Ministerio de Ciencias, Tecnonogía y Medio Ambiente, Cuba (CISAT), Cuban Ministry of Science, Technology and Environment (CITMA), Cuba

Jorge Calvera, Departamento de Arqueología, Ciego de Avila, CITMA, Cuba

We summarize here some of the results of recent collaborative archaeological research at and around the site of Los Buchillones in northern Cuba. The excavation of wooden structural posts at the site reveals aspects of house size and structural design. A coastal survey indicates the potential size of this coastal site. A survey and excavation of islands in the Jardines del Rey archipelago provides extensive evidence of indigenous marine resource and subsistence exploitation on these offshore islands. Assemblages from island sites are compared with those from Los Buchillones. Radiocarbon dates provide evidence for the chronology of human activity at these different sites.

> Aquí presentamos los resultados de unas investigaciónes recientes en el sitio de Los Buchillones, en la costa norte de Cuba. La excavación de viviendas nos proporciona nueva informacion sobre el tamaño y el diseño de estas estructuras. Un recorrido a lo largo del littoral indica el tamaño arqueológico del sitio. Recorridos y excavaciones en las islas del archipiélago Jardines del Rey proporcionan evidencias nuevas sobre la utilización de recursos marinos en estas islas. Los artefactos de los sitios isleños se comparan con los de Los Buchillones. Fechas radiocarbónicas proporcionan evidencias sobre la cronología de las actividades humanas en estos sitios.

In this paper we discuss recent archaeological fieldwork at Los Buchillones, located on the north coast of the modern province of Ciego de Avila, Cuba (Figure 7.1). Preliminary information from the recent surveys and excavations provides a picture of an indigenous settlement that includes previously unknown details.

Archaeological evidence and radiocarbon determinations indicate economic and chronological ties between Los Buchillones and sites on offshore islands up to 32 km distant.

The site of Los Buchillones in northern Cuba provides a rare opportunity for Caribbean archaeologists to study a site with good levels of organic preservation. The site was first excavated in the 1980s with archaeological investigations conducted by the Cuban Ministry of Science, Technology and Environment (Calvera and Febles 1984). These excavations, carried out in the 1980s, yielded large quantities of ceramics (Mesa et al. 1994) and evidence of a permanent settlement that included a number of distinctive artifacts such as a quartz pendant and *Xancus angulatus* shell hammer (Calvera and Febles 1984). In the 1990s the discovery of a wetland part of the site, which contained a large quantity of preserved wooden artifacts, raised the profile of the site both nationally and internationally (Calvera et al. 1996).

This led to collaborative archaeological investigations by CITMA and the Royal Ontario Museum (ROM) in 1997, 1998, and 1999 (Calvera et al. 2001; Jardines and Calvera 1999; Pendergast et al. 1999, 2002, 2003). These excavations produced an assemblage of hundreds of wooden artifacts that reflected intensive woodworking at the site. During this fieldwork two structures also were identified, each of which was excavated and found to contain evidence of extensive roof thatching, stringers, and rafters. Stratigraphy was not preserved in the boggy wetland conditions, but the discovery of these structures indicated the preservation of an indigenous settlement in the coastal wetlands at Los Buchillones.

Recent Archaeological Research

In 2003, a collaborative institutional agreement was signed by Professor Peter Ucko, director of the Institute of Archaeology (IoA), University College London (UCL) and Celso Pasos Alberti, minister for the Ciego de Avila department of CITMA. Under this agreement, all parties agreed to cooperate to the maximum level possible in advancing the scientific study of Los Buchillones archaeological site in Ciego de Avila under the management of project directors Jorge Calvera, Gabino La Rosa (CITMA), David Pendergast and Elizabeth Graham (IoA) and field directors Roberto Valcárcel (CITMA) and Jago Cooper (IoA). This collaborative partnership has led to consecutive years of archaeological fieldwork, scientific analyses, and publications. The first collaborative CITMA-IoA excavation in 2004 had the primary aim of investigating wood house construction techniques, building upon previous investigations by CITMA-ROM in the 1990s.

The Indigenous House

The indigenous wooden house is a topic that has intrigued Caribbean archaeologists for many years. Work by Curet (1992), Drewett (2003), Delpuech et al. (1999),

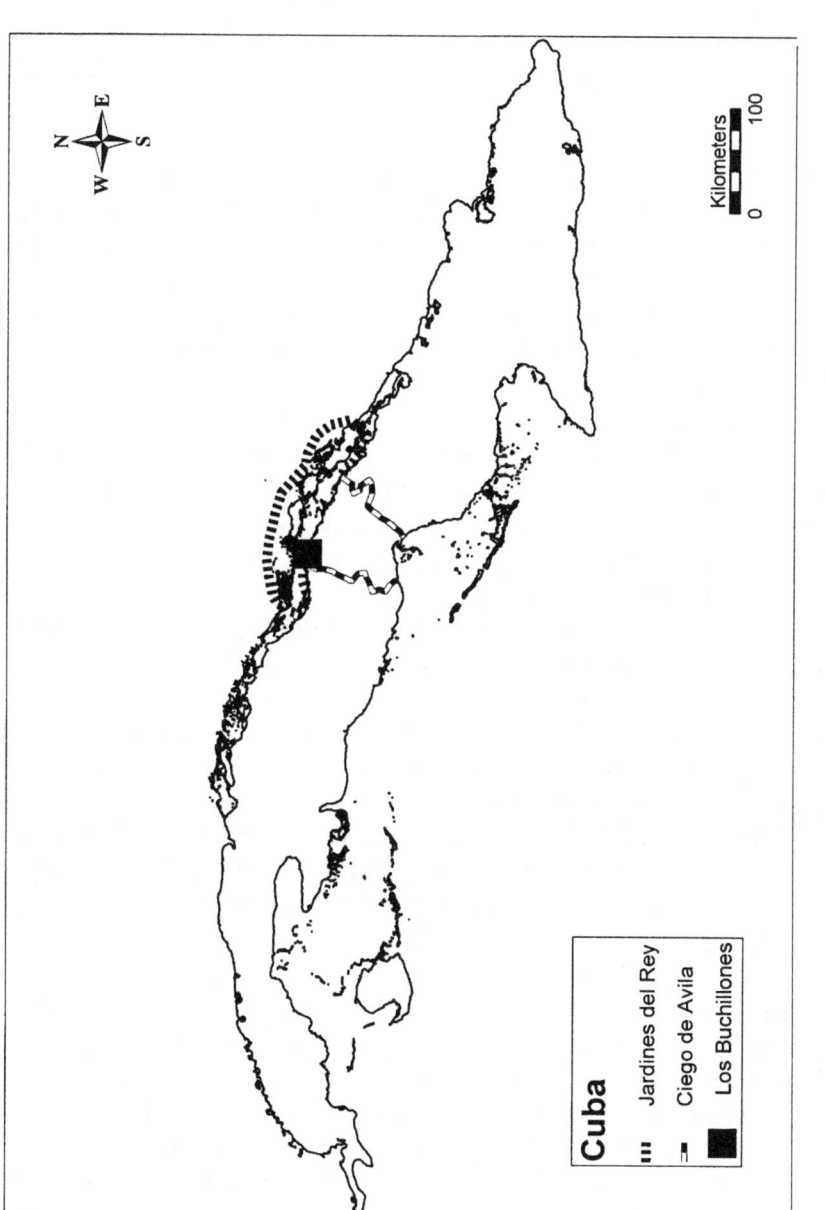

Figure 7.1. Map of Cuba showing location of Los Buchillones, Ciego de Avila, and the Jardines del Rey archipelago.

Bartone and Versteeg (1997), and Schinkel (1992), among others, has provided a wealth of data from elsewhere in the Caribbean. However, the available data are often restricted by the poor preservation of the structural timbers; thus models of house design and construction often are based upon postholes and posthole molds (Curet 1992). Therefore, Los Buchillones provides a perfect place to further investigate house forms because of the exceptional preservation of wooden elements at this site.

In 2004, the area for excavation at Los Buchillones was selected based on the observation of a cluster of wooden posts that were visible underwater, emerging from the seabed 12 m north of the spit of land that separates the lagoon from the open sea. The excavation area was 22 m in diameter and enclosed a cluster of 17 visible wooden elements emerging from the seabed and labeled in 1999 as area D2-6. This area was coffer dammed with sandbags and plastic sheeting and drained in order to facilitate excavation.

As the excavation developed it became apparent that unlike previous excavations in the 1990s, the roof and possible floor of this structure had already been eroded by the action of the sea, leaving the main structural posts and a collection of associated artifacts embedded in the seabed sediments. This excavation led to the eventual discovery of 28 large structural posts and 29 smaller supporting posts. Once the top of each post had been recorded on plan, a 180-degree arc of sediments was excavated in sections to reveal the stratigraphic location of each post and its angle of inclination. Each post was then fully excavated and extracted in order to record the post dimensions, surface condition, and tool marks, and to extract a sample of wood for species identification. The posts were then replaced in order to maintain their continued preservation in the anoxic environment.

A spatial pattern in the distribution of the posts was determined through nearest neighbor analysis. This spatial pattern included a hexagonal series of structural posts within an outer octagonal series of structural posts. The validity of this spatial pattern was further supported by the distinctive typologies of the posts used in each group. The posts that made up the internal hexagon all had diameters between 18–24 cm and lengths between 65–86 cm with roughly finished angular bases. The posts that composed the external octagon all had diameters between 23–33 cm and lengths between 80–168 cm, with tool marks showing that the bases of these posts had been deliberately worked to provide a rounded or flat base.

One hypothesis to explain this observed variation in larger post size and base shape is that it increased the stability of the outer octagonal ring of structural posts. An additional piece of evidence in support of this notion came from the angles of inclination of each post, as they all lay in opposing directions, suggesting that the posts had once been held together in tension. When the unifying force was released, arguably by the collapse or erosion of the superstructure, the posts settled back at an angle.

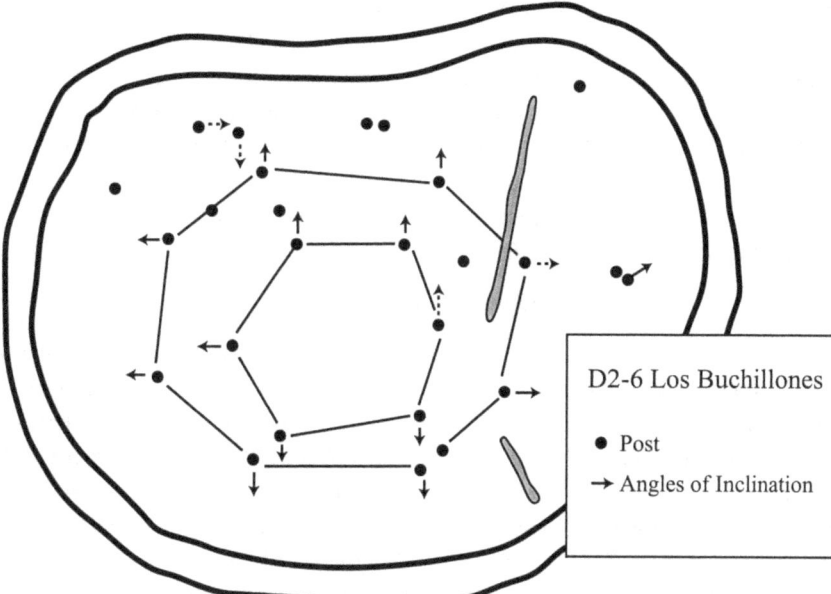

Figure 7.2. Plan of posts excavated in 2004 with spatial patterns of associated posts, based on comparative analysis of post size, base type, and spatial distribution including the internal hexagon, the external octagon, and the two lines of posts running east-west to the north of the structure.

The preservation quality of the timbers and paleoenvironmental data (Peros 2005:156) from the site indicate that it is likely that the stilted structures excavated at Los Buchillones were standing in a waterlogged environment at the time of their occupation. Another pattern that was observed in the spatial distribution of the posts of D2-6 was the presence of two broadly parallel lines of posts running east-west across the north of the structure (Figure 7.2). One hypothesis that may explain this double line of posts is that they are the remains of a walkway that provided a path between the different structures above these wetland conditions. This possibility, along with many other research questions, remains to be investigated through further excavations at the site.

The material assemblage from all the excavations conducted at Los Buchillones indicates long-term domestic occupation at the site. Artifacts include seats *(duhos)*, household effigies, rafter hooks, wooden vessels, and cooking griddles *(burens)*, as well as shell and lithic ornaments. Therefore the structures at Los Buchillones appear to have been viable domestic units.

Excavation of structure D2-6 in 2004 revealed that this domestic unit was an oval structure that measured 8.5 m in length and 6.2 m in width, covering a total of 45 m². The size of this structure can be compared to the estimated sizes of structures found at Taíno period sites in Puerto Rico. There, Robinson and Espenshade (cited in Curet 1992:163) tentatively identified a structure measuring 8-x-6 m at the site of El Bronce. At Playa Blanca 5, in eastern Puerto Rico, Curet (1992:163) identified a structure measuring 7.14-x-6.64 m. The sizes of these structures are similar to the structure identified at Los Buchillones. Valcárcel et. al (2006) provide the most complete publication to date on excavation methods and interpretation of structure D2-6.

Settlement Size and Location

In order to determine the size and shape of the settlement at Los Buchillones, a coastal survey was conducted along a 10-km stretch of coastline around the site. Archaeological and environmental data were collected from 2 m² survey squares at 100-m intervals along the coast (Cooper and Valcárcel 2004). The artifact distributions recorded in this survey, predominantly ceramics and lithics, provide evidence that the settlement size of Los Buchillones extended 2.2 km east-west along the coast. The site appears to be truncated to the west by the modern village and marina complex of Punta Alegre. The northern boundary of the settlement is currently under water and is consequently more difficult to establish, but the excavation of D2-6 indicates that the settlement extended at least 28 m north of the current coastline, and clusters of wooden posts have been identified further along the coastline during previous fieldwalking by Calvera and colleagues (Calvera et al. 2001).

Excavations in 1984 and 1989 provided evidence that the settlement extended at least 40 m to the south of the current coastline, but modern road developments, the lagoon, and agricultural farming have obscured further indications of the southern boundary of the settlement. Therefore it is only through additional survey and excavation that a detailed plan of the exact settlement size at Los Buchillones can be established. However, based upon all available data, the settlement spanned at least 68 m north-south from dry land out into the sea and 2.2 km east-west following the coastline (Figure 7.3). Paleoenvironmental research carried out by Peros (2005) indicates that while there might have been localized coastline morphology it is likely that the current wetland portions of the site were also wetland environments during the indigenous occupation of Los Buchillones. Therefore this settlement appears to have straddled the liminal edge, with both dry and wetland occupation.

The spatial patterning of the excavated houses and identified post clusters indicates an extensive stretch of structures ranging between 6 and 10 m in diameter. It is premature to estimate the number of structures at the site, but if the density of structures throughout the site is comparable to the area of the excavated structures to date, there may have been more than 80 structures at Los Buchillones.

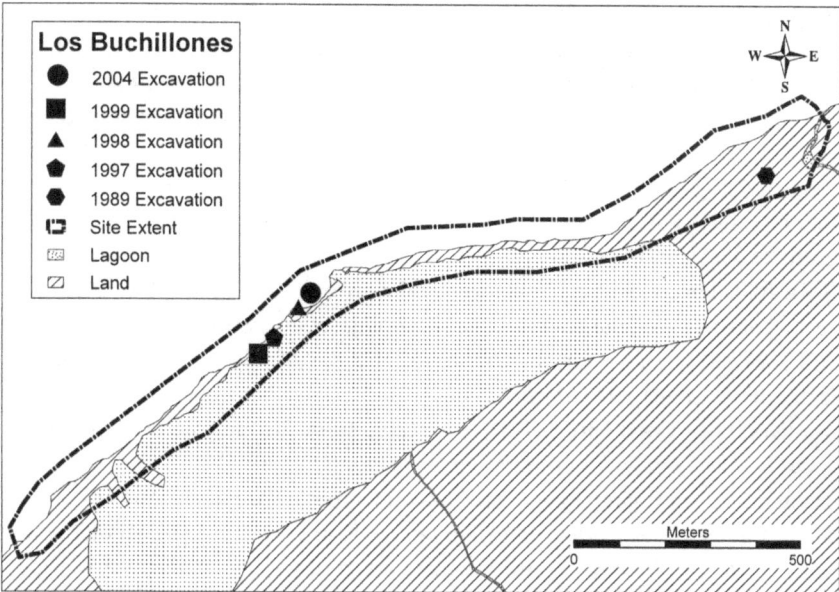

Figure 7.3. Plan of site extent of Los Buchillones based on the archaeological evidence recovered during the coastal survey and excavations at the site.

Los Buchillones Chronology

This large site evidently had a long occupation. The artifact typologies from all of the excavations indicate a Taíno period assemblage with a broad potential chronological range based on established chronological frameworks for occupation spanning of cal A.D. 900–1500 (Febles 1991; Guarch 1978; Rouse 1992). This broad chronological range for artifact typologies is a common problem in Cuban archaeology that restricts more tightly defined chronological phases of occupation.

In order to resolve some of these chronological questions, a number of samples were submitted for radiocarbon dating. Twelve wood samples were taken from the structural timbers of House 1, D2-1 in 1998. All radiocarbon dates provided in this paper are calibrated dates to two standard deviations with 95 percent confidence. The wood samples from D2-1 produced a calibrated date range of ten dates from cal A.D. 1295–1435 to 1460–1665, with two samples producing earlier dates of cal A.D. 540–690 and 635–780. Six wood samples were taken from the structural timbers of House 2, F1-1. The samples from F1-1 were dated and produced six dates ranging from cal A.D. 1390–1490 to 1610–1690 (Pendergast et al. 2002).

Further discussion of these dates highlights some of the potential problems with taking samples from structural elements of houses in the Caribbean. Issues include the fact that some trees may live up to 100 years, especially some of the hardwood species used in house construction such as Caoba *(Swietenia mahagoni)* and Guayacán *(Guaiacum sp.)* (Valcárcel et al. 2006:83). There is also the possibility of reuse of old wood either taken from the local environment or cannibalized from previous and potentially older structures. These factors might obtain in the two samples from D2-1 that produced the early dates of cal A.D. 540–780. However, the chronological ranges interpreted for these structures were cal A.D. 1290–1635 for D2-1, and cal A.D. 1390–1690 for F1-1. These date ranges clearly fall within the limits of Taíno period occupation.

In 2004, ten additional samples were taken from D2-6 as part of a wider radiocarbon dating project to compare the chronological relationships between Los Buchillones and other sites in the region. All of these samples were taken from artifacts with assumed short animal/plant lives, short death-to-use periods, and short use-lives. Both wood and shell samples came from the same archaeological contexts in order to provide comparative date ranges.

All of the wood samples were calibrated to two standard deviations (2σ) against the IntCa104 atmospheric calibration curve (Reimer et al. 2004). All of the shell samples were calibrated to two standard deviations (2σ) against the Marine04 calibration curve (Hughen et al. 2004), following comparisons between the regional deltaR offsets from the marine reservoir correction database (Reimer 2005). The calibrated radiocarbon dates of the ten securely dated samples taken from structure D2-6 provide a chronological range between cal A.D. 1264–1376 and cal A.D. 1512–1667. This date range for D2-6 is compatible with a date range for F1-1 of cal A.D. 1390–1690 and D2-1 cal A.D.1290–1665 (Pendergast et al. 2002:69). Further radiocarbon determinations of structures from different areas of the site are required to see if the entire area of the site was occupied concurrently or whether there were phases of occupation. However, the results of this dating project indicate that these structures had extended and contemporaneous phases of occupation during the Taíno period potentially spanning between the thirteenth to as late as the seventeenth centuries.

Island and Marine Environment Interaction

A study of the faunal assemblage from Los Buchillones reveals a strong marine focus, based on the minimum number of individuals (MNI), with marine animals accounting for 80 percent of the faunal assemblage (shell 58 percent, fish and marine mammals 18 percent, turtle 4 percent), terrestrial animals 13 percent, and unidentified species 7 percent (Rosario Pérez et al. 2003). In addition, the known habitats of the wide variety of fish, shell, and marine mammals found in this assemblage were analyzed. These include mangrove, shallow water, turtle grass beds, reefs, and pelagic waters (Newsom and Wing 2004:24). These data indicate that a number of different habitats were being exploited, not all of which are found in the immediate coastal environment around the site. Therefore a survey was

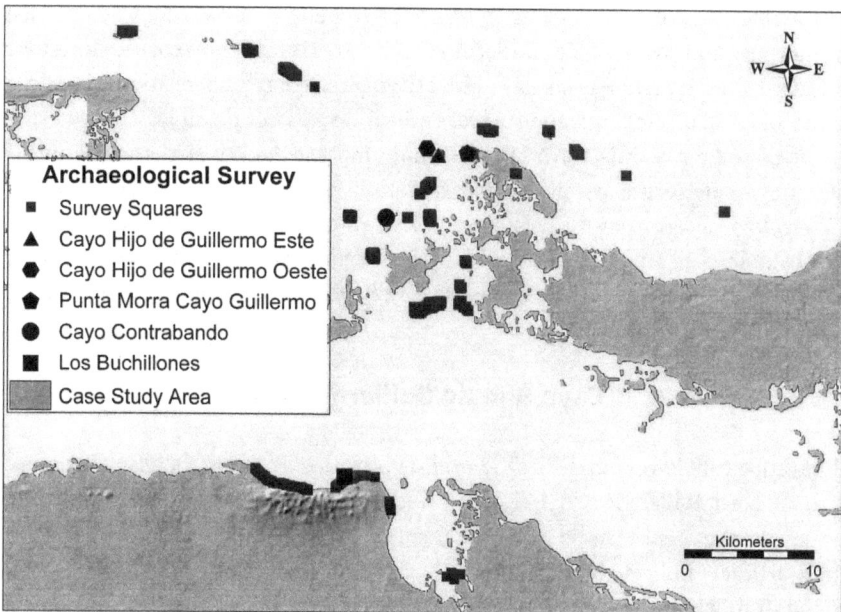

Figure 7.4. Map of coastal and island survey that shows the location of islands where sites with archaeological evidence for potential links with Los Buchillones were found.

planned that could help to identify the wider patterns of marine interaction from the site (Cooper 2007).

In 2004 and 2005 a survey was conducted to investigate the nature and extent of archaeological evidence for human activity in the Jardines del Rey archipelago, a chain of islands stretching into the Bahama Channel (Figure 7.4). This island survey (Cooper and Valcárcel Rojas 2004; Cooper et al. 2006) focused on an investigation of archaeological evidence for maritime-based interaction within a designated study area of 200 km². In total 22 different islands were intensively surveyed over a two-year period. Archaeological evidence for indigenous human activity was found on 10 islands. Most of this evidence consisted of anthropogenic shell deposits in association with shell, ceramic, and lithic artifacts.

These middens varied greatly in the quantity and nature of archaeological materials. Excavations were conducted in order to collect a substantive body of archaeological material with which to make comparative analyses. Sites with archaeological evidence of potentially contemporaneous activity with Los Buchillones were found on four islands: Cayo Contrabando, Cayo Guillermo, Cayo Hijo de Guillermo Este, and Cayo Hijo de Guillermo Oeste.

A sample was taken from a surface deposit on Cayo Contrabando for radiocarbon dating, but this site, on the edge of a mangrove swamp, was not excavated.

The archaeological deposits with evidence of contemporaneous activity on Cayo Guillermo and Cayo Hijo de Guillermo Oeste were situated on exposed limestone surface deposits; there was no way of identifying the contextual relationship of the archaeological assemblage, and further excavation was not possible.

Of these four islands, Cayo Hijo de Guillermo Este had the largest assemblage of contextually secure artifacts; thus excavations were carried out there. The rich archaeological record at this island includes two cave sites and three rockshelters that contained stratified deposits with archaeological materials that do not appear to have been subjected to the same erosive taphanomic processes as the surface deposits on the other islands.

Cayo Hijo de Guillermo Este

Excavations at Cayo Hijo de Guillermo Este provided over two thousand artifacts. Lithic materials include two limestone grinding stones and a number of small flint fragments that appear to be waste fragments from tools used on the island. While these artifacts indicate human activity and the movement of resources out to the islands, unfortunately there were no diagnostic artifacts that could be used comparatively to establish links with the lithics from Los Buchillones.

The faunal assemblage from the top stratigraphic layers of Cave 1 and Cave 3 (Table 7.1) revealed a pattern of marine-based subsistence. This evidence was similar to the assemblage from Los Buchillones. Analysis of the faunal data, based on number of individual elements (NIE) from stratigraphic layer 1, Cave 1, indicated that marine animals account for 85 percent of the assemblage (shell 78 percent, fish and marine mammals 5 percent, turtle 2 percent), terrestrial animals 13 percent, and unidentified species < 2 percent.

Marine animals accounted for 99 percent of the faunal assemblage from stratigraphic layer 1, Cave 3. This evidence was compared to published records for the faunal assemblages from excavations of F1-1 and D2-1 at Los Buchillones (Rosario Pérez et al. 2003). The data from F1-1 and D2-1 are based on Minimum Numbers of Individuals (MNI) and thus are not quantifiably comparable to the NIE counts from the cave sites, but they provide a qualitative comparison that indicates similar species exploitation at all three sites, as illustrated in Table 7.1. Faunal studies from coastal sites occupied throughout different periods in Cuba provide evidence of these same shell species being exploited, but not with such similar patterns of species selection (Angelbello et al. 2002; Navarrete 1990; Reyes 1997). The examination of the shell artifacts from these sites was done using established Cuban shell artifact classification methods (Dacal 1978; Guarch 1978; Izquierdo and Rives 1993; Tomé 1994).

Some of the collected shells reported in these studies were reused expediently for different practical purposes without substantive modification. *Codakia orbicu-*

Table 7.1 Shell Species from the Top Stratigraphic Layers of Excavations in Caves 1 and 3, Cayo Hijo de Guillermo Este; also D2-1 and F1-1, Los Buchillones on the Cuban Mainland

Shell Species	Cave 1 NIE	Cave 1 %	Cave 3 NIE	Cave 3 %	Buchillones MNI	Buchillones %
Strombus gigas	477	57	258	59	20	24
Strombus sp.	179	21	70	16	5	6
Cittarium pica	48	6	9	2	1	1
Xancus angulatus	32	4	14	3	2	2
Codakia orbicularis	25	3	70	16	34	41
Oliva reticularis	15	2	—	—	8	10
Murex brevifrons	12	1	9	2	2	2
Fasciolaria tulipa	8	1	2	<1	1	1
Pinctada radiata	5	<1	—	—	2	2
Nerita sp.	4	<1	—	—	—	—
Nerita peloronta	2	<1	—	—	—	—
Strombus costatus	2	<1	—	—	5	6
Arca zebra	1	<1	—	—	—	—
Tellina radiata	1	<1	1	<1	—	—
Chiton sp.	1	<1	—	—	—	—
Diodora listeri	1	<1	—	—	—	—
Fissurela nimbosa	1	<1	—	—	—	—
Chama sp.	—	—	1	<1	—	—
Lucina pectinatus	—	—	—	—	1	1
Menipe mercenaria	—	—	—	—	1	1

laris valves show use-wear signs on the ventral margin, indicating that they had been reused as scrapers. The columnella of some *Strombus gigas* gastropods have use wear indicating that they functioned as hand picks. Typologically similar tools also are reported at sites from different chronological periods (Dacal 1978:7).

Examples of selective shell part use include *Xancus angulatus* and *Strombus costatus* lips of mature specimens that were broken off and reused as hand hammers. More skillful shell working is exhibited in the abundant *Strombus sp.* point collection. There are a number of detailed studies of shell point technology in Cuba (Izquierdo Diaz and Sampedro Hernández 2002), and several different point types can be identified in the artifact assemblages. These carefully worked shell tools provide some diagnostic typological indications of cultural and chronological affiliation.

At Cayo Hijo de Guillermo Este the most prominent form in the shell assemblage is a penetration point that probably was used as a hafted harpoon point for fishing. There is also evidence of targeted selection of certain shells for decorative jewelry. *Oliva reticularis* shells are found on Cayo Hijo de Guillermo Este with evidence of modification into beads and pendants. Ornately carved examples of these beads and pendants are also found at Los Buchillones. All of the shell tools found at sites on Cayo Hijo de Guillermo Este were found to have typologically similar examples in the excavated assemblages at Los Buchillones (Figure 7.5).

Ceramics, the Islands, and Los Buchillones

The indigenous ceramics in our assemblages provide only a broad chronological range for the archaeological deposits. In the published literature this range is traditionally defined as cal A.D. 800–1500. The chronology of Cuban ceramics is currently undergoing further revisions, especially with the discovery of early ceramic traditions in Cuba (Jouravleva 2002; Ulloa 2005; Ulloa and Valcárcel 2002). Yet ceramics are useful, in a preliminary sense, for establishing interactions between the islands and Los Buchillones.

Ceramics were found on the four islands of Cayo Contrabando, Cayo Guillermo, Cayo Hijo de Guillermo Este, and Cayo Hijo de Guillermo Oeste. The majority of these sherds were significantly eroded and not large enough to indicate vessel form or decorative style. One sherd from Cave 1, Hijo de Guillermo Este, was large enough to provide a vessel shape typology. This sherd came from a closed globular vessel with a small-incised line around the top edge. This is a common vessel type found at Los Buchillones. One sherd from Cave 3, Cayo Hijo de Guillermo Este, was identified as a double-edged griddle *(buren)* rim. The presence of griddles at archaeological sites in Cuba, as found at Los Buchillones, has traditionally been considered an indicator of cassava-based agriculturalist societies, though recent residue analysis of *burens* from Cuba and Puerto Rico demonstrates a wider range of cooking activities (Pagan-Jiménez and Oliver 2006; Rodriguez and Pagan-Jiménez 2006).

Superficial studies of the unidentified sherds indicate that they have similar superficial qualities to indigenous ceramic sherds found at archaeological sites elsewhere in Ciego de Avila (Mesa González et al. 1994). These macroscopic observations were supported by the microscopic study of thin section samples made from ten sherds collected at sites on Cayo Hijo de Guillermo Este, two sherds from Cayo Contrabando, and nine sherds from Los Buchillones (Barclay 2001). Microscopic analysis of the paste mineralogy indicated that the sherds from Cayo Hijo de Guillermo Este and Cayo Contrabando, as well as those from Los Buchillones, were made of a similar yellow brown clay with unsorted subangular quartz, feldspar, and olivine inclusions and no evidence of intentionally added temper. Possibly, the clay in all of these sherds came from a single source. Although the data

Artefact Comparison

Jardines del Rey Archipelago
Hijo de Guillermo del Este
Excavations 2004-2005

Cuban Mainland
Los Buchillones
Excavations 1996-2004

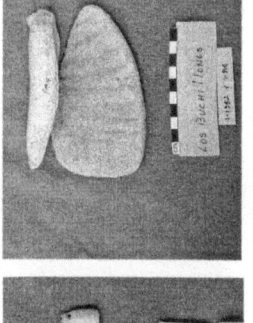

Shell Beads
Oliva reticularis

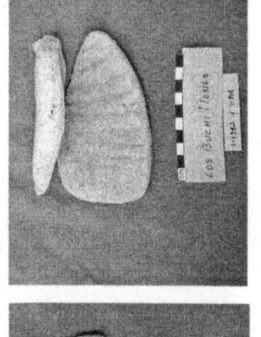

Shell Beads
Oliva reticularis

Shell Hammers
Strombus costatus

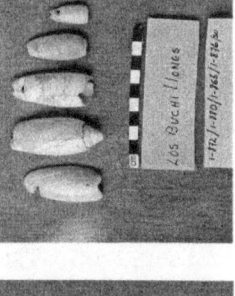

Shell Hammer
Strombus costatus

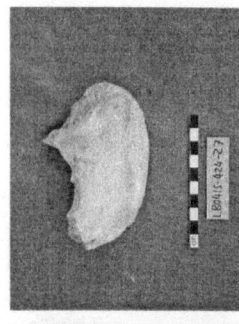

Shell Scrapers
Codakia orbicularis

Shell Vessels
Strombus gigas

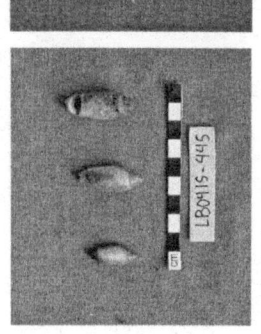

Shell Vessel
Strombus gigas

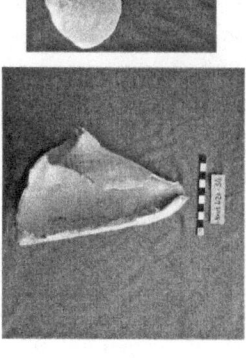

Shell Scrapers
Codakia orbicularis

Figure 7.5. Photographs of shell artifacts from Cave 1, Cayo Hijo de Guillermo Este, and Los Buchillones showing similar species selection and artifact typology.

are very preliminary, vessel forms, clay sources, and ceramic pastes from the island sites seem comparable to the ceramics found at Los Buchillones.

Temporal Links between Los Buchillones and Sites on the Off-Shore Islands

Although there is evidence for a cultural connection between these sites, it is necessary to establish firmer chronological links that go beyond relative dating based on ceramic and shell artifact typologies. Due to the absence of wood or charcoal samples from the sites on Cayo Hijo de Guillermo Este, six shell samples from three stratigraphic levels in Cave 1 and one from the top stratigraphic layer of Rockshelter 1 were submitted for radiocarbon dating. The calibrated dates from these shell samples reflects an extended period of human activity in the cave, with evidence of chronologically sequenced stratigraphic layers.

Four shells from Cave 1 provided a date range between cal A.D. 1232–1323 and cal A.D. 1517–1670. In addition, a shell sample taken from the top stratigraphic layer from Rockshelter 1 provided a date of cal A.D. 1475–1639, and the *Strombus gigas* sample taken from Surface Deposit 2 on Cayo Contrabando provided a date range of cal A.D. 1429–1506. Considered together, these six radiocarbon determinations provide a chronological range for human activity at sites on the islands of the Jardines del Rey archipelago of cal A.D. 1232–1670. Thus the island chronology is closely correlated with the previously discussed date range of cal A.D. 1264–1690 from Los Buchillones (Figure 7.6).

Conclusions

The survey and excavation data discussed above provide a picture of a coastal community with marine and island interaction. The map (Figure 7.6) of known archaeological sites contemporaneous with Los Buchillones shows a direct route from the mainland site into the open sea. The small ceramic assemblage and lack of other domestic artifacts at the sites on the offshore islands, combined with the absence of evidence for fresh water sources, may mean that these sites were occupied temporally.

Another clear difference between the artifact assemblages from Cayo Hijo de Guillermo Este and Los Buchillones is the large quantity of shell debitage and shell tools that were discarded during the process of manufacturing on the islands. Possibly the sites in the Jardines del Rey archipelago were used as base camps or staging posts for marine resource exploitation and shell artifact manufacturing (Cooper 2008). The environmental context of the islands supports this hypothesis.

The bathymetric data from this region indicate that there were different marine environments in the region. Cayo Hijo de Guillermo is located close to the

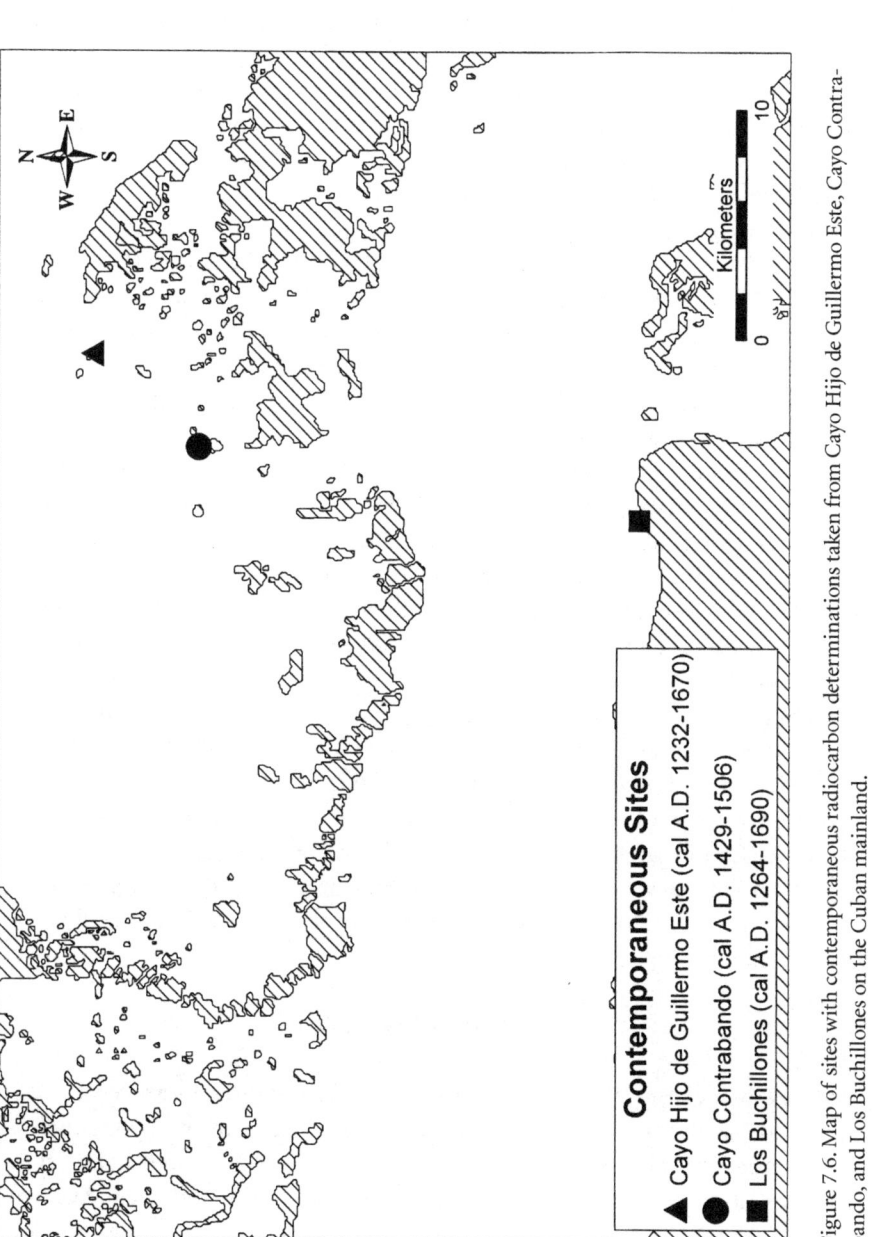

Figure 7.6. Map of sites with contemporaneous radiocarbon determinations taken from Cayo Hijo de Guillermo Este, Cayo Contrabando, and Los Buchillones on the Cuban mainland.

edge of a reef that drops off into the Bahama Channel. This environment provided the rich marine ecosystem from which fauna were exploited. The faunal evidence from Los Buchillones suggests that the journey to procure these fauna was undertaken on a regular basis.

Wider interactions can only be inferred from comparative similarities in material culture between Los Buchillones and other sites elsewhere in Cuba and the wider Caribbean. There are a number of examples of stylistic influences that might be associated with wider regional interaction. One of the most striking is found in basketry-impressed griddles *(burens)* at Los Buchillones that are more commonly found in the Bahamas (Berman and Hutcheson 2000). Four sherds with basketry impressions have been found at Los Buchillones, and the weave types were identified as wickerwear patterns that are similar to those found at Palmetto Grove and Pigeon Creek on San Salvador in the Bahamas (Hutcheson 2001).

The good preservation of organic materials such as wood at Los Buchillones has allowed the preservation of a larger spectrum of materials that can be used to identify wider cultural influences. A number of ornately carved duhos, effigies, and vessels have been found at Los Buchillones. The elaborate styles and expressive faces with shell inlays reflect a tradition often associated with highly stratified Taíno chiefdoms. These characteristics are more commonly identified in the more durable ceramic and lithic assemblages from other sites in eastern Cuba and Hispaniola (Dacal and de la Calle 1996; Olazagasti 1997; Ostapkowicz 1997; Robiou-Lamarche 2005; Veloz 1977).

The Los Buchillones ceramic assemblage does not contain the same ornate ceramic styles associated with eastern Cuba and Hispaniola, indicating that a site's ceramic assemblage may not always reflect the full detail of cultural influence and artistic expression of an indigenous community (Mesa González et al. 1994). Certainly it appears that the people of Los Buchillones were more culturally expressive while working in wood. While the style of these wooden artifacts suggests interaction in broader Caribbean spheres, we are only beginning to understand where Los Buchillones fits in this panorama.

Future Research

Radiocarbon chronology ranging between the thirteenth and seventeenth centuries at Los Buchillones raises the issue of the potential for post-1492 indigenous settlement at the site (Domínguez 1995; Valcárcel 1997). Despite radiocarbon dates as late as cal A.D. 1610–1671, only one majolica sherd and one indigenous vessel with a form that seems European, collected along the littoral at Los Buchillones during a survey carried out in the 1990s, serve as possible evidence of interaction with the Europeans.

This paucity of evidence for direct Indo-Hispanic interaction at Los Buchillones stands in contrast to the evidence from chronologically contemporaneous indigenous sites elsewhere in Cuba (for example, see Valcárcel et al. this volume). Investigating the wider spatial and temporal evidence for interaction with other Taíno sites, and with the Europeans, is an important aim of ongoing archaeological research at Los Buchillones.

Acknowledgments

We would like to thank those involved in organizing and conducting recent archaeological research at and around Los Buchillones, including Celso Paso, David Pendergast, Gabino La Rosa, Liz Graham, Odalys Brito, Pedro Cruz, Nelson Torna, Ana Celis, Marcos Labrada, Rhiannon Williams, Paul Wordsworth, Roberto Melo, and Adrián García.

8

Turey Treasure in the Caribbean

Brass and Indo-Hispanic Contact at El Chorro
de Maíta, Cuba

Roberto Valcárcel Rojas, Departamento Centro Oriental de Arqueología,
Ministerio de Ciencias Tecnología y Medio Ambiente, Cuba

Marcos Martinón-Torres, Institute of Archaeology (IoA),
University College London, UK

Jago Cooper, Institute of Archaeology, University College London, UK
Thilo Rehren, Institute of Archaeology, University College London, UK

Based on the interpretive possibilities offered by a group of European metal assemblage found in association with an indigenous cemetery, we present an analysis of Indo-Hispanic contact at the archaeological site of El Chorro de Maíta in northeast Cuba. In an area with very few ethnohistorical or historical descriptions of the processes of contact, archaeology enables us to discover a local population influenced by elements of European culture. Funerary practices were modified, although the local population maintained its capacity for decision making and cultural expression. We perceive a dynamic interaction with multiple facets, in which local elite individuals played key roles in both indigenous society and the Hispanic project of domination.

> A partir de las posibilidades interpretativas que ofrece la identificación de un grupo de objetos metálicos europeos encontrado junto a entierros indígenas, se presenta un análisis del contacto indo-hispánico en el sitio arqueológico El Chorro de Maíta, en el nororiente de Cuba. En un área con muy pocas referencias etnohistóricas o históricas sobre estos procesos de contacto la arqueología descubre un caso de población local fuertemente influenciada por elementos de la cultura hispana, que modifica sus prácticas funerarias aunque mantiene capacidades de decisión y expresión propia. Se percibe una interacción dinámica y con múltiples facetas en la cual también se insertan individuos de la elite local en razón de su papel clave, tanto para la sociedad indígena como para el proyecto de dominación hispano.

Analyses of the links between indigenous groups and Europeans, and an examination of the processes of change both populations confronted in the Antilles as a

Turey Treasure in the Caribbean / 107

result of their encounter, are key to understanding colonial history and many aspects of modern sociocultural structures as well. Lamentably, the historical vision of the processes of contact is incomplete due to the exclusively European perspective and the imbalance in the ethnohistoric and documentary coverage of the different events and locations in the Caribbean during this period. Under these circumstances archaeological investigation appears to be an important tool in the task of establishing a picture of greater objectivity, since it offers information that allows us to evaluate diverse spaces and social behaviors, including those that pertain to disenfranchised groups ignored in the written record or incapable of expression via written means (Deagan 1996; Lightfoot 1995).

Conceived from that perspective, our research offers new information on Indo-Hispanic contact in Cuba, based on a study of European metal materials obtained from the archaeological site of El Chorro de Maíta, in the modern province of Holguín, northeast Cuba (Figure 8.1). This chapter is based on part of an extensive investigation under the direction of the first author.

Indo-Hispanic Contact in Cuba: Archaeological Studies

The study of Indo-Hispanic contact in early Spanish settlements is underdeveloped in Cuba. Nevertheless, there exists a long tradition of investigation at indigenous archaeological sites, where distinct relationships with the Spaniards or with their material world are reported. Studies such as those carried out by Rouse (1942) in the highlands of Maniabón used the presence of European materials—or indigenous copies of European objects—as chronological markers to define the "historic" character of the sites where these appeared, linking them to documented events for the zone vis-à-vis the conquest and colonization of the island.

Other investigations (García 1949; Morales and Pérez 1945) extended the analysis and reporting of this evidence, noting quantity and type of materials and emphasizing their value not only in verifying contact between the two cultures but also in considering the intensity of contact and the possibility of perceiving processes of transculturation—an exchange of influences in which elements are gained and lost, giving way to the development of new cultural expressions (Ortíz 1983:90). With advances in excavation and recording methods this focus was improved, establishing a specific classificatory methodology (Domínguez 1978) for identifying two different contexts. Sites of contact were those at which European material was superficial, not very abundant, and unmodified. At sites of transculturation, in addition to abundant European objects with traces of use, modification, or reuse, objects indicating a mix of European and indigenous cultural influences appear.

Later studies have made clear the necessity of going beyond simple contextual classification (Rives et al. 1991); today we focus on analytical schemes that permit

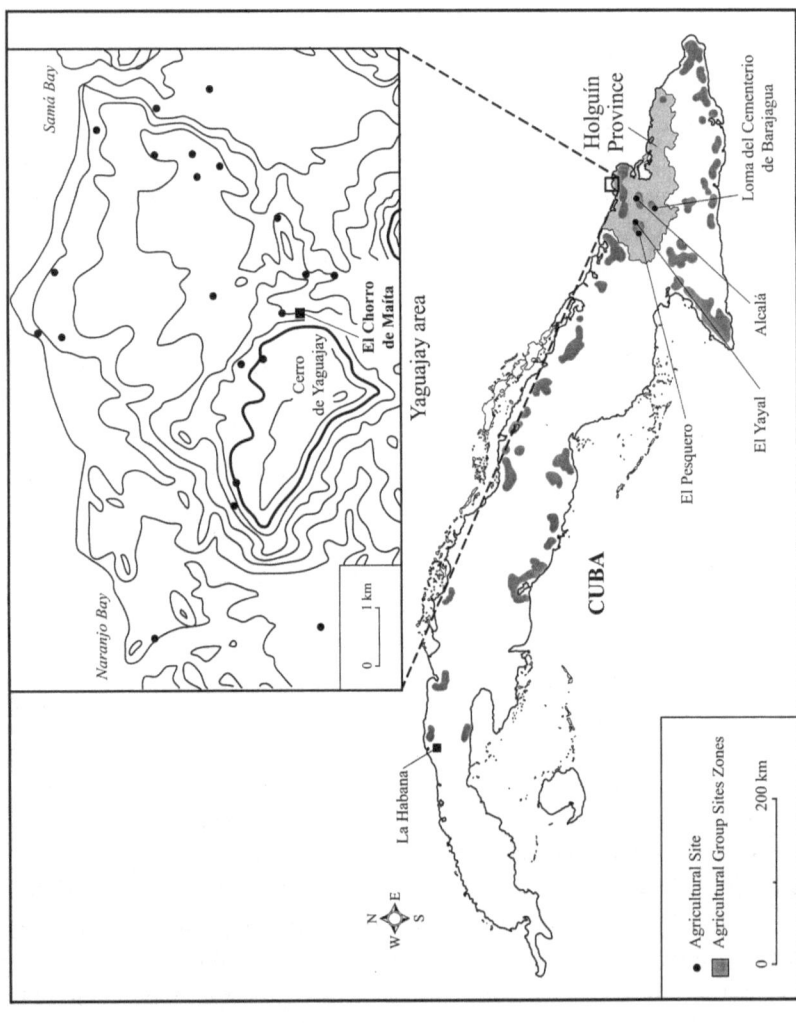

Figure 8.1. Reported agricultural-ceramicist sites in Cuba, including sites referred to in text, with detail of the Yaguajay area showing the location of El Chorro de Maíta.

the determination of changes in indigenous cultural behavior generated by links to the Europeans, as well as the detection of indigenous presence in periods later than the first half of the sixteenth century. To that end researchers have considered modifications in utilitarian artifacts (Rives et al. 1987; Tomé and Rives 1987), economic changes including modifications in diet, specialized production of certain goods, and variations in ceramic decoration (Domínguez 1984).

The idea that the disarticulation of the indigenous society was neither uniformly fast nor complete has been supplemented by the view that profound cultural exchanges were generated via transcultural processes as well as through diverse circumstances of survival and indigenous integration. However, to date these ideas remain largely in conceptual terms (Domínguez and Rives 1995).

In general, previous approaches focused solely on the processes of change, leaving many themes unexamined, including the motives that sustain indigenous practices in the process of adopting European elements, and the peculiarities of interaction at the level of context and social actors. In this chapter we propose an approach to these issues. The investigation offers a rereading of the Indo-Hispanic relationship in El Chorro de Maíta based on the interpretive possibilities of a situation in which metal elements used in European clothing in the fifteenth and sixteenth centuries were encountered in the context of native burials. This research is focused on the symbolic meaning behind the materials through an examination of the dynamic responses to the arrival of European metals, where observed changes in material meaning are neither immediate nor simplistic. The symbolic influences that determined the use of European metal were the result of dynamic interaction in which change was neither immediate nor total. The evidence also reveals some characteristics of indigenous social structure, especially traces of hierarchy, which are not clearly recorded in ethnohistorical texts and only rarely examined in Cuban archaeology.

The Indigenous Peoples of the Contact Period

At the moment of European arrival, Cuba was occupied largely by indigenous communities of the ethnolinguistic Arawak group, related to the so-called Taíno culture (Rouse 1992). Cuban archaeologists do not generally use the term "Taíno," instead employing classifications based on economic factors or archaeological indicators: *Etapa Agroalfarera* (Agriceramic stage [Tabío 1984:39]); *Fase Agricultores* (Agricultural phase [Guarch 1990:31]); *Comunidades neoliticas* (Neolithic communities [Domínguez et al. 1994:29]); or *Comunidades tribales agroceramistas* (Agriceramic tribal communities [Torres 2006]). Although important cultural similarities exist across the Antilles, recognized even by the Spaniards (Fernández 1992:115), archaeological and historical data indicate that the populations that settled in Cuba had not reached the higher demographic densities found in Hispaniola and Puerto Rico, and that ceremonial and political expressions in Cuba also were different in character (Domínguez et al. 1994:46).

The principal distribution of Arawak ceramic agriculturalist sites concentrates in the center of the Antilles archipelago; in Cuba, these settlements cluster in the eastern portion of the island (Figure 8.1). It is widely believed, although some authors (e.g., Keegan 1992:4–89; Knight this volume) question whether there is archaeological support for this idea, that at the moment of European contact the western part of Cuba was populated only by fisher-gatherer groups.

The agricultural occupation of Cuba clearly began by the ninth century A.D. (Valcárcel 2002a:20), though calibration of the earliest dates indicates that it might have begun 200 years earlier, stretching it back to the seventh century A.D. (Torres 2006:36). Agricultural contexts include utensils of ceramics, wood, shell, bone, and stone; very rarely do archaeologists recover the textiles and items of vegetable fibers mentioned by the Europeans. Ceramics are predominantly related in some measure to what Rouse (1992:96) calls the Meillacan ostionoid subseries, although they clearly are Cuban variants (Valcárcel 2002a). Ceramics linked to Rouse's Chican subseries are also found, though these are restricted to the extreme eastern end of the island and also have a clear local profile. These ceramics were made by sedentary societies that depended heavily on land animals and marine species as well as plant resources; agriculture was centered on the cultivation of tubers.

Agricultural-ceramic sites are very abundant in the archaeological area of Banes (Valcárcel 2002a:26), situated in the northeastern part of the island in the modern province of Holguín. Within this area are groups of sites delimited to some degree by accidents of geography (Valcárcel 2002a:65, 85), the densest of which are found in the hilly zone known as Yaguajay. El Chorro de Maíta is the largest and most fertile of the known sites in this region (see Figure 8.1).

In Yaguajay, as in other parts of the Banes area, archaeologists have located indigenous sites with early European materials (Rouse 1942; Valcárcel 1997). Nevertheless, historical references to indigenous presence in this zone or to the situation that generated these contexts are very rare. Several authors have assumed a possible link between this territory and the "provincias indias" of Baní and Cubanacan (García 1941; Rouse 1942:157), the first visited by Diego Velázquez in 1513 (Pichardo 1971:70). We also know, based on the fragmentary document of a judgment of residence applied to Gonzalo de Guzmán in 1530 (Mira 1997:425), a bit about the transfers and allocations of Indians in Baní and of the existence of an encomienda. Rouse (1942:157) correlated some of these very general dates and references on the process of conquest and colonization in northeast Cuba with the material record of the archaeological zone of Banes. However, his conclusions are questionable given the lack of precision in the available historical information and the very limited level of analysis vis-à-vis the processes of Indo-Hispanic interaction at the sites he considered.

El Chorro de Maíta

This site is located 4 km from the north coast, on the eastern slope of Yaguajay hill, at a height of 160 m above sea level. Rouse (1942:103–106) explored and provided a written description of the site, which he considered the most important in the Yaguajay zone. He reported abundant archaeological material and mentioned the collection of numerous ceremonial objects and body adornments.

Between 1979 and 1987, personnel from the Department of Archaeology of Holguín, under the direction of J. M. Guarch Delmonte, explored the site and excavated several deposits of possible domestic refuse and an ample burial grounds (Guarch 1988:162). From the absence of domestic or workshop waste (Guarch 1994:13), the abundance of burials, and the observed continuity of burial practice in one location, Guarch (1996:20) considered this zone to be a cemetery, the only one reported to date at an agricultural site in Cuba. The investigation carried out by the Department of Archaeology of Holguín and successive studies related to the material collected from that project concentrated on the funerary context. Beyond that, there have been only a few limited excavations.

In Excavation Units 2 and 5, located near the cemetery, archaeologists encountered refuse deposits containing faunal remains and abundant fragments of indigenous ceramics with ash lenses and carbon from cooking hearths. Guarch (1996:16) thought they were part of an indigenous village established around the cemetery. In both units fragments of European ceramics and domesticated pig bones *(Sus scrofa)* were recorded in superficial strata and in small quantity.

The contents of Excavation Unit 6, to the west of the cemetery (Figure 8.2), included faunal remains, ceramics, and various indigenous pieces for body adornment and ceremonial use (Guarch 1994:37). Also recovered in this unit were a thin sheet of metal with a perforation, a fragment of Columbia Plain mayolica pottery, also perforated, and a small, round European bell. Other items from the extension of Unit 6 included pig bones *(Sus scrofa),* more sherds of Columbia Plain (white and green-on-white varieties), sherds of ordinary Spanish lead glazed coarse earthenwares (Melado and Bacín Verde), fragments of the "early style" (ca. A.D. 1500–1570) olive jars, and a ceramic vessel with designs very similar to those on pieces made in Concepción de la Vega, Hispaniola (Guarch 1994:37–38), a settlement established in 1494 and abandoned in 1562 (Ortega and Fondeur 1978:11).

Excavated from the cemetery in a controlled fashion were 106 skeletons provisionally identified as indigenous individuals, one intrusive modern burial, and a quantity of disarticulated human remains tentatively identified as being from indigenous individuals.[1] In addition excavators recovered the skull of an individual with features some investigators (Rivero et al. 1990:85) consider to be Europoid; the skeleton to which it belonged could not be identified (Guarch 1996:17–20). A great variety of burial positions were noted, although supine burials with the

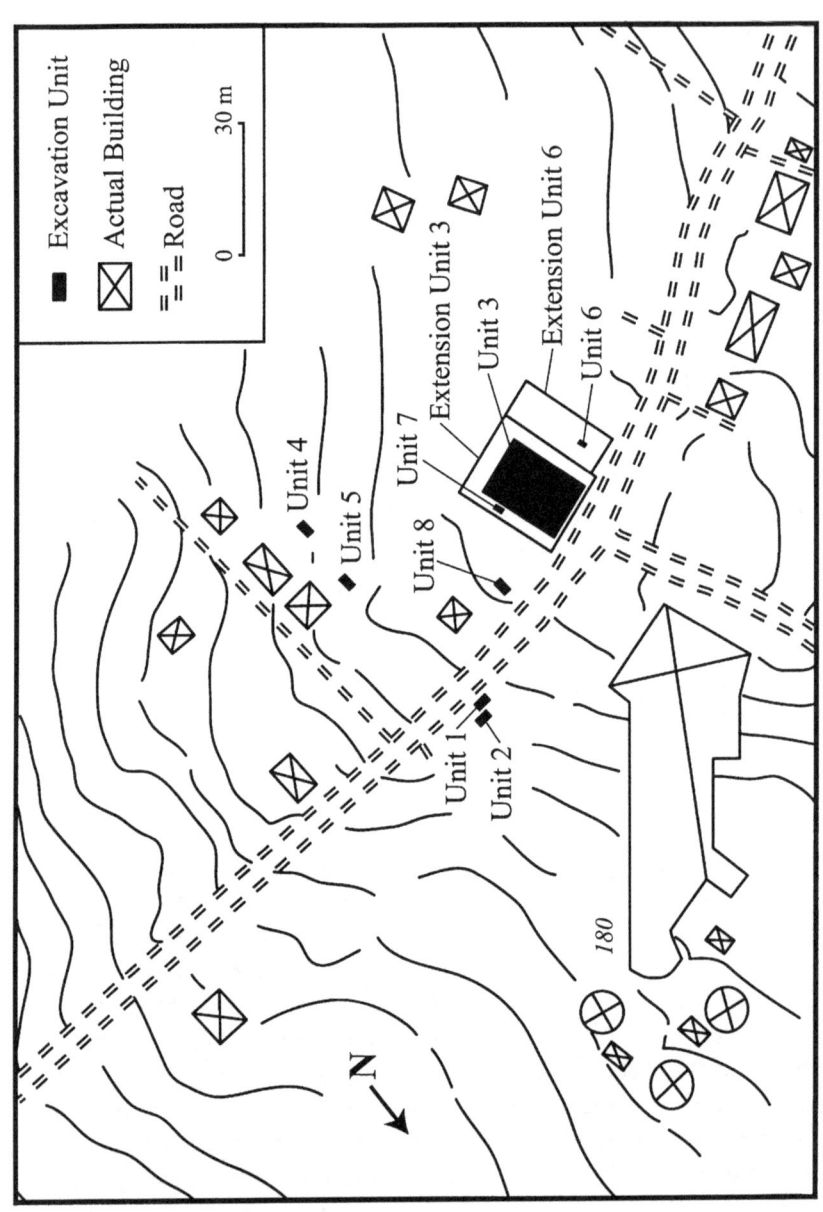

Figure 8.2. Plan of El Chorro de Maíta.

legs flexed to varying degrees was the most common burial position. In most of the preserved skulls, fronto-occipital tabular oblique deformation was present, although, according to Guarch (1996:21), the skulls of one adult skull and some juveniles were not deformed.

Radiocarbon dates were obtained on bone from two of the skeletons: burial No. 25 (conventional radiocarbon age 870 ± 70 B.P., Beta—148956; d 13c/12c = –19 percent; 2 Sigma calibration: cal A.D. 1020 to 1280 [cal 930 to 670 B.P.]) and burial No. 39 (conventional radiocarbon age 360 ± 80 B.P., Beta—148955; d 13c/12c = –19 percent; 2 Sigma calibration: cal A.D. 1420 to 1670 [cal 530 to 280 B.P.]). In addition, we have a date obtained on wood carbon taken from Excavation Unit 5 (Valcárcel 2002a:142), which indicates the pre-Columbian use of parts of the site for food preparation (conventional radiocarbon age 730 ± 60 B.P.; Beta—148957; d 13c/12c = –25.0 percent; 2 Sigma calibración: cal A.D. 1200 to 1320 [cal 750 to 630 B.P.] and cal A.D. 1350 to 1390 [cal 600 to 560 B.P.]). Unit 5 also contained an indigenous skeleton.

Some of these burials contained body adornment objects—ear spools, necklaces, and bracelets—made of stone, coral, and vegetal resins (Guarch 1996:21). But the cemetery's largest, most complex assemblage of ornaments (Figure 8.3) was buried with skeleton No. 57, a female between 19 and 21 years of age (Guarch 1996:21). Beads of gold, quartzite, coral, and pearls, as well as pendants made of an alloy of gold, copper, and silver were recovered. Other objects made of these ternary alloys included a small bell and a bird's head. The bell and bird's head are clearly not Antillean; in the case of the latter, Oliver (2000:201, 207n.37) and Juanita Saenz Samper (personal communication to Roberto Valcárcel 2004) suggest that the bird's head came from Colombia given its similarity to Tairona pectoral ornaments from the Caribbean coast of that country.

Small metallic tubes (Figure 8.4) also were found with this burial, as well as with 16 other skeletons in the cemetery (Valcárcel and Rodríguez 2005:137). Five of these tubes (Figure 8.5) were excavated with skeleton No. 25, these tubes were found in association with a metal disc covered with cotton cloth forming a single ornament (Guarch 1996:20). Few adornments were found with the rest of the burials, although these objects were of great value in the indigenous world (Guarch 1994:8; Valcárcel and Rodríguez 2005:139). A certain degree of complex craftsmanship was involved in the elaboration of some of these objects, including the manufacture of quartzite beads as small as 1.5–2 mm.

For Guarch (1994:37, 1996:22), who directed the first studies of these materials, this site was clearly one of "Indo-Hispanic contact," as indicated by the objects, animal bones, and human remains of apparent European origin, as well as the local modification of European materials and the elaboration of a vessel that copied, with native techniques and materials, Hispanic ceramic forms of indeterminate type. Guarch (1988:177, 1996:22) considered the extended position of some

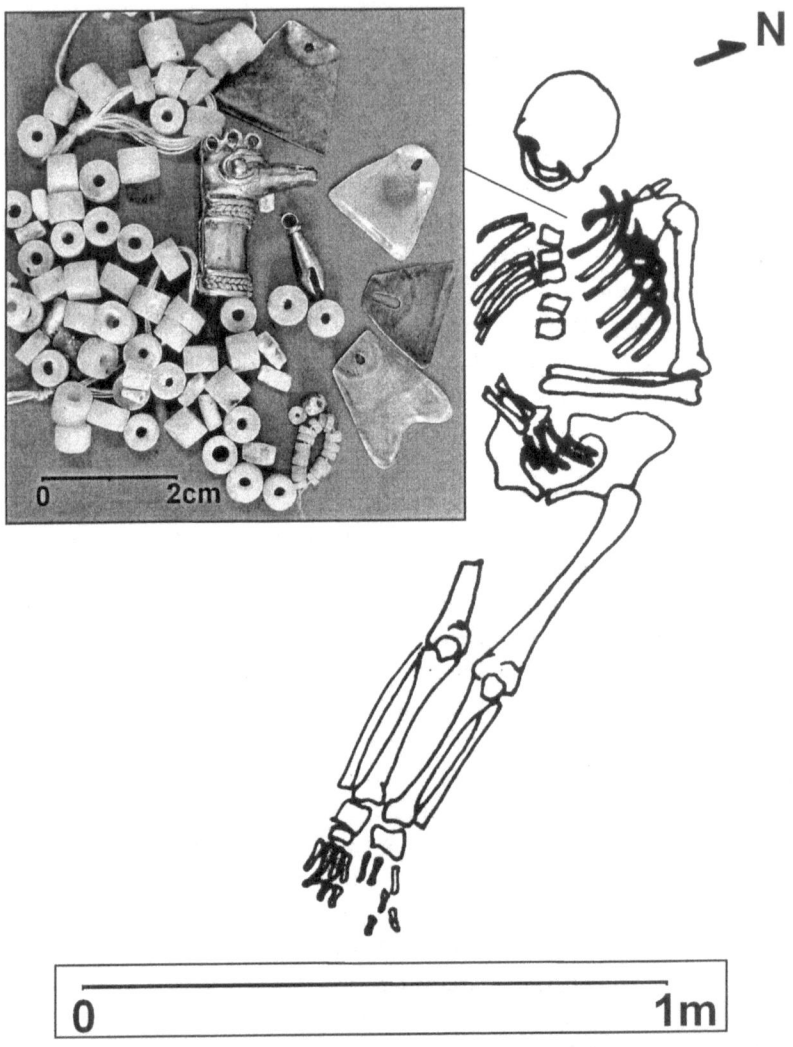

Figure 8.3. Burial No. 57 with some of the reported objects.

of the burials, along with the existence of individuals lacking cranial deformation, as probable indications of contact between indigenous peoples and Spaniards, although he admitted the difficulty of determining the nature and depth of this link given the absence of both adequate chronology for the burials and historical references to the site.

This conservative focus was appropriate, since compared to other indigenous sites with the reported presence of European materials in northeast Cuba (see Figure 8.1), including El Yayal (Domínguez 1984; García 1938), Alcalá (Valcár-

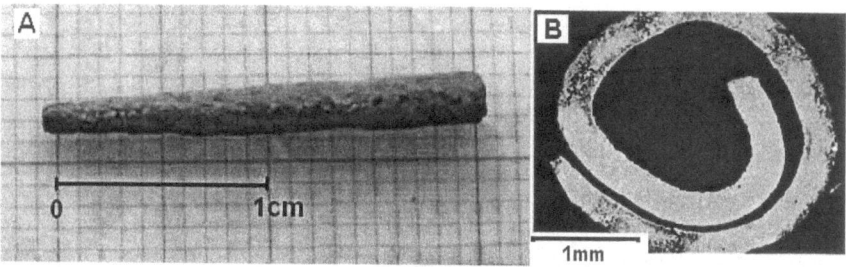

Figure 8.4. Brass tubes (lacetags); (a) photograph of a complete piece, (b) transverse view.

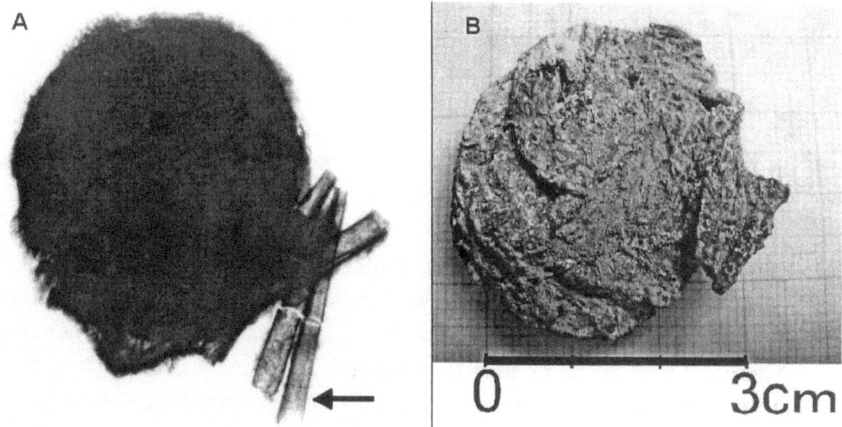

Figure 8.5. Ornament from burial No. 25; (a) radiograph, (b) photograph.

cel 1997), or El Pesquero (García 1940), the level of contact at El Chorro de Maíta seemed notably moderate (Valcárcel 1997:73). However, without a reliable chronology, the absence of cranial deformation and the extended burial position are not, by themselves, sufficient evidence to assume that they were the direct result of European influence.

Brass, Lacetags, and Turey

The tubes found with the skeletons are made of very thin metal sheets rolled around themselves, creating a hollow structure. Through the tubes passed the string that served to suspend them or insert them into other objects. The average dimensions of complete specimens are 29 mm (length) with a diameter of 2 mm at the narrowest end and 3 mm at the widest part (Figure 8.4). From the moment of discovery researchers believed, probably because of the green tones present on some pieces and spots of the same color on the bones upon which the artifacts rested, that these tubes were made of copper (Guarch et al. 1987:29). One of the tubes was submitted to laser microspectral analysis with an LMA-10 microprobe, which determined that the composition of the metal was largely copper with other unidentified elements (Guarch et al. 1987:31).

In 2002 and 2003 Valcárcel (2002b) coordinated new studies on the metal objects from El Chorro de Maíta, carried out at the Center for Technological Applications and Nuclear Development of the Ministry of Science, Technology and Environment in Havana. X-ray fluorescence determined the presence of copper in the perforated piece from Excavation Unit 6 and of gold in one of the beads from skeleton No. 57. In addition 19 tubes (or fragments thereof) were analyzed and determined to be composed of brass (Valcárcel 2002b; Valcárcel et al. 2007). Nevertheless, this method of analysis provided information only on the composition of the objects' surfaces; given the high grade of corrosion in most cases, quantification of the elements present was not thoroughly reliable, and evaluation of various aspects of the technology used in creating the artifacts was impossible.

Ultimately some contradictory evidence emerged. Although apparently there are cases of accidental production of low-zinc brass in pre-Columbian America (Craddock 1995), its presence on the continent fundamentally began with European importation. The unexpected identification of brass in one of the ornaments from skeleton No. 25, dated to the pre-Columbian period, necessitated both an evaluation of this chronological placement and additional analyses of the metal composition of the objects found in the cemetery.

Thus in 2005 the authors of this article carried out new studies on the tubes in the Wolfson Archaeological Science Laboratories at the Institute of Archaeology at the University College London (Martinón-Torres et al. 2007). Six tubes, some already analyzed in Cuba, were analyzed by scanning electron microscopy with energy dispersive spectrometry for composition and structure. This examination revealed that they were made of brass with relatively high concentrations of zinc. The microscope also revealed evidence of various episodes of hammering, followed by brief periods of annealing. The composition of these tubes is very similar to brass produced in large quantities by cementation processes used in central Europe in the fifteenth and sixteenth centuries, especially in Nüremberg, Germany (Martinón-Torres et al. 2007:8).

If we take into account the preceding analysis in Cuba and the similarity among all of these objects, it seems possible that all of the tubes were made of brass. Thus the tubes must have arrived at the cemetery via some type of contact between the local population and Europeans. The form of the pieces also supports this interpretation; an examination of pictorial sources, archaeological data from fifteenth-century Europe (Martinón-Torres et al. 2007) and information on early colonial contexts in the Americas (Deagan 2002:174–175) reveals that the tubes were elements used in European clothing during the fifteenth and sixteenth centuries, known as *agujetas* in Spanish or aglets, lace chaps, or lacetags in English (Deagan 2002:175).

Deagan (2002:175, Figure 8.24) and Martinón-Torres et al. (2007, 2008) show paintings from this period in which the use of lacetags is illustrated. They were placed on cords used to adjust or close items of clothing; when the tube pressed the end of the cord it prevented the closure from coming undone. Deagan (2002:174–175) describes such cords as the most common clothes-closing devices in the Spanish colonies until the second half of the seventeenth century. They have been recovered archaeologically at La Isabela, a fifteenth-century site in the Dominican Republic (Deagan and Cruxent 2002:155); at sixteenth-century sites including Concepción de la Vega, Dominican Republic (Deagan and Kulst 1998:14), Puerto Real, Haiti (Marrinan 1995:193), and several sites in the United States including Santa Elena, South Carolina; St. Augustine, Florida; and Jamestown, Virginia (Deagan 2002:174–175; Kelso and Straube 2004:173–174).

Deagan (2002:175, Figure 8.23) depicts archaeological lacetags from Saint Augustine that are very similar in form and dimension to those from El Chorro de Maíta. Elsewhere in Cuba, lacetags have been found at the indigenous site of Alcalá and in sixteenth-century archaeological contexts in Old Havana (Valcárcel et al 2007). Lacetags of this kind are rare after 1650 and have not been reported in eighteenth-century contexts (Deagan 2002:174–175).

At El Chorro de Maíta, some indigenous individuals may have been buried in European clothing. Cloth fragments found in burial No. 57 seem to support that idea. Nevertheless, the available evidence is insufficient to draw that conclusion, at least for now. The location of the tubes on the skeletal remains indicates that originally they were placed on the wrists, near the neck and chest, or at the waist. These placements coincide with those of lacetags in European clothing of the sixteenth century, but these are the same body parts on which the natives wore ornaments (Alegría 1980). Thus we cannot exclude the possibility that the lacetags were placed apart from clothing and were used as items of adornment rather than as clothes-closing devices. In fact, the Spaniards on Columbus's first and second voyages (Álvarez 1977:92; Colón 1961:149) used lacetags to barter with the indigenous communities.

The above-described, complex ornament on skeleton No. 25 from El Chorro de Maíta (Figure 8.5), in which the lacetags appear associated with a cotton-wrapped metal disc, was located on one of the individual's legs, a location evidently related to traditional ornamentation practices. Below the knees, the indigenous peoples used cotton cords that girdled the legs, making them look thicker. Also the design of this object resembles indigenous ornaments: tubes of amber and gold suspended from belts, and ornaments made of gold discs probably encrusted in cotton bases are described at Hispaniola (Alegría 1980:12, 22–23).

The skeletal remains with which this particular ornament was found belonged to a man who in life must have been very robust in any event and whose height (172 cm) distinguishes him in a mortuary sample in which the average height of men seems not to have exceeded 159 cm (Rodríguez 2003:87, 90). This information suggests that the person in question may have had certain status, a detail that underscores the importance of the object. The reuse of lacetags in this piece may be explained if we examine the significance of metals in the indigenous societies of the Antilles, especially that assigned to brass.

Metals, Indigenous Societies, and Brass

Archaeological (Siegel and Severin 1993) and ethnohistoric (Vega 1988) evidence indicates that long before the arrival of Europeans, the indigenous peoples of the Greater Antilles used objects of gold or an alloy of gold, copper, and silver called *guanín*. Pure gold, obtained from placer deposits, was hammered into sheets of varying thickness and occasionally embossed. The prepared sheets were made into body ornaments, parts of religious images, and luxurious ritual implements (Oliver 2000:204).

References pulled together by Vega (1988:37–38, 42–44) mention that the indigenous peoples perceived in guanín a special odor. They preferred it to gold, recognizing it as an extremely valuable material. The Europeans, taking advantage of this situation, began bringing *guanines* from other places to trade for gold in Hispaniola (Oliver 2000; Vega 1988). Its use in the Greater Antilles dates back to pre-Taíno times (Siegel and Severin 1993:76), although its elaboration seems not to have been local since the indigenous peoples of the Antilles lacked the smelting techniques necessary to produce this alloy. In fact, we lack archaeological evidence of furnaces where this process could have been executed (Siegel and Severin 1993:77). Vega (1988:43), citing the opinion of Rivet and Arsandoux (1946) on the possible Guayanese origin of the pieces held by the Taínos of the Antilles, suggests that the material was obtained via contacts on the continent (see also Oliver 2000:202; Rouse 1992:9). Still, we lack archaeological confirmation of the source; it is possible that Venezuela and Guyana received these metals from further afield, potentially from Colombia.

In various descriptions of caciques' vestments the presence of guanín and gold contrast with the simple image of the common Taíno (Oliver 1998:67). The foreign origin of guanín and its limited availability are factors in its great worth, as highlighted by its noteworthy role in Taíno mythology. Arrom (1975:154) points out its religious value, finding it mentioned in important mythological passages about the origins of Taíno social practices. Oliver (2000:209–215) offers a more detailed analysis of these passages defining the social order, establishing guanín as a sacred unifying principle among the symbols of chiefly power.

With the Spaniards came new metals, some of which were incorporated into in-

Turey Treasure in the Caribbean / 119

digenous society for use as body ornamentation. Among these are objects of copper, bronze, and, in most cases, brass. Vega (1988:36) cites an illustrative comment made by sixteenth-century Spanish cleric Bartolomé de Las Casas (1965:281), in which he clarifies the meaning of the indigenous interest in brass objects, including the lacetags: "All things of brass they esteemed more than any other, and for this, for a piece of a lace chape, they gave without difficulty everything they had, calling it *turey*, like something from the sky, because they called the sky *turey*."

The term *turey* could designate diverse objects of European origin, as Diego Álvarez (1977:93) indicates, although some investigators (Oliver 2001:198; Vega 1988:35) relate the term in particular to brass. For Oliver (2000:198) the most appropriate translation of *turey* is "the brilliant part of the sky, excluding the clouds." Las Casas (1965:281), cited in Vega (1988:36), specifies that in brass the indigenous peoples perceived a special odor, just as they did with guanín. Like guanín brass was shiny and golden hued, and the remoteness of its origin[2]—Spain—as well as the strangeness of its providers, individuals considered immortal by the indigenous communities (Cassá 1992:190, 227; Crespo 2000:125), loaded this metal with sacred values. These qualities (Oliver 2000:199) determined its rapid insertion in the symbolism of power, creating a demand for brass analogous to that of guanín that the Europeans took advantage of, exchanging it for pure gold.

This information confirms that the act of reusing the lacetags for the adornment found with skeleton No. 25 goes beyond the passive acquisition of a foreign object. Instead, the evidence indicates precise selection, based on native symbolic codes that generated a cultural reordering of the metal. The lacetags of turey were a valuable resource, containing special qualities. The complexity of the ornament from skeleton No. 25—and the decorative concept with which it was designed and used— distinguishes it not only as an object of great importance but also as a creative act structured by local concepts.

This interest in brass was not isolated; the presence of guanines in burial No. 57 is another case that illustrates the interest in valuable metals; the large cache of precious goods, especially metals (a lacetag and seven guanines, as well as beads of pearl, gold, quartzite, and coral) apparently mark a hierarchical context, although we cannot know whether the symbolic meaning of the brass in burial 57 is similar to that of the metals from burial 25 discussed earlier.

Brass and Indo-Hispanic Contact

The identification of the lacetags provides new insights on the universe of European objects (in this case, elements of clothing) to which the indigenous individuals buried at El Chorro de Maíta had access. We now understand something of the processes of reutilization of these objects according to native symbolic codes. In addition, the data from these burials provide a valuable chronological and cultural reference that lets us reevaluate aspects of this cemetery, including certain funerary practices and the temporality of the burials themselves.

The clearest case is that of the 16 burials Guarch (1996:16) encountered in extended position. Our reevaluation diminishes that number to 14 (13 supine, one prone). Of the 13 supine burials, 9 were found with their hands crossed and placed on the chest or abdomen; the arms of two were extended along the sides of the body; on one skeleton one arm was extended along the side of the skeleton, the other toward the head. The arm position of the remaining skeleton could not be determined because the remains were deteriorated.

The extended position is extremely unusual in burials of indigenous agriculturalists in Cuba. It is found in groups of fisher-gatherers in Cuba and other parts of the Antilles, and occasionally in early sedentary communities with Saladoid ceramics (Sannen 2006); but extremely rare at sites associated to "Meillacan ostionoid" or "Chican ostionoid" ceramics (Rouse 1992) such as those present in Cuba. In these cases the bodies were usually supine or placed on the side, with the lower extremities flexed to varying degrees (Crespo 2000:119; Guarch 1978:182; Jiménez 1979:268; Veloz et al. 1976:314, 317n.4). The flexed position does not register clearly in the ethnohistoric record of the Greater Antilles, although some confusing descriptions of Taíno burials referred to in the European chronicles might pertain to this type (Crespo 2000:136). Nevertheless, given the persistence and frequency of flexed burials they must be strongly related to religious beliefs and should have figured largely among groups that attributed a great deal of importance to acts related to death.

Thus the presence of extended burials in pre-Columbian contexts in the Greater Antilles is often considered atypical (Veloz et al. 1976:314n.4) or interpreted as an isolated event unrelated to funerary rituals (Crespo 2000:157). At the site of El Atajadizo, in the Dominican Republic, the extended burial position is reported for individuals who may have met a violent death and were buried hastily, without regard for traditional burial practices (Veloz et al. 1976:313–314). At early European burial sites in the New World, however, extended burials prevail, even when indigenous individuals were laid to rest in such contexts, such as at La Isabela, in the Dominican Republic (Guerrero 1999:108), or Puerto Real, Haiti (Marrinan 1995:179). The typically Christian extended position at these sites is supine, legs extended, hands crossed over the chest or abdomen, and laid out along an east-west orientation so that the individual, awakening on the day of judgment, could see the face of God in the east (Parker Pearson 2003:6).

In Cuba, a strong tendency toward flexed-position burials prevails even in places where there is evidence of relations with the Europeans (Miguel 1949; Rouse 1942: 136). Only in indigenous settlements where this relationship was very intense and prolonged, such as El Yayal or Barajagua (Figure 8.1), do some native burials appear extended (Rouse 1942:136).

At El Chorro de Maíta, over half of the 106 burials exhibit some degree of flexed lower extremities (this excludes the 14 extended examples and 33 cases in which the position of the legs could not be determined due to deterioration or alteration of the remains (Guarch 1996:18, Table 2). The lone prone burial (No. 97) does not fit the Christian norm. In two of the remaining extended burial cases all of the characteristics of Christian burials are present; 10 examples comply with two or three Christian practices. In 6 of these burials, all laid out with hands crossed over chests or abdomens, brass was present. This consistent pattern establishes a clear relationship between the extended position and European influence. The discovery of brass in almost half of the extended burials provides a cultural and chronological reference that confirms Guarch's original interpretation and complements a picture in which, in addition to incorporating foreign materials, the local communities were abandoning established cultural traditions in favor of new funerary practices.

Spatially, the extended position burials marked by the presence of brass artifacts are concentrated in the central part of the cemetery, where the tentatively identified European skull also was found. This spatial link suggests some degree of temporal proximity among the burials and indicates, above all, an interconnection among these individuals that expresses, without excluding other motivations, the genesis of a shared process: changes in local culture determined by interaction with Europeans.[3]

The confirmation of the relationship between extended burial position and European influences increases the number of inhumations that clearly post-date the arrival of the Spaniards. If we consider all of the extended burials without brass, but with two or more elements of the Christian burial pattern (there are 6 of these), and add them to those with brass (17), we have a total of 23 post-Columbian burials. This does not exclude the possiblilty that many of the nonextended burials lacking brass are also post-Columbian. Although we lack a full chronology for the cemetery, the large number of deceased could be related as much to a long period of use after European arrival as to a post-Columbian increase in use in the location, or an increase in mortality during this period.

The presumed pre-Columbian origin of the cemetery was based on the dates from burial No. 25 and the carbon from Excavation Unit 5 (Valcárcel and Rodríguez 2005). The presence of brass with skeleton No. 25 highlights the problem with this assumption and forces us to evaluate with caution the relationship between the rest of the human remains in Unit 5 and the skeletons found in the central zone of the cemetery (Unit 3; see Figure 8.2). Moreover, if we consider the absence of cemeteries at known pre-Columbian indigenous agriculturalist sites in Cuba, and the ample number of burials post-dating the arrival of the Europeans, the notion of pre-Columbian origins for this cemetery requires further scrutiny. We are looking at either an indigenous burial ground transformed into a cemetery at the start of European contact, or even a cemetery that originated during the contact period.

In this context of strong post-Columbian use with clear evidence of modifications to local funerary practices, the lack of cranial deformation may also be related to European influence. In a preliminary consideration of the burials containing undeformed skulls, we noted one individual (skeleton No. 45) with brass also buried in extended position. Cranial deformation functioned as an ethnic identifier associated with the beliefs, rituals, and aesthetics (Crespo 2000:227–230) of agricultural, ceramic-producing groups. At least in Cuba, the absence of cranial deformation in burials recovered at agriculturalist-ceramicist sites is rare.

The high degree of change we see in these groups resulting from European pressures undoubtedly influenced this particular situation. Since the deformation process began in childhood, the practice may have been ended by indigenous peoples protecting children born after European arrival. However, sixteenth-century documentary references to the prohibition of cranial deformation in Peru (Dingwall 1931:215) illustrate the conquistadors' eagerness to modify the aspects of indigenous culture they saw as opposed to the canons of civilization and religion, including those related to the body. The adult with an undeformed skull—skeleton No. 45—was approximately 25–30 years old at time of death; even if this adult came from another area, the additional presence of subadults of varying ages (Guarch 1996:21) lacking cranial deformation points toward the presence of strong Spanish influences for at least several years.

Persistence and Change

The presence of brass with burial No. 25, assigned a pre-Columbian date in the original radiocarbon assays, and the wide range of calibration on the date for burial No. 39 (see above) are unresolved problems. However, during recent fieldwork in nonfunerary contexts at El Chorro de Maíta carried out by Valcárcel, Knight, and Persons (2007; also Persons et al. 2007), we identified an indigenous context dated to the first half of the fifteenth century, as well as strata containing diverse types of European ceramics ranging in date between 1490 and 1650. If we assume the existence of some contemporaneity between the use of the cemetery and of the surrounding spaces, we have a potentially long period of post-Columbian use, related to diverse moments and situations of Indo-Hispanic contact. In these circumstances the lacetags distinguish a group of individuals of certain chronological proximity, although the exact period of their use is difficult to determine.

Except for burial No. 25, in which the ornamental use of brass is clear, we do not know if we are seeing clothing with lacetags or independent ornaments. Still, we can distinguish some basic elements of culture and the exercise of power, evident in the selective capture of European objects, funerary patterns that persist or change, and elite individuals inserted into the ambient interaction. In the case of burial No. 25, the presence of brass implies the specific use of European materials and their reordering according to local ideological norms, in terms of both the indigenous symbolic universe and native mechanisms of legitimizing rank.

The use of brass in this case reflects an independent, active perspective from which the metal is adopted and adapted to indigenous ornamental practices. The extended burial position provides a different perspective, underscoring the loss of deeply ingrained cultural practices related to ritual schemes and indigenous identity and their replacement by new practices linked to Christian burial rituals. It is difficult to know if these changes respond to real ideological adjustments, since the available historical evidence refers to communities that even in conditions of complete subjugation remained attached to their rites and ceremonies (Pichardo 1945). We might be looking at a population that accepted changes to survive, using these as a means of protection through which autochthonous beliefs were maintained. In any event, in the case of extended burials the subordinate position of the indigenous population and their receptivity to European norms related to the imposition of religion is clear.

The entry of the European burial position may mark distinct incidents and levels of Hispanic pressure or domination. It may even be related to inherent aspects of the social rank of the indigenous individuals or their personal relation with the material or religious world of the Spaniards; perhaps for this reason the pattern is not generalized. Yet the majority of the burials with brass follow indigenous burial customs (10 of these burials are semi-flexed or very flexed). Although we still lack a diachronic perspective, these burials suggest the persistence and continuity of local patterns. The position of skeleton No. 25 was very flexed. This is the best example we have of the confluence of post-Columbian moments with indigenous practices, pointing to circumstances in which certain prerogatives and possibilities of indigenous expression were maintained even while changes determined by European influence were present.

The use of ornaments that include brass probably reflects the existence of post-Columbian indigenous elites (Valcárcel and Rodríguez 2005). As a case in point, one of the individuals in our sample (burial No. 57) contains mortuary objects of interest to the Europeans, including the gold beads and guanín. Perhaps the Spaniards gave differential treatment to the chiefly levels of society, since the recognition of their political importance, established even by colonial legislation, was a key element in ordering their relations with the indigenous communities (Deagan and Cruxent 1993:70; Moscoso 1986:319–324). In addition, burial No. 57 is one of the best examples of Christian burial in our sample, a phenomenon probably linked to Spanish interest in the development of ties to local elites as a means of promoting acceptance of Catholic beliefs. In fact, there are very early historical references to the Christianization of caciques in Cuba, as well as indications that children of native families of high rank were sent to Spain in 1526 to be instructed in the Catholic faith in order to diffuse this belief system among their own people (Pichardo 1945). Nevertheless, the potential for elites to maintain a certain level of local autonomy, visible in the maintenance of symbolic and mortuary customs, probably was determined by a situation in which relationships with the Europeans were not coupled with total disarticulation from indigenous society and its institutions.

The selective use of European elements, and the changes this generated, calls attention to elite strata reiterating their key role in the panorama of Hispanic/indigenous interaction. We cannot ignore the fact that the important personage in the case of burial No. 57 was a young woman, which bears reference to the recognized feminine protagonism in indigenous spaces of power and to the important role played by women in the processes of contact with the Europeans (Sued-Badillo 1989).

Conclusions

The identification of the use of brass lacetags in the cemetery at El Chorro de Maíta rectifies earlier ideas about the metallic composition of these objects and determines the precise nature of their European origin. This new evidence brings about a radical change in the way we understand Indo-Hispanic contact at this site, and provides new insights into the post-Columbian character of many of the burials. The results of our investigation underscore, here as at other contact-era sites in the Antilles (Deagan 2004), the need to focus on methodologies directed toward questions of interaction rather than depending on the typical investigation strategies used in pre-Columbian contexts.

At El Chorro de Maíta, the level and characteristics of the cultural connections were discovered not just through an assessment of the quantity of European material or the presence of transcultural objects. Rather, we explored the possibilities these items offered for achieving an integrated evaluation of diverse elements within the burial contexts and recognizing the give and take among indigenous attitudes and the reality of the imposition of Spanish practices. Thus consideration of the nature and intensity of Spanish contact as expressed in the objects of transculturation is but one element in the larger task of understanding the development and results of cultural interaction.

The lacetags, in a modified mortuary environment, help us perceive strong links between the native population and elements of European culture, both material and ideological, as well as variations in important aspects of local cultural practices. The lacetags demonstrate intense use of the cemetery in post-Columbian times and force us to reevaluate our original notions of its pre-Columbian origins. In a place where historical documentation is scant and imprecise, we discovered through archaeology a cemetery that contains evidence of great interest regarding Indo-Hispanic interactions. Despite changes in important native cultural practices the indigenous peoples maintained their capacity for self-expression. The elite appear central in actions of cultural continuity as well as in changes regarding their key roles in local society within the project of Hispanic domination. With these data, Indo-Hispanic interaction appears as a highly dynamic process in which change was neither immediate nor comprehensive. Indigenous communities were not the passive receivers of influences and elements as portrayed in earlier historical visions, but rather active agents living through a unique period of cultural interaction in the Caribbean.

Acknowledgments

For their suggestions, comments, and information shared we would like to thank José Oliver, John Merkel, Salvador Rovira, Juanita Saenz Samper, Roberto Lleras, Glenis Tavares, Roger Arrazcaeta, Lourdes Domínguez, Lisette Roura, Iosvany Hernández, Osvaldo Jiménez, Antonio Curet, Alex Bayliss, Daniel Torres Etayo, Alice Samson, and Susan Kepecs. The technical assistance of Renata Peters, Simon Groom, Kevin Reves, and Stuart Laidlaw has been invaluable, as has the support of specialists from the Laboratory of Chemical Analysis at the Center for Technological Applications and Nuclear Development of the Ministry of Sciences, Technology and Environment in Havana. We also owe a debt of gratitude to the Holguín Provincial Monuments Commission, the National Vicepresidency of Monuments, and the National Subcommission on Archaeology in Cuba. The available radiocarbon dates were obtained thanks to the help of Dr. Betty Meggers. The investigation at the Wolfson Archaeological Science Laboratories and the use of other facilities of the Institute of Archaeology at University College London was made possible thanks to a Marie Curie grant for Early Stage Training of Researchers, contract MEST-CT 2004, 2005, No. 514509.

Notes

1. According to Valcárcel and Rodríguez (2005:134), the number of aboriginal skeletons could reach 110. This possibility is based on unconfirmed information concerning remains found during the construction of a museum at the site.

2. The concept of Spain as a distant place is an important factor. Objects from distant points of origin, as is the case with guanín, may be linked to the notion that in traditional societies cosmological distances are perceived as equivalent to geographic distances; thus goods or people from far away are perceived as possessing supernatural powers (Helms 1993).

3. Valcárcel and Rodríguez (2005:141) suggest that the selection of this space may also express hierarchical distinctions.

9
The Archaeology of Escaped Slaves
Utensils for Resistance

Gabino La Rosa Corzo, Sección de Historia de la
Unión de Escritores y Artistas de Cuba

This chapter is based on a study of 30 archaeological sites used by escaped slaves (maroons; *cimarrones* in Spanish) in the region known as the uplands of Havana—Matanzas, Cuba. I evaluate the potential of historical archaeology as a scientific tool for reconstructing the daily lives, defense tactics, and subsistence resources of the people who took shelter in these locations. In practice, I aim beyond the simple material inventory of these sites; my goal is to refine the discipline's ability to decipher the degrees of African-ness and creolization that appear in the traditions, habits, and customs of the human groups produced as a consequence of plantation slavery but living in liberty in the hills.

> Sobre la base del estudio de las características de los sitios y de las evidencias arqueológicas colectadas en treinta refugios de cimarrones en las Alturas Habana-Matanzas, Cuba, se evalúa el potencial de los recursos de la arqueología histórica como disciplina científica para reconstruir la vida cotidiana de los cimarrones, sus tácticas defensivas y recursos subsistenciales. El artículo se propone superar el simple inventario material de los sitios de cimarrones y evalúa las perspectivas de la disciplina, en especial sus recursos para apreciar el grado de africanía y criollización que en las tradiciones, hábitos y costumbres de estos grupos humanos, se había producido como consecuencia de la esclavitud de plantaciones y de su vida en libertad en los montes.

During the last decades important variations have arisen in the field of historical archaeology. Its terrain has been broadened, from the spaces of elites to questions about the popular sectors and the mechanisms of domination and resistance (Little 1996; McGuire and Paynter 1991). A review of the discipline is revealing. Without abandoning the objectives of investigations in urban zones and great, museum-class architecture, researchers have extended their interests to rural zones and essential questions about American history, including slavery. And within this topic, attention has begun to turn from the living quarters of hacendados to the spaces of slaves, especially the infirmaries, barracks, and cemeteries on the plantations. Among numerous contributions to the study of slave spaces we have the works of Ferguson (1992), Delle (1998), and Orser (1990), as well as three important edited volumes (Farnsworth, ed., 2001; Haviser, ed., 1999; Singleton, ed., 1999). These last in particular are examples of interest in the study of slaves in the Caribbean.

Nevertheless, efforts aimed at the study of the spaces of fugitive slaves are still relatively few in number. Among the most significant works along this line are those of Kofi E. Agorsah (1990, 1993), who, from an archaeological perspective, has rescued episodes of slave resistance in Jamaica. Other archaeologists have considered the issue in Brazil (Funari 2006; Orser 1992; Orser and Funari 2001). In this field, as the cited authors have shown, the tools of historical archaeology permit an effective critique of the documentary sources generated in the centers of colonial power. These sources currently constitute the basis of information on which our knowledge of this part of American history rests.

Like the above-cited authors, I have long been convinced that historical archaeology can facilitate a comprehensive, detailed approach to fugitive slaves, their lifeways, and above all the process of cultural transformations in which they found themselves immersed. Through this lens, in 1983 I began a search for information linked to this issue in the Cuban National Archive and various provincial archives. I found hundreds of documents containing denouncements of escapes and assaults, slave hunters' diary entries, and even references to geographic accidents that had acquired fame by serving as refuge sites for the cimarrones.

Thus my archaeological explorations were directed toward determined regions, where I paid attention to oral traditions that facilitated the identification of localities that do not appear on maps today. With this information I was able to identify about 50 seasonal refuges in caves and rockshelters, plus five large settlements at high elevations in eastern Cuba. Here I discuss only the results of the work I carried out at the 30 sites in the Havana-Matanzas uplands region, which had, during the first half of the nineteenth century, the greatest concentration of slaves on the island. The material evidence obtained via controlled excavations allowed me to establish not only a chronological framework for the occupation of the sites used as refuges or camp grounds, but also, and above all, to demonstrate that fugitive slaves survived thanks to the combination of habits, abilities, and traditions that mixed African elements with experience on the haciendas and the necessities of life on the run in the hills.

General Information on the Archaeology of Escaped Slaves

Testimonies from the epoch under consideration—the first half of the nineteenth century—make it clear that the material resources of escaped slaves in Cuba were fundamentally those of the haciendas. Nevertheless, a comparative study of the archaeological evidence collected via controlled procedures from the sites that served as hiding places or observation points for the fugitives discloses a rich variety of artifacts and instruments that goes far beyond the simple appropriation of objects from the overlords. It is worth noting that in this chapter I only discuss fugitivism, which is only one of the forms that slave resistance took. As fugitives, one or various escaped slaves wandered in the hills near the haciendas from which they came, depending, in large part, on barter or robbery from those same rural establishments. I am not concerned here with another form of slave resistance, the establishment of palenques—runaway slave settlements set up in isolated spots, at which the cimarrones survived essentially on a subsistence-based economy. This distinction is important, since the theoretical suppositions and field practices for each are very different (La Rosa 1991a, 1991b, 2003). In addition to my own work in eastern Cuba, Pedro Funari's studies (1999) of escaped slaves in Los Palmares, Brazil, lay out theoretical aspects and peculiarities of fieldwork demanded by the conditions of fugitive slave settlements in open spaces.

The archaeological complex that marks the fugitive slave sites of Havana-Matanzas, and the study of artifact function in relation to the life of persecution to which the runaway slaves were submitted, allow the reconstruction of important aspects of the daily life of the cimarrón. A descriptive list of the evidence, with emphasis on brand names, provenience, and technology, would be irrelevant for my proposed objectives. Nevertheless, the artifacts resulting from the adaptation or use of late-colonial potsherds for distinct uses—the inventions of escaped slaves to solve their material necessities—require analysis and evaluation.

These artifacts are the material carriers of the information necessary for approaching these groups, and for beginning to understand their survival tactics, lifeways, and customs. By asking not only what evidence characterizes cimarrón sites, but also why and how these artifacts were used, we can begin to untangle the ways in which the people who made them subsisted, and how they managed to evade the slave hunters who pursued them. Further, by studying the artifact complexes at these sites—which contain both artisanal objects and those obtained via robbery or exchange at haciendas or rural stores—we can begin to measure the degree of dependency fugitive slaves had on the slave-based haciendas from which they came.

Numerous testimonies of the period confirm the existence of this dependency. The Reverend Abiel Abbot from Massachusetts, who visited Cuba in 1821, wrote (1965 [1829]:98) that the cimarrones "sometimes do not go far from the hacienda of their owner and come to drink water from his reservoir, and they provision themselves from his crops and stables." The North American doctor J. G. Wurdemann, who arrived in Cuba in 1841, noted (1989 [1844]:316) that the fugitive slaves passed the day in some secret cave and their nights "prowling around the borders of the haciendas." Similarly, the Swiss visitor Frederika Bremer, writing in

1851 (1980:120), affirmed that "these uplands have deep caves and isolated spots that serve as refuge for the escaped slaves . . . at night, the fugitives come down from the mountain to the planted fields, to get food from the hands of the negros on the plantation."

But the cimarrón assemblage also points in other directions. The information I use to consider the possibilities of fugitive slave life, obtained through the archaeological study of the selected sites, is grouped in two categories—the sites and the artifacts. Thus this chapter contains two separate sections on the archaeological information at hand. In the first, I analyze the characteristics of the sites and their possibilities for defensive tactics on the part of the cimarrones. In the second, I examine the presence and frequence of artifacts destined for the transport, conservation, and use of liquids and foods, as well as their potential use as utensils or tools. Finally, in the conclusions I evaluate the role of these two kinds of evidence in the context of the groups' survival.

Characteristics of the Sites

In the western portion of Cuba, between the provinces of Havana and Matanzas, two mountain ridges of relatively little height extend east to west.[1] The northern ridge is Alturas del Norte; to the south sits Alturas del Centro. The greatest number of archaeological sites selected for study in this chapter (Figure 9.1) are located in these two hilly chains, although six sites are in caves on nearly flat plains that were heavily wooded in the nineteenth century. All of the sites considered here are rockshelters or caves containing archaeological remains of seasonal occupation.

Despite the expansion of the slave-based plantation economy in the region between 1790 and 1850, with the corresponding rise in the slave population, the uninhabited parts of the territory—the hilly, wooded ridges—remained practically unknown.[2] The proximity of this unused land stimulated the flight of slaves from the haciendas. Of the 30 sites in this study (Table 9.1), only 18 are located in places that are difficult to access. Nevertheless, the sites are all situated in abrupt topography and surrounded by vegetation; thus most of them are barely perceptible even in an intentional search (Figure 9.2). Among the sites situated in caves, 17 have several entrances. Nine of the 30 sites are rockshelters—open spaces, partially protected against bad weather. Only 3 sites have natural water sources, although at 2 of these water availability was limited to the rainy season. None of the other sites is close to arroyos, rivers, or lagoons.

This pattern of site selection can be interpreted as a manifestation of life on the run. It demonstrates the dependency these fugitive slave groups must have had on material means to transport and conserve water in their hiding places. The search for water often became a risky enterprise, since it had to be obtained from nearby sources, including haciendas, as some entries in slave hunters' diaries attest (Vil-

Figure 9.1. Map of the region, with the general locations of the sites mentioned in text.

laverde 1982:37). In fact, at all of the refuge sites I encountered the remains of containers for liquids.

All of the caves and rockshelters contained rustic hearths, set directly on the floor. These consist of three stones laid in a rough triangle over the ash lenses, which served as support for the cooking containers. Many of these hearths were rich in archaeological evidence—dietary remains, temporally diagnostic ceramic sherds, and rustic pipes for smoking tobacco were concentrated therein. In contrast, the fragments of containers for liquids—botijas (olive jars), bottles, and demijohns—were more irregularly distributed.

At 12 of the sites I identified more than one hearth; among these, one was always larger and thicker than the rest. The larger hearths were used for cooking, but the fires also may have been maintained through the night for heat and for repelling the insects that abound in these caves. Where there were multiple hearths, some completely lacked food remains, supporting the notion that fires were used for these ends.

Numerous testimonies from the period seem to confirm this idea. The nineteenth-century regionalist writer Cirilo Villaverde (1961 [1891]:18) noted that "the affinity of the people of this race for the hearths, like the Indians, although without

Table 9.1 Site Characteristics

Sites	Difficult access	Camouflage	Various entrances	Rock shelter	Number of hearths	Diet: number of species identified*
1.-Cimarrón 1	X	X			2	1,2,3,4,5, y 8
2.-Cimarrón 2	X	X	X		2	1,2,3,4,5, y 7
3.-Cimarrón 3	X	X	X		1	1,2 y 3
4.-Cimarrón 4	X	X		X	1	1,2 y 6
5.-Cimarrón 5	X	X	X		1	1,2y 6
6.-Cueva del Indio		X			1	1 y 2
7.-Cueva de las Avispas		X			1	1 y 2
8.-Cueva del Búho		X				
9.-Cueva de los Muertos		X	X			1, 2 y 4
10.-Cueva del Aguacate		X	X		1	1 y 2
11.-Cueva del Toro-Matojo-Jía		X	X		2	1,2 y 7
12.-Solapa 1 de las Lomas de Diago		X		X	1	1 y 2
13.-Solapa 2 de las Lomas de Diago		X		X	1	1 y 2
14.-Cueva de La Habana		X	X		1	1, 2 y 3
15.-Solapa de las Lomas de Javier	X	X		X	1	1 y 2
16.-Cueva del Gato		X	X		2	1, 2, 3 y 4
17.-Cueva de la Casa de Purga	X	X	X		2	1, 2, 3y 6
18.-Cueva de la Cachimba	X	X	X		4	1, 2,3y 5
19.-Solapa 1 de la Cueva del Tambor	X	X		X	1	1, 2, 9 y 10**
20.-Solapa 2 de la Cueva del Tambor	X	X		X	1	2
21.-Solapa 3 de la Cueva del Tambor	X	X		X	1	2
22.-Cueva del Tambor	X	X	X			
23.-Cueva del Indio de la Sierra del Grillo		X	X		2	1, 2,4 y 7
24.-Cueva de la Caja	X	X	X		2	1,2,3,4 y 6

Continued on the next page

Table 9.1 *Continued*

Sites	Difficult access	Camouflage	Various entrances	Rock shelter	Number of hearths	Diet: number of species identified*
25.-Cueva de las Piñas	X	X	X		2	1 y 2
26.-Cueva del Jagüey	X	X	X		4	1,2,3 y 6
27.-Solapa de las Horma	X	X		X	1	1 y 2
28.-Cueva del Pan	X	X	X		3	1,2,3,5 y 6
29.-Solapa de la Cueva de Sanguily		X		X	1	1 y 2
30.-Cueva de Sanguily	X	X	X		2	1,2 y 8

*Species identified: 1. Cerdo (Sus scrofa); 2.Jutía (Capromys sp.); 3.Vaca (Bos taurus); 4. Gallina (Gallus gallus); 5. Pato (Cairina moschata); 6. Majá (Epicrates angulifer); 7. Caballo (Equus caballus) ; 8. Perro (Canis familiaris); 9. Jicotea (Pseudemys sp.) 10. Pez (sin identificar).

**Corn cob fragment.

shrewdness, as in summer as in winter, they light them constantly; and not on few occasions, the smoke they dispatch in the middle of the mountains has been cause for their discovery when they wandered as fugitives, apprehending them or destroying them the parties that the government paid to pursue them." The above-cited Swiss writer Bremer (1980:84, 190) wrote in one of her letters that on entering the ranch of a free black she found the door open and a fire on the ground: "secure sign that an African lives here!" And referring to the slaves of the barracks, she noted that inside the hearths glowed and that the African "cannot live without fire, even in the midst of the greatest heat; and they like to light them on the ground."

Among tools I found at the cimarrón sites—often on or near the surface—were machetes, knives, hoes, shackles, buttons, and above all containers—of glass (bottles and demijohns), grès stoneware (flasks), and as expected, coarse earthenware botijas. These assemblages, and the spaces in which they were found, unaltered except for the hearths, speak to the precarious nature of the daily lives of the people who used them—people who did not construct houses but preferred to shelter themselves in the most rustic, seasonal shelters, consuming their food by the hearths into which they tossed the remains of their meals.[3]

Based on all of the above evidence, I conclude that these hidden, naturally camouflaged caves and rockshelters offered vital possibilities for the withdrawal of these fugitives from life in captivity. The use of such sites for the preparation and consumption of food, as well as for sleeping, makes good sense in the context of the marginalized, persecuted existence of runaway slaves.

Figure 9.2. The inaccessibility of the sites is still one of their distinguishing characteristics. Cueva de La Jía. (Photo by G. La Rosa Corzo)

Tools for Resistance

The study of the material evidence collected from the 30 sites described above further illustrates the precarious nature of the lives of the individuals or small groups that subsisted in these spaces. At the same time, the artifact types and frequences provide insights into the cimarrones' cultural characteristics. In total, I collected 1,632 pieces of evidence, within which 360 kinds of artifacts or tools are represented. Among these remains (Figure 9.3), 84 percent belong to some type of container, and 16 percent to instruments, tools, and other metal objects. In the container category, 142 artifacts were associated with carrying, preparing, storing,

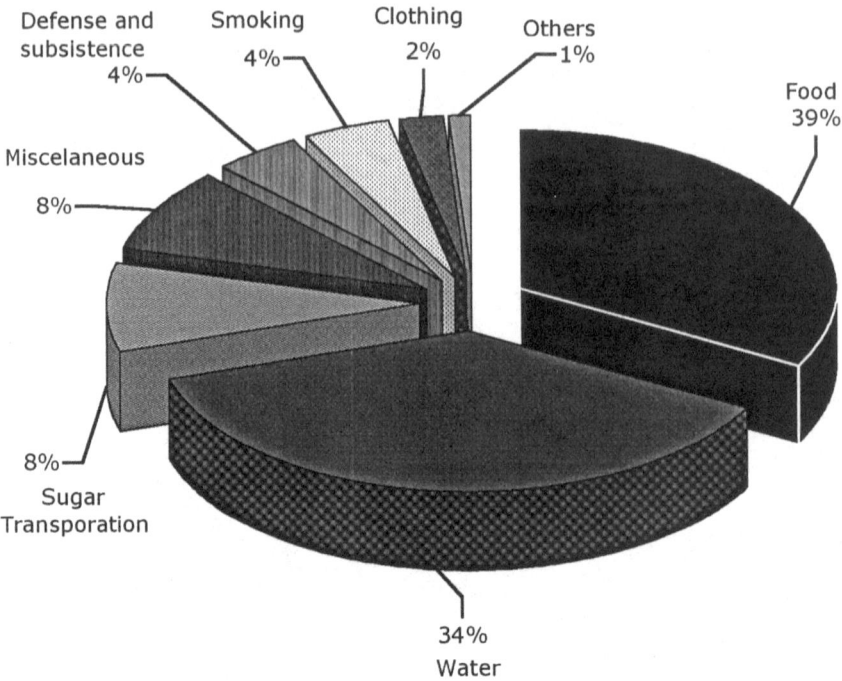

Figure 9.3. Percentages of artifact and tool types, by category.

and consuming food; 124 were used for the transport, storage, and consumption of liquids (fundamentally water, given the lack of nearby sources at most of the sites). Among the remaining containers, 28 are associated with the transport of sugar from the plantations to the refuge sites, 10 with smoking tobacco, and finally, a single chamber pot, the function of which, within the hideaway in which it was found, remains unknown.[4]

Containers for Solid Foods

The containers destined for the storage, preparation, and consumption of solid foods included earthenware and porcelain plates and various kinds of pots. Fifteen round cast-iron pots with three feet, called *trébedes,* and a single kettle of the same material, are included in this category. Trébedes were common in the nineteenth century, and generally came from the United States. Although imported, these pots were very cheap since they broke easily and were impossible to clean. Thus they are always associated with very humble segments of society. They were typical receptacles in slave barracks. Those collected in the refuge sites generally were quite large.

Glazed ceramic pots, also very common in nineteenth-century Cuba, in both urban and rural kitchens, could be acquired by escaped slaves through robbery or barter in rural stores. Fragments of 110 vessels of this type are included in the artifactual inventory from the 30 sites in consideration. These data, taken together, support the notion that the cimarrón assemblage was taken largely from the haciendas.

Nevertheless, the fugitives who took refuge in the rockshelters and caves of the Habana-Matanzas uplands did not depend solely on containers stolen from the wealthy or bartered for in the back woods. The presence of 14 locally produced pots and plates are the most important archaeological evidence in this study. At sites across the region (Cimarrón 5, Solapa de las Lomas de Javier, Solapa 2 de la Cueva del Tambor, Cueva de la Caja, and Cueva de Sanguily), the inhabitants made clay pots for cooking food and rustic pipes for smoking tobacco.

The fabrication of clay containers by escaped slaves is mentioned in various sources. In a document from 1885 that describes a cimarrón community in Surinam, women made clay pots for cooking (Price 1981:238). Clay containers of local manufacture are reported at archaeological sites linked to slave resistance in the Dominican Republic (Arrom and García 1986:50) and Brazil (Allen 1999; Funari 1999; Jacobus 1996). In Cuba, the first report of a ceramic pot of local manufacture in the context of cimarrón sites was written in 1946 by archaeologist Eladio Elso, who collected artifacts in a rockshelter of difficult access in Pinar del Río. In the diary of his expedition he also described large pottery fragments in a rustic stone hearth set on the ground. Among food remains in the hearth, he noted bones of land tortoise *(Pseudemys sp.)*, dogs *(Canis familiares)*, and wild pigs *(Sus scrofa)*. In Elso's (1946:10) judgment, "Easily I can identify this place as a shelter for one or several cimarrones, which is why I baptized it with the name 'Cueva del Cimarrón.'"

Despite the fact that Elso recognized the local manufacture of the above-mentioned pot, in the collections of the old Center for Anthropology in Havana it was classified as aboriginal. In a recent study carried out in the laboratory at the Cuban Institute for Anthropology by ceramics specialist I. Jouravleva and myself (La Rosa 1999), all available samples of this type of pottery, including the example from Elso's collection, were reanalyzed. We determined that the sherds in question were made with coils and molded, then cooked on an open fire. Although these pieces are easily confused with indigenous pottery because both were fired in open hearths, the formation techniques of the cimarrón pottery are distinct from any native ceramics known in Cuba.

While it is true that unslipped pots incorporating techniques used by both indigenous groups (Domínguez 1980) and Africans (Ferguson 1980) were made in the ovens of haciendas, what is important in this case is that the fugitive slaves of Cuba did not depend totally on the material resources of haciendas and stores. In the pots they made at their temporary shelters we find the imprint of the slaves' African origins. Although it is quite possible that servants acquired or strengthened their ceramic skills during their years of captivity on the plantations, it is

Figure 9.4. Bowl from a rustic pipe for smoking tobacco, from Cueva de la Cachimba. The star decoration is a recurrent motif in Bantu artifacts and tatoos. (Photo by G. La Rosa Corzo)

well known that the Yoruba and numerous groups from the great linguistic Bantu family were able artisans. The Yoruba, it is important to note, made coiled ceramics and fired them in open hearths (Forde 1965:188).

Moreover, the great majority of the Africans introduced to the New World became habituated to tobacco consumption, using pipes of wood, seeds, bone, and ceramics. The decorations on some of these pipes recall African motifs (Figure 9.4). And in studies of various plantations, archaeologists have described the African origins of the decorations on ceramic implements made by slaves (Emerson 1999; Handler 1983; La Rosa 1999). For these reasons, the rustic pipes known for centuries in Cuba as "cachimbas" constitute one of the best archaeological indicators we have of cimarrón contexts.

Also among unglazed ceramic containers found at the sites in this study are the open-ended clay cones *(hormas)*, introduced in the first moments of the Spanish sugar industry that took root in the Antilles. All of the sugar mills had a tile shop where hormas were made, since they usually broke in the process of extracting the loaf of sugar inside. Thus the *tejero* (in charge of the tile shop, where the hormas were made) was an indispensable figure on the sugar plantations, along with the carpenter and the sugar maestro. By 1850, metal hormas began to substitute for the clay ones; thus horma sherds are reasonably good chronological markers.

The manuals that were used to direct the production of sugar during the period in question provide guidelines for strict control over the hormas during the extraction of the sugar loaves. It was much easier for a slave to steal a sugar loaf, complete with horma, during the production process, than to do so once the product was separated from the mold and stored under lock and key (La Rosa and Ortega 1990). "During the drying operation do not leave the drying drawers, taking care that the Negro workers do not break the hormas and that these are not turned upside down, but laid on their sides instead, to avoid this damaging traffic," one manual insists (Vásquez 1837:14).

Yet the slaves on sugar plantations developed the habit of consuming high quantities of sugar, which they could acquire in the field (by consuming cane), or during the fabrication process, in the boiling and filtering houses. The cimarrones had a great affinity for sugar and guarapo (cane juice),[5] and the calories mitigated the long, hard workdays. Thus in inventories taken by slave hunters who assaulted the palenques, sugarcane is listed along with coffee and tobacco plants. While it could be said that the presence of the remains of hormas at fugitive slave sites does not constitute resounding proof of sugar consumption on the part of the cimarrones, the difficulty of stealing and transporting these containers was great, and because of their open ends they could not be used as water containers.

In sum, the food containers in the cimarrón site assemblages reveal dependency on the plantations or rural stores, yet persistent traces of African cultures in the fabrication of pots, plates, and smoking pipes of unslipped fired clay also are demonstrated. The hormas, on the other hand, are indicators of habits acquired on the plantations.

Containers for Liquids

The 124 examples of containers used for transporting and conserving liquids collected from the 30 sites in this study constitute 34 percent of the total artifactual inventory. Most abundant were glass bottles (n = 52), within which an ample range of manufacturing techniques are represented, all dating to the first half of the nineteenth century. Most of these bottles originally were used for wines and liquors, though their reuse as containers for water, honey, or milk in humble homes, especially on rural estates, is well known. Also in this category are 18 grès stoneware flasks originally containing beer.

In numeric terms bottles represent 56 percent of the liquid containers in the sample. Their abundance is due to the fact that they were easy to obtain after they were thrown away in the stores and on rural estates and also to their easily transportable nature. Because of their frequency, bottles might be seen as the typical vessels used for liquids by runaway slaves. Yet the best storage jars were demijohns—great globular, long-necked containers with a capacity of about 17 liters.

In the total artifactual inventory from the Havana-Matanzas project there are 27 demijohns, recovered at 20 of the 30 sites. Demijohns came to Cuba filled with gin. They are common at nineteenth-century archaeological sites because they were so often reused for water storage in contexts both rural and urban.[6] They abound at sites linked to mercantile activities—ports, garbage dumps used by stores, warehouses, boats, and sites used by contraband runners. The demijohns, plus the botijas (among which the smallest had capacities of over 6 liters), make a total of 47 large containers. Taken together, the capacity of these large jars is over seven times that of the bottles and flasks.

Artifacts and Objects of Wood and Vegetable Fiber

Wooden artifacts are reported at some fugitive slave sites in Cuba. In particular, decorated wooden combs, rustic beds, and containers cut from short, thick tree trunks that may have served as basins (for water) or mortars (for grinding food) were reported in a cave at Sierra de la Güira, east of Havana, by Ortega and Azcuy in the newspaper *Juventud Rebelde* (October 13, 1985:3). At Kalunga, a palenque in eastern Cuba, during surveys I carried out in 1987 (La Rosa Corzo 1991b), I found a great wooden basin that clearly was used for grinding coffee. I also had the opportunity to study rustic beds at Solapa de la Rinconá in Pinar del Río.

Nevertheless, I found no wooden archaeological remains at the sites under consideration in this chapter. I did, however, find fragments of a spoon made from a gourd (güira[7]) at Cimarrón 5 and four tubes for smoking pipes[8] made from Tibisí reeds[9] at Solapa 1, Cueva del Tambor—a high, dry site that, based on the disposition of the evidence, appears not to have been altered since the moment it was abandoned. The pipe tubes were no surprise, since in the hearth of this refuge I collected two pipes, one rustic, the other imported. And, between the bottom ash lens and the sterile surface of a hearth, I recovered a small fragment of corncob.

The singularity of this find—there are no other reports of corncobs in similar archaeological contexts—is difficult to explain. Possibly it represents the remains of a meal, since slave hunters reported corn at fugitive slave refuges; it may also have been used as fuel for the hearth, as it is today in some rural zones. The conservation of these organic artifacts is due to their proximity to the hearths and to the high, dry atmosphere of these sites.

Tools and Utensils of Metal

Metal utensils include the cast-iron pots discussed in the section on food containers, as well as nails, spurs, a bridle bit, and a key, which could be circumstantial finds—in any event their function within the context of escaped slave hideaways is difficult to interpret. I classify them as miscellaneous objects of uncertain use; they comprise 7 percent of the entire artifactual inventory.[10] The rest of the utensils I collected underscore the already discussed characteristics of the fugitive groups that used these hideaways.

Knives, machetes, an iron stake, an adze, and five flints—7 percent of the total inventory—are clearly linked to vital activities including defense, hunting, and the procurement and preparation of food. The flints, found at both Cimarrón 1 and Cueva de Avispas, indicate the use of firearms, as reported in the testimonies of slave hunters (Villaverde 1982:57). The use of firearms by the cimarrones is testimony to the transcendental needs of life on the run.

Five buttons and a buckle might be the remains of the fugitives' clothing. The shackles found at the entrances to both Cimarrón 1 and Cueva del Búho link these places with the passage from life in captivity to the life of freedom as an escaped slave. The discovery of shackles in caves also has been reported in Matanzas (Alvarez and Vento 1996). Abiel Abbot (1965:98) wrote in a letter of 1821 the story of a cimarrón who, to remove his shackles, "had filed them with the juice of sour orange and his machete; and one of the sections, which was too big to cede to this method, was broken between two stones."

Dietary Remains

As with the rest of the archaeological evidence, the dietary remains provide firsthand information about the social, economic, and cultural characteristics of the individuals who used these natural refuges. Although faunal analysis has become important in the historical archaeology of urban contexts (Gutiérrez and Iglesias 1996; Vergara 2002), mine is the first study of the food resources that formed the subsistence base of the fugitive slaves of the Habana-Matanzas uplands (see La Rosa Corzo 2005 for additional information). The faunal data strengthen the discussion of food-related potsherds presented above.

As in the case of tools and utensils, the faunal sample demonstrates that the cimarrones were dependent on the haciendas in the region, but only partly so. The remains of wild pigs *(Sus scrofa)* were present in 28 of the 30 sites, and thus the most prevalent animals consumed. They are followed by *jutía* rats *(Capromys sp)* at 26 sites and cattle *(Bos taurus)* at 10 (Figure 9.5). Less frequent remains include hen *(Gallus gallus)*, recovered at 6 sites, *majá* boa constrictor *(Epicrates angulifer)* at 6, and Muscovy duck *(Cairina moschata)* at 4. Horse *(Equus caballus)* remains appeared at only 3 sites; dog *(Canus familiaris)* at 2, and *jícotea* land tortoise *(Pseudemys* sp.) and unidentified fish remains at one site each. Thus the escaped slaves of the region relied largely on hunted species; cattle and horses are the main exception.

Conclusions

As demonstrated above, historical archaeology facilitates a more comprehensive anthropological approach to the sites of slave resistance than simple typological studies. The selection of the sites used as camps or refuges was governed by principles linked to the survival of persecuted human groups, including inaccessibility,

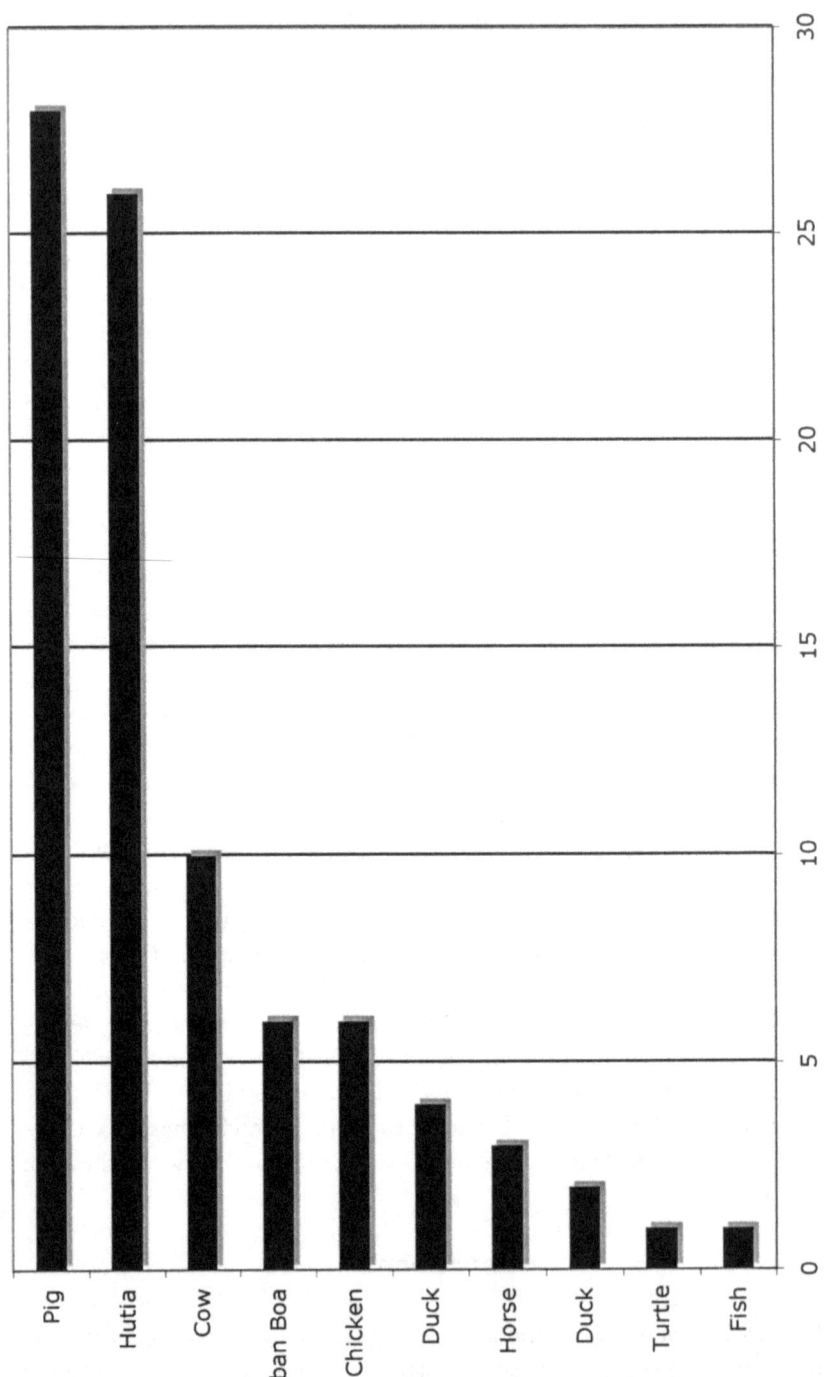

Figure 9.5. Presence of faunal species, by number of sites at which they appear.

natural camouflage, and opportunities for withdrawal in case of unexpected assaults. The cimarrones, by selecting the most inaccessible sites for their hideaways, often gave up ready access to natural water sources and were obliged to carry in quantities of the precious liquid. Thus they reutilized or made containers for this purpose. Further, the evidence collected from these sites demonstrates that the individuals who used them did not depend totally on the slave haciendas from which they came. In addition to resources stolen or bartered for, the fugitives utilized resources from the woods. They also practiced skills acquired in captivity and maintained African traditions carried from their homelands.

Finally, some of the archaeological materials, such as the hormas, allow the establishment of the occupational chronology of these sites. All were used between the final decade of the eighteenth century and the middle of the nineteenth, which coincides with the slave plantations' greatest stage of development and the period in which the largest number of slaves came to western Cuba. The spaces occupied by fugitive slaves during the days of slavery on the plantations constitute a crucial source of information that allows us to deepen our understanding of the events that mark the genesis of the New World.

Acknowledgments

This investigation could not have been realized without the support of the National Counsel of Cultural Patrimony under the Provincial Office of the Patrimony of Havana, as well as the Municipal Museums of Culture of Havana and the Cuban Institute of Anthropology; and it could not have been concluded without the aid of my colleagues Antonio Curet and Susan Kepecs. To all, many thanks.

Notes

1. From west to east, the highest ranges are Sierra del Esperón (250 m above sea level), Loma del Grillo (231 m ASL), and El Pan de Matanzas (381 m ASL). These ranges present a morphology fundamentally defined by abrupt slopes in which caves and rockshelters abound.

2. In 1817, Havana Province contained the territory from the extreme west of Pinar del Río to Santa Clara and Trinidad. Within were 625 sugar mills and 779 coffee plantations, concentrated mostly in the departments of Guanajay (122 mills, 295 coffee plantations); Jaruco (133 mills, 81 coffee plantations); Güines (78 and 35, respectively); and Matanzas, with 95 and 83. These departments surrounded the hilly ranges of Havana-Matanzas (Archivo Nacional de Cuba [ANC], Gobierno Superior Civil Leg. 864 no. 29229). In 1841, during a decade of great plantation development, this western region contained 73.6 percent of the total number of slaves on the island (*Comisión de Estadísticas* 1842).

3. In very isolated cases the existence of small protective stone structures have been

reported. One was found in a cave in Viñales, Pinar del Río. On a visit to the site I noted that this small wall was partially covered with secondary limestone formations in the process of creation, attesting to the feature's antiquity. Another example was found in San José de las Lajas (Garcell 2002:48). Nevertheless, great care is required in identifying possible structures associated with nineteenth-century cimarrón sites, since hunters of *jutía* rats today often seal the entrances of caves and rockshelters with small stone walls, in order to trap the animals.

4. Domestic slaves had access to chamber pots in the homes of their owners, and slaves in the field used them in infirmaries. But their presence in a fugitive slave refuge is baffling, given their principal function.

5. An illustrative example is that of the Yoruba priest Francisco, from Bauta in Havana, who was killed in March 1831 when he visited the stockpile in search of hot guarapo and tobacco for smoking (Ortega 1982:187).

6. The use of demijohns as water storage jars by a group of slaves cutting sugarcane is depicted in an oil painting by Victor Lanaluze, "Corte de Caña," which portrays an everyday scene at a Cuban sugar mill. In the center of the scene is a slave with a wicker-wrapped demijohn on his head, and a rustic smoking pipe in his mouth. There is a reproduction of this painting in the National Museum of Cuba, and in the 1990 catalogue of this institution (*Museo Nacional de Cuba* 1990).

7. Gourd (güira) remains were reported by the Guamá group of archaeological investigators in La Gloria, an aboriginal mound (Pérez 1943:48). During the colonial period güira provided "to the poor their most important domestic objects . . . cups, plates, spoons and everything imaginable. Güira is the most important domestic object, especially for the blacks" (Bremer 1980:40).

8. Spoons of gourd and tubes for pipes made from Tibisí reeds are amply documented in the historic and ethnographic records.

9. Tibisí is the popular name of various species of graminacaes that are very abundant in Cuba's woods, especially in the mountains and around arroyos. Its hollow canes are still used for making birdcages, and at least in the nineteenth century it substituted well for pipe stems. This last function is amply supported in the literature (Pichardo 1976 [1836]:576). Pioneer archaeologist García y Grave de Peralta (1938:29), examining a rustic clay pipe discovered east of Havana in 1893, inserted a tibisí reed for drawing smoke, just as the slaves had done years before.

10. Unexpected objects often are found in slave hideaways. The Reverend Abiel Abbot (1965 [1829]:98) described a bag, a fetish, two keys, a paper bearing the name of an escaped slave, a candle, and other items. In 1848 *(Archivo Nacional de Cuba [ANC], Real Consulado, Leg. 145, no. 7151)* a band of cimarrones assaulted in the hills of Hacienda Curajaua, in Puerto Príncipe, Camagüey, left behind a chisel, a compass, straw sombreros, and shoes.

10
Built Patrimony and Historical Archaeology
Problematic Relations in Working with the Past

Iosvany Hernández Mora, Gabinete de Arqueología,
Oficina del Historiador de la Ciudad de Camagüey, Cuba

In this chapter I analyze the problematic relationships that can occur between the practices of archaeology and restoration, if we admit the current demands of disciplinary development and take into account the notion of minimum intervention proposed in international documents that set standards for working with national patrimonies. Toward this end I consider the contract between archaeology and restoration, based on the history of historical archaeology in Cuba as well as direct empirical experience in the practice of archaeological investigation in the historic center of Old Havana.

> En este artículo se realiza un análisis de la relación problemática que puede tener la práctica arqueológica con la restaurativa, si se admiten las exigencias actuales de desarrollo disciplinar y se atiende la noción de mínima intervención, que proponen los documentos internacionales para el trabajo con el patrimonio. Para esto me he fundamentado en la contratación entre trabajos arqueológicos y restaurativos, tanto desde el conocimiento de la historia de la arqueología histórica en Cuba, como de la experiencia—referente empírico directo—en la práctica de la investigación arqueológica en el centro histórico de la Habana Vieja.

> The American architect is obligated to follow closely a formidable artistic tradition whose historical roots should be clarified by the archaeologist, the erudite, the specialist in a field that if well-tied in certain ways to architecture, offers unsuspected possibilities for the scientist and the historian. This suggests, almost without wanting to, the problem of the relations between the architect and the archaeologist.
>
> —Luis Bay Sevilla (1939:17), at the Eighth International American Conference on the Conservation and Preservation of Natural Regions and Historic Places

In the conservation of the built patrimony in Cuba various disciplines come together, among them archaeology and architecture. In this interconnection, the theory and objectives of different disciplinary praxis provide incongruent grounds for restoration. This incongruency works against both the respectful rehabilitation of the historical legacy (or authenticity) of buildings and urban spaces and complete archaeological knowledge. Below I attempt, without realizing a detailed analysis, to make explicit some considerations of the problem and to suggest some immediate, theoretically grounded alternatives.

Today any planned intervention in the built patrimony incorporates multidisciplinary teams that attend different aspects of the rehabilitation of buildings and urban spaces. In these groups, architects and archaeologists, among other professionals, participate in a context in which their actions should be coordinated, given the tasks and proposals involved in the restoration project. It is up to the archaeologists to determine the historical elements, not only based on the study of horizontal deposits within the structure, but also in the determination of the building's vertical development. In Europe, especially in Italy, since the seventh decade of the twentieth century, archaeologists have taken experimental steps toward understanding historical edifices as multistrata totalities that are impossible to break up for archaeological and restoration purposes.

This perspective has been aided by the application of the method of analysis for the organization and interpretation of the stratigraphic sequence of buildings developed by Edward C. Harris at the end of the 1970s. The Harris matrix (Harris 1979, 1991) began a revolution that is changing our understanding of urban archaeological contexts, opening the way, among investigators worldwide, for the comprehension of buildings as units containing various levels of cultural materialization. Nevertheless, the international charters for the conservation of cultural patrimony did not reflect this great advance until the late 1990s. The central theme of the *Charter of Architectural Survey* (Bustamante 1999:323), hammered out in April 1999, in Naples, Italy, is significant for its recognition of the increase in methodologies and techniques that make it possible to read with increasing detail the histories of buildings in the material record.

Today in Cuba, however, understanding the relevance and character of archaeology for restoration is still oriented toward international documents produced prior to 1999. Fundamentally, the principles for excavation adopted by the General Conference of the Organization of the United Nations for Education, Science and Culture, in 1956, fail to consign the development of architectural archaeology to the analysis of the built patrimony. Among other relevant documents are the *Charter of Venice* of 1964 and the *International Charter for the Administration of the Archaeological Patrimony* of 1990 (Bustamante 1999:339, 403). It is worth noting that the relatively recent *Charter of Krakow* (2000) is limited to a request for less destruction in the process of excavation.

In Cuba, meretorious works that take an archaeological, stratigraphic perspective to the study of architecture have been carried out. Some of these works are not only pioneering, but also classic examples of this approach. The forward-looking study by the architect Aquiles Maza y Santos, during the 1940s, in the Main Church of San Juan Bautista de Remedios, in northern Villa Clara province, stands out. In 1974 and 1983, the historian Angela Peña developed in Holguín an archaeological investigation in two stages for the restoration of the house in which the eminent independence fighter General Calixto García was born (Rodríguez and Hernández 2006:5–6). And in Havana, from the end of the 1970s through the next decade, studies were carried out with a very original vision that linked archaeology to architecture through what was then called structural archaeology, a field subsumed within colonial archaeology. This practice brought together, for the purposes of historical construction analysis, historical, architectural, artistic and archaeological investigations.

In the archaeological realm there were two directions—the study of structures, construction materials, and all types of architectural components, and the study of residual evidence of human activities underground (Ramos 1988:9–10), which relied on traditional stratigraphic methods. These analyses began at the initiative of Rafael Valdespino, based on the meticulous registration of construction elements at the Triunvirato sugar mill in the province of Matanzas (Morejón 1978:93). Later, such studies extended to Morro Castle at the entrance of Havana Bay, and to buildings Nos. 314 and 414, among others, on Calle San Ignacio in Old Havana (Ramos 1988:16–17). I discuss some of these studies in more detail, below.

A Change in Perspective: The Problem

In 1996 the Harris method was introduced into the methodological repertory of the Cabinet of Archaeology in the Office of the Historian of the City of Havana. At the end of the 1990s Edward C. Harris visited Cuba for the first time, giving several lectures on the applications and practice of his method. His teachings were timidly incorporated in fieldwork beginning in the year 2000, with the goal of achieving more holistic investigations in the city's historical center. Today the implementation of the practice Harris devised is in full development, though not without obstacles and lack of professional comprehension on the part of some researchers who find themselves absorbed in traditional methods or alienated from current trends in historical archaeology.

The current practice is based on the stratigraphic principles proposed by Harris (1991, 2004) for the differentiation, dating of phases, and sequence of stratigraphic elements of buildings. In the Harris method both the vertical (construction) and horizontal (depositional) components are taken into account. These two stratigraphic dimensions are simply the results of additions and subtractions at different levels, expressed archaeologically in superimposed and interfacing contexts. The objective is to situate the units of stratification in relative sequential order, paying attention to interfaces (units of use) and deposits (units of dis-use). This practice presupposes a conception of the archaeological record as essentially differentiated and heterogeneous (Figure 10.1), rather than as simple deposits of objects.

The employment of the Harris method in interventions in Old Havana has demonstrated its instrumental value, permitting the ordering and registering of information for thousands of stratigraphic units in urban contexts. Now that they can differentiate deposits and interfaces (Harris 1991:51–54), archaeologists are moving away from the traditional practice of excavating in arbitrary strata. The contrasts between the Harris method and the practice of traditional stratigraphic excavation are becoming evident, necessitating a reconsideration of archaeology done previously in Cuba, in rural zones as well as urban contexts (Hernández 2006).

Roger Arrazcaeta, director of the Gabinete de Arqueología that exists under the auspices of the Office of the City Historian of Havana, is the author of an article, "Habana Vieja: arqueología en edificios históricos" (2002), that represents the first attempt to apply the Harris method to the archaeology of architecture in urban contexts in Havana. Arrazcaeta aimed to address archaeological contexts holistically, from the Harris perspective, although in essence his analysis was directed toward the deposits' horizontal elements, much like the many excavations that had been carried out previously by personnel from the Gabinete. In terms of the vertical dimension, the expression of the new method was fundamentally limited by concerns about destruction to the structure's walls or interior elements (Arrazcaeta 2002:20, 22).

Destruction often accompanies attempts to access the third (vertical) dimension in historic buildings, since the methods of intervention can undermine these elements of the construction. This is highly problematic, since the interior walls of the great majority of historic buildings in Old Havana present stucco finish topped with layers of historically important mural paintings. In general the problem of conserving the paintings competes with the conservation of significant original elements that make buildings and urban spaces into invaluable archaeological and historical entities. Yet the elements of traditional architecture, sometimes represented in dozens of stratigraphic levels, should nevertheless be investigated for the valuable information they contain.

These are only a few manifestations of a real scientific and intellectual conflict that demands examination of the purpose of archaeology in historic urban centers. Thus it is necessary to reconsider the objectives of study and the change that the methodological criteria demand in these spaces. If holistic, complex archaeological investigations that produce valuable knowledge for the conservation of the

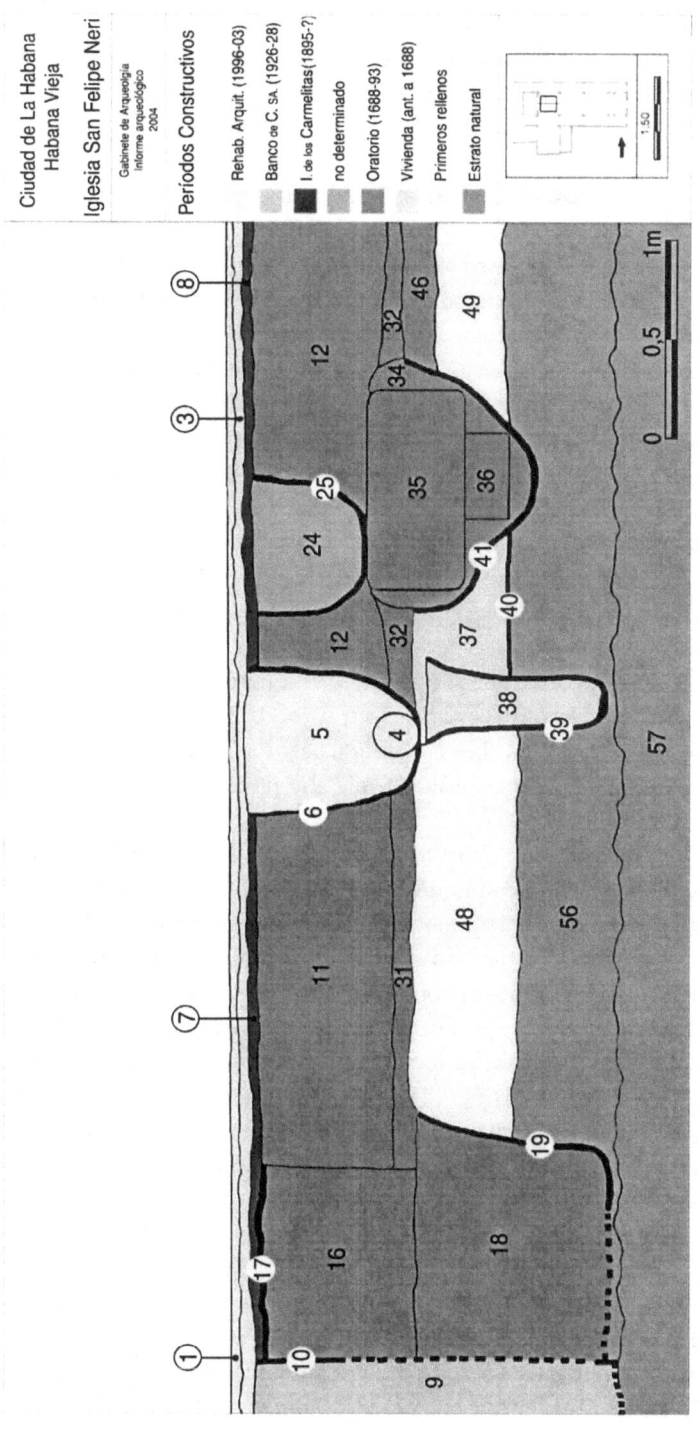

Figure 10.1. Section of a recent excavation by the Archaeological Cabinet of the Office of the City Historian, in the church of San Felipe Neri, Old Havana. This example shows how the stratigraphic sequence changes completely if attention is paid to the interfaces (units of use) and the evidence is properly utilized as an essential element of the deposition. The drawing shows the different construction periods, materialized diachronically, although the associative links among all of the encountered materials have yet to be made.

built patrimony cannot be carried out because archaeological practice destroys the foundations that sustain these historical buildings—and thus archaeology conflicts with the restoration of these structures—what is the point of archaeological studies?

Development: The Focus

My concern in this article is oriented toward interrelating the sociocultural necessities of conserving the built patrimony: minimal intervention, architectural restoration, and archaeology. Archaeology in this case must be understood as the discipline with which trained specialists investigate the material record in order to create representations of the past. When there are agreements among interpretations posited by investigators from multiple disciplines, organized institutionally around the project at hand, archaeological interpretations become a key to the reevaluation of the cultural patrimony.

With this in mind I take into account the concrete social conditions, the subjectivities in play, and the paradigmatic particularities of the participating disciplines in creating a holistic approach (Trigger 1993:369-370) toward urban historical archaeology. In this context I consider the distinctive methods of archaeology, the finalities of the act of restoration and the principle of minimal intervention. In the process, I hope to answer an old question (Crejo 1976:74): how can we rescue and preserve archaeological sites and objects (cultural patrimony) adequately and in a manner congruent with their social value, while also protecting the information they contain?

My methodology involves an effort to maintain a relatively open mind, independent of a disconcerting dilemma involving universal criteria versus the national perspective on the administration of the patrimony of a specific place (López 2002:163). In principle, in the critical analysis of shared social patterns it is crucial to the recognition of three factors: (1) the heterogeneity and multiplicity of individual conceptions; (2) the peculiarities of the different disciplines involved and the final actions taken for the restoration of buildings, based on a fictitious homogeneity of objectives overlying different and not necessarily collegial attitudes; and (3) the multiple internal perspectives on the problem, recurrent in all participating disciplines, which determine the dialectic on the margins of transdisciplinary discourse. In this way the social dimensions of the investigation are operationalized—made active rather than passive in the society in which the project is carried out. Thus, from the classic exposition of the subject-object problem, we can extend a practical methodological concept without ruptures between what we understand as objectivity and subjectivity (Sotolongo 1998:144, 155).

Without abandoning the focus on external examination, I attempt to provoke theoretical reflection on the links in the system (Bunge 1972:50), based on a singular reading, translatable in the realization of the whole and its parts (Bunge 1999:29–30; Harris 2000:49, 56; Morin 1996:11). That is, each part depends on its functional interrelations within the totality (Delgado 2002a:8–9). I assume for the purpose of this argument that the totality is the realization of the trilogy of restoration, minimal intervention, and archaeology; at the same time, this is part of the set of activities that can be developed to conserve a historic urban center.

On Patrimony and Archaeology

The *Charter of Krakow*[1] (2000:5) provides a universal, holistic definition of patrimony: "A set of works of man in which the community recognizes specific and particular values with which it identifies." In correlation with previous international declarations (the 1965 *Charter of Venice,* the *Restoration Charter* of 1972), this dictum essentially reflects concrete, contextual laws.

In the case of Cuba, the rule for the execution of the law of protection of the patrimony (declared in 1983) establishes this definition of the national cultural patrimony: "All urban historic centers, constructions or sites that merit conservation for their cultural, historical or social significance" (Consejo de Ministros 1998:7–8). Further, from the perspective of sociocultural anthropology, patrimony has been understood as "the normative models that orient actions and experiences, through which men, women and groups, in a definable social and historical locations, react to their environments and reduce their complexity" (Arnold 1991:81). In other words, in the above-cited concepts, the products of the daily activities of groups and individuals, as objectified in artifacts, structures, and institutions perceptible at various levels, play active roles in society, guiding tradition in every way.

The actors, individual and collective, are subject to these demands in dynamic fashion as the terms are continually translated and changed. In consequence, the ideas that define patrimony and guide our attempts to restore and conserve it are significantly related to the regular production of meaning from both familial and professional environments; the discourse and consequent actions, in the measure in which they become repetitive, create the customs that inform definition. Further complicating this concept is the existence, in all social groups, of "patrimonial" models that interact with what professionals call the "built patrimony." Thus what is patrimonial constitutes a duality impossible to tease apart, as much material as ideational, an organic totality, a synthesis of objective and subjective (Pupo 1990:107).

The study, restoration, and revaluation of the built patrimony must take into account this dual reality, considering present and future objections and depending, pragmatically, on how (in terms of perceived reality) and why (in terms of interpretation) we aspire to restore the past for the societies of today. In this sense, although "why" and "how" are closely related and mutually relevant, if we consider the customary significance of "why," it is much more urgent to attend the "how," since every answer to this question supposes an orientation to the importance of patrimony. The question of "how" is essentially realized in restoration. It is a vital element that presupposes an attitude toward shared representations that are continually updated and that tangibly affect the interventions and hermeneutic technologies used to give the past meaning, via a surviving notion of approximation and appropriation through typological classifications that serve as a direct passage to the past.

In the reproduction of this posture, archaeology, among other disciplines, has played a fundamental role, legitimizing narratives of the past based solely on material objects. Yet in the twentieth century these rhetorics contributed little to the discourses on patrimony that created the traditions and expectations involved in operationalizing archaeological practice (López 2002:158). The conceptual definition of historical archaeology (or archaeology of the colonial period) remains problematic in that there are no unified criteria for its practice (Orser 2000:8); thus it is necessary to create specific methodologies that capture realities at the conjunction of archaeological and historical processes.

Toward this end, in Cuba the stratigraphic record, as interfacial units, has gained importance in both interventions and results (Harris 2004:84). The exhaustive search for historical sources, oral as well as written (South 1977:1), deemed the unavoidable starting place for colonial archaeology in the 1980s (Ramos 1988:14), has been invariable. Perhaps, by paying greater attention not only to the results of the direct historic method, but also to everything that can help to define and explain the course of history in its multiple varieties, we can arrive at some useful conclusions (Schmidt 1975:144).

One facet of historical archaeology is the archaeology of historic sites. Robert Schuyler (1978a:2) defines this practice as "the study of the material manifestations of the expansion of European culture in the New World, which begins in the sixteenth century and ends with industrialization or with the present, depending on local conditions." To decodify and operationalize this definition, we can agree that this kind of archaeology occupies those temporal and symbolic spaces that contain the concrete results of the social processes of transculturation occasioned by European expansion. Among these spaces it is useful to highlight those places that demonstrate urban values with concentrated populations, esteemed as historic centers, where sociopolitical relations, constructive logics (methods, techniques, materials, and special legislation), and styles (aesthetic and functional) flowed and reproduced, affecting everything from the design of the city to the buildings and artifacts.

The focus of restoration and rehabilitation of the built patrimony in these historic centers should have two dimensions, impartially assessed and understood.

Built Patrimony and Historical Archaeology / 151

The first is the analysis of the material nature of the spaces and structures, which provides decisive information about the forms and techniques of past construction as well as about the art and the history of the community, with its systems of production, its customs, and its social logic. The other is an analysis of use, from the present to the representation of the past (Azcárate 2002:57), in accordance with the necessity of each restoration project to calculate the underlying cultural, social, political, and economic interests of the present.

The restoration procedure is estimated through the investigator's self-comprehension and a reaffirmation of differences in relation to the other (the idea of the past and its objective representation) in time, while at the same time she or he constructs a notion of the past. The object, site, or city should be understood simultaneously in expressions of its own context and in terms of the present, a problematic connection when we take into account the constant flux between relativism and realism. Nevertheless, this perspective is made possible through a set of cultural profiles mobilized by socially determined cognitive images. Gadamer (1975:271) proposes that each response to "the other" (the idea of the past and its objective representation) leads to new self-awareness and new questions in the present. In this way the objective of restoration is framed as an operation of conservation, though also as a unique and irrepeatable occasion for knowledge and self-definition. These premises are consubstantial and indissolvable (Azcárate 2002:58).

The practice of restoration is inconceivable without the most complete knowledge possible about that which one desires to restore. The indissolvability of these components proceeds from the historicity of the object and is a consequence of the restorer's cognitive framework. Ultimately archaeology possesses a fundamental role in the studies applied to the restoration of the built patrimony, in virtue of the empirical support it provides for the conservation of the material aspect of human life.

One must remember that the application of archaeological knowledge is only possible if archaeological studies are done prior to the moment of restoration. The chronological order should be as follows: archaeological study, intervention project, restoration. If we admit that the archaeological investigation provides the source and the instrument for bringing significance and values to the built patrimony, thus socializing it, contrary to what many in Cuba believe, these investigations must methodologically surpass the type of case studies (isolated or not) that are an end unto themselves.

The implementation of scientifically affiliated projects should allow us to overcome procedures that privilege a solo voice. This integrated approach should facilitate the logical resolution of complex problems that today are discussed in academic circles both within Cuba (Domínguez 1999:66; Hernández 2006:199–200; La Rosa 2001:43–44) and beyond (Ewen 2001:21). This perspective brings about a point of departure that allows for systematic contrasts and integral knowledge that ultimately will be applicable to any concrete problem or objective in the realm of patrimony.

The demands to which archaeology must respond include the following: First, the proclaimed ethical and ideological neutrality of archaeological science—that is, its objectivity, so questioned today by postmodern theorists—is little more than a myth of production compromised (implicitly or explicitly) by a socioeconomic base and strong colonialist traditions. The contours that underlie this misleading notion of science are revealed in its politically motivated tendency to exclude ample sociocultural sectors. Like all human activity, the political-social strategies that sustain this posture are not free of ideological concerns.

Archaeology in urban historical centers is thus an ideological manifestation of the discipline's values. Part of its reason for existence is the search for a coherent practice that frames patrimonial restoration as a legitimate social demand. This issue is inseparable from the elements that constitute archaeological practice, which need rethinking—it seems euphemistic to redesign methodologies when ontological and epistemological concerns are more urgent.

Second, the epistemic logic of historical archaeology as a social science must be based on the realities of the past as understood via the cognitive dialectic of analysis/synthesis. In this pursuit it is necessary to develop activities that are not far from the peculiarities of individuals and societies to which the patrimony under consideration belongs, given the obvious connection between what is considered past or present and the phenomenon of authenticity that historical archeologists aim to conserve, at least within the context of current use.

On Restoration, the Authentic, and the Archaeological

Different international documents, with universal rationality, have attempted consensus or the establishment of norms to follow that conform to what the authors consider to be the notion of restoration. In the ninth article of the above-cited *Charter of Venice*, we find this statement: "The goal is to conserve and reveal the aesthetic and historical values of the monument, and it is based on respect for original material and authentic documents" (Bustamante 1999:340). In the *Restoration Charter* of 1972, restoration is understood as "any intervention undertaken to maintain validity, to facilitate the reading and to transmit entirely into the future the works and objects of art." Further, in the instructions for the execution of architectonic restorations, this point is made: "A fundamental demand of restoration is to respect and safeguard the authenticity of the constructive elements. This principle should always guide and condition the selection of operations" (Brandi and D'Ossat 1972:3, 11).

At the Nara Conference, tied to the 1994 World Heritage Convention in Japan, it was agreed that authenticity is the principal qualitative factor for the assessment of cultural patrimony. This principle plays a fundamental role in scientific studies, conservation, and restoration plans and inventories of built patrimony and inscriptions on the list of world heritage sites (Bustamante 1999:323). In the set of definitions annexed to the *Charter of Krakow* (2000:5), restoration is defined as "an operation directed on a heritage property, aiming at the conservation of its authenticity and its appropriation by the community." Authenticity, as defined in this document, means the sum of "substantial, historically ascertained characteristics: from the original up to the current state, as an outcome of the various transformations that have occurred over time."

In diachronic terms, what holds constant in the idea of restoration is the conservation of authenticity of the object, taking into consideration its various temporal additions. I propose then that every study should pay attention to all of the historical periods represented in the architecture. But unconsciously, this attention is limited by the ever-present intention to restore a structure in order to highlight a given historical period, selected according to the building's particular potential. This factor obligates archaeologists studying historical centers to carry out secondary projects that provide the most complete knowledge possible of the sociohistorical processes that will not be represented in the final restoration.

Nevertheless, archaeological practice in Old Havana demonstrates that in principle, these considerations are counterproductive given the emergency of carrying out restoration. In this domain the discipline usually concentrates on rescue and salvage, commensurate with the temporal limits established by factors of deterioration and urgent intervention. Further, these structures are inhabited, often by families—an inconvenience that limits the practice to creating a photographic register, carrying out documentary investigations and/or studying the building's façade. The results now are known: the great majority of this work is partial and particular, given the difficulty of developing more integral and systematic investigations.

A recent study carried out by my colleague Beatríz Rodríguez and myself (Rodríguez and Hernández 2006) that began with the façade of a still-inhabited structure, No. 602 on Calle San Ignacio at the corner of Acosta in Old Havana (Figure 10.2), revealed the instrumentality of Harris's stratigraphic method as an appropriate approach to the evolution of the building. The initial investigation, despite being focused on the particular, revealed, based on the contrast between primary documents and the archaeological reading of the walls, how much the temporal additions complicated the concept of the original or authentic structure. This situation led to physical investigations designed to go beyond the obsession with appearance and typological horizons. In studying the façade the elements corresponding to the colonial period were assumed to be original, in correspondence with the building's potential. Architectural components of the seventeenth and eighteenth centuries were observable, and, in lesser proportion, those dating to the nineteenth

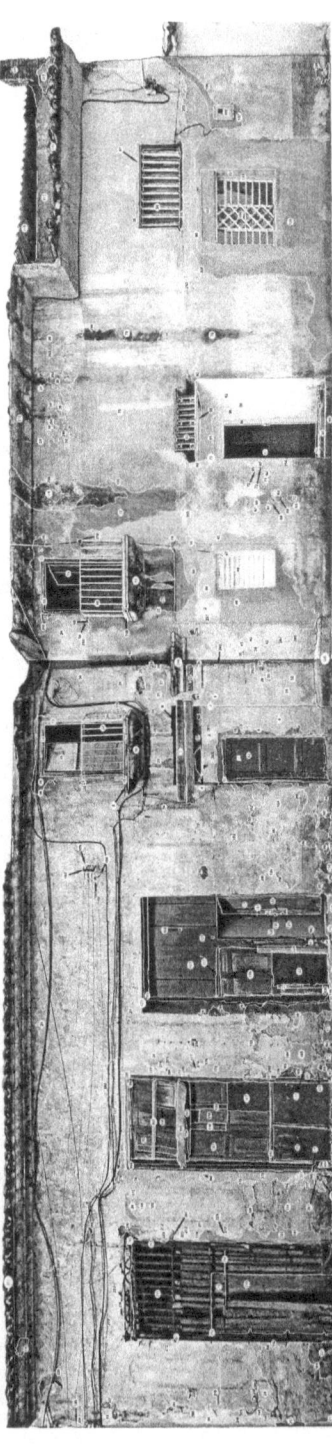

Figure 10.2. Montage of two images of the façade of the corner house at No. 602 San Ignacio. The most recent and significant anthropic changes include the closing of door and window openings, the use of modern construction materials, including the fills and finishes of gray cement. The building's current physiognomy is a result of profound changes in the interior. Any restoration project with the intent of returning the house to its colonial appearance must take these transformations—interior and exterior—into account. Thus holistic studies that include archaeology are of utmost importance.

Figure 10.3. Wall on the second level of the house, which was completely stripped of its surface finish and other transformations, a subtractive action that provides a detailed stratigraphic reading on the evolution of this part of the house. We can observe different moments of the life of the building in the filled-in windows and traces of stair landings and hydraulic systems.

century as well. Changes to the structure accelerated vertiginously thereafter, beginning with the first years of the twentieth (Figure 10.3).

To create a restoration plan respectful of authenticity (original legacy), should the evolutionary elements of the twentieth century (and of the start of the twenty-first) be taken into account and inevitably eliminated because the structure has a history of architecture in the domestic cannon typologized for the seventeenth and eighteenth centuries (Rodríguez and Hernández 2006:14)? In the case of No. 602 San Ignacio this question became especially problematic when we confronted the fact that in the third and fourth stages of its development (beginning in the early twentieth century), major transformations were executed in terms of the distributions of space, evidence of a continual functional reordering projected in the façade that obeys the radical changes in the social structure of the country that began in 1959 (refer to Figure 10.2; also see Rodríguez and Hernández 2006:8–9).

The investigation was not aggressive in terms of using destructive methods; instead it was based on small observations of the changing functionality of the home. We were left with a considerable margin of incertitude, having been unable to test some parts of the masonry structure. This raises a key question: should stratigraphic readings, the central axis of archaeological analysis (Quirós-Castillo 2002:28), and a current key to understanding building modifications, be detailed and systematic? The methods of excavation and registration, which archaeologists have applied in horizontal and vertical form for these studies, work against the maintenance of original components that should be used to achieve authenticity. Thus the principle of minimum intervention—that is, the reduction, as much as possible, of the destructive aspects of interventions, as laid out in the fifth article of the 1990 *International Charter for the Management of Archaeological Patrimony* (Bustamante 1999:405)—is undermined.

As noted earlier, one of the problems that impedes integral stratigraphic analysis in Cuba is the restriction imposed by the presence of superimposed layers of fresh plaster and mural paintings in the great majority of the buildings considered to be patrimonial. This issue is inherent in the conceptual and technical positioning of the various disciplines involved in the project, and the ways in which its consequences are manifested depend on the fundamental cosmovision of the project—whether the building is conceived as a historical (archaeological) phenomenon or an architectural (technical) one (Caballero 1996:56). The positions investigators take vary, depending on whether the plastering is considered an independent stratigraphic element or part of the accumulated historical stratigraphy of the building. In other words, the plaster is part of a totality constituted by different elements, but one in which every element is realized in correspondence with the conceptual actions fused in the whole (Rodríguez and Hernández 2006:7). The notion that the plaster is an independent element makes sense within a theoretical framework that individualizes the function of all the parts, but this is a reductionism that overlooks related elements arbitrarily discounted as not being central to the realization of the totality.

Further, the intelligibility of the stratigraphic sequence alone does not guarantee the conclusion of the study. The analysis of artifacts and sedimentary information from the subsurface, as well as the materials and techniques of construction employed and decodified, constitute an investigative continuum essential to understanding a unit that cannot be fragmented if the desired outcome is a coherent approximation of a concrete reality (Francovich and Bianchi 2002:105). Thus the technologies employed under the principle of minimum intervention, such as photogrammetry, planimetry, and topographical and geotechnical recording methods, considered semidestructive or not destructive, do not, in themselves, help investigators obtain the data necessary for sociocultural and historical knowledge of the past. These essentially technical data must be coordinated with real archaeological data to achieve adequate rehabilitation. To follow this reasoning, it seems indisputable that the destructive methods used by archaeologists are nevertheless essential for the goals of the discipline.

The history of historical archaeology in Cuba demonstrates an essential disjuncture: works based on destructive processes make much more progress than those that are subordinated to the objectives of conservation. The work I cited early in this chapter by the architect Aquiles Maza y Santos in the Main Church of San Juan Bautista de Remedios demonstrates the distance between placing priority on archaeological knowledge or on respect for the structure's physical evolution. The criteria of authenticity that Maza (1952:288) employed can be recognized in his insistence on restoring the building to a past in which it reached its highest artistic level—the mid-eighteenth century—a stylistic restoration, in virtue of the coherence among the structure's architectural elements.

Maza's procedures (1952:289), in the vanguard of the times, concentrated on "methods of direct investigation on the object itself, on the building, to save the gaps or the deficiencies in written interpretation." With the objective of recovering the greatest amount of information possible on the distinct stages of the building's evolution, in terms of both historical period and changes to the structure, "the plaster finish that covered [the building] was totally removed, explorations in the ceilings and also the floor were made, and within the closed perimeter of the walls distinct test pits were cut to the necessary depth" (Maza 1952:299). With these procedures important alterations to the structure were detected, and pertinent changes to the restoration design were realized.

Based on these techniques, unusual for the epoch in which he worked, the architect was able to approach the constructive logic of the building's temporal modifications, and to interpret, by way of the spatial distribution of the elements, the goals pursued in those changes. At the same time, Maza recreated lost components with traditional materials, the same ones he had observed in his investigations, orienting his restorations on a base of archaeological knowledge.

A similar process occurred when Ramos (1988:15) began his "problematic restoration" of an old building at No. 314 Calle San Ignacio in Old Havana. The historical documents on the house, valuations that spanned the eighteenth to nineteenth centuries, could only be used to draw a set of partial changes within a complex of unknown transformations. It was necessary to implement excavations below ground and employ other techniques of horizontal intervention, which Ramos (1988:3) called "parietal test pits" of different types and sizes, aimed at establishing morphological stratigraphy.

The results of this investigation led Ramos (1988:16) to conclude that it was "not adequate to give immediate credit to the exterior reality, to the visible, when there are interpretive problems in a monument of long existence. It will be, then, an archaeological task to penetrate farther than what is apparent to reveal objective knowledge of the multiple changes and superpositions not detectable to the naked eye."

In contrast to Dr. Prat Puig's earlier (1947) study of the same house, which was based on typological conventionalisms and the above-cited valuations, Ramos (1988) detected changes for which no written references existed. Ramos's discoveries were incorporated into the restoration with the objective of recuperating the primary architectural image of the structure at the start of the eighteenth century. If he had instead merely executed a morphological/descriptive study, the primary architectural image surely would have been different than the one reproduced in this restoration on the basis of his detailed archaeological data.

In the above-mentioned archaeological project executed by Angela Peña in 1974 and 1983, subordinate to the restoration of the birthplace of General Calixto Garcia in Holguín, archaeology and restoration were carried out as parallel practices. This house dates to the second half of the nineteenth century. Test pits were opened in the walls and floors, and the plaster finish was removed, respecting those elements identified as originals according to the proposed chronological horizon (Peña 1987:60). In this case the objective was not the construction of historical knowledge, per se, but the identification of architectural elements in the service of authenticity. The archaeologically discovered relationships between the outer masonry walls and the rest of the components in the ground and in the vertical plane allowed the reproduction of the building's partially lost appearance. The importance of this example rests on the fact that the restoration plan began with archaeology, which made it possible to create a representation of the past at the home in which the distinguished Cuban was born.

The principal contrast between this paradigm and some of the current restorations going on in Old Havana is manifest in the decentralized position that archaeology is given with respect to making decisions in the historic center of the island's capital. The directions for rehabilitation often are made by investors and planners who work at the margins of archaeological knowledge. The reason can be found in the lack of concrete regulations at the local level, though the issue is further complicated by the fact that the economic object of the businesses in charge of these restorations is not patrimonial conservation. Builders are investing in the substitution of historical, sometimes useable elements, for the new—that is, the replacement of the authentic by more modern solutions. In this context archaeology does not bear full responsibility for aggressive actions against the patrimony; instead, the practice of archaeology is directed by requirements alien to the discipline.

The studies carried out over five years ago at the old Palacio de los Condes de Cañongo, Calle San Ignacio Nos. 350 and 356, in Plaza Vieja, demonstrate the destructive nature of both the archaeological investigations and the actions of the restorers. Excavations in this mansion began in the central patio, with the goal of finding a reservoir, an objective solicited by the investors. Twenty-nine units were excavated in the subsurface and countless exploratory test pits were cut into in the walls; in some places these were totally stripped of their plaster finish, destroying murals and other evidence in the process.

The difficulty in analyses like these begins with the master plans for rehabilitation. Such plans exist everywhere in the country, in historical centers decreed world patrimony sites like Trinidad, Old Havana, and, most recently, the old city of Camagüey. These plans are not based on fundamentals revealed through basic archaeological investigations; instead, archaeological studies continue to be ruled by the traditional norms of the discipline—typology and description—which yield results that have little to do with reaching the full potential of this type of research.

Final Considerations

The characteristics of archaeological practice in historical centers can bring about confrontations with other disciplines involved in the conservation of the built patrimony that do not share archaeology's updated procedures and cognitive objectives. In today's Old Havana, many restoration projects still rely on surveys of artistic styles or comparative typologies, in line with the most traditional historiography of architecture or art. Nevertheless, we have known for a long time that styles and architectural types do not overlap in time and that this disjunction cannot be taken lightly (Ramos 1988:16–17), given that change has complex causes linked to both objective conditions and cultural subjectivity. In too many cases the monument is sanctified as a fetish that embodies a style physically frozen in time. But the complexities and responsibilities involved in restoring the built patrimony demand that this activity not be the domain of a single discipline (Quirós-Castillo 2002:34; Ramos 1988:5).

Since techniques, methods, and norms are internal to theoretical positions (Hughes and Sharrock 1999:194), can we hope to find common ground? Scientific disciplines are cultural phenomena—partial, local, and susceptible to consensus. But interdisciplinary incompatibility is circumstantial or insurmountable to the degree to which each discipline is flexible or wed to uncompromising criteria. The key to vigorous interdisciplinary and transdisciplinary restoration (with the aim of retaining the authenticity of spaces and buildings) will be found in the confluence of criteria, within which prejudices must be mutually canceled. The contradictions between disciplines indeed may be fictitious, or at least nonexistent, for most of the actors and their interactions with the past in terms of their own fields.

In the search for a better way to deal with conservation there are no Archimedean realities. The archaeologist and the architect-restorer, as social individuals, belong to groups that provide resources for understanding what is correct within their particular frameworks. Mutual understanding can result from consensual disciplinary actions, changes in the interpretation of "what is correct," and approaches to the built patrimony driven by shared motives and shared reasons.

Our challenge is to overcome disciplinary barriers through an understanding of reality as a diverse and complex entity; we must surpass the limits of reductionism to achieve results that are archaeological as well as conservational (Delgado 2002b:124). Current discussions are centered on how architects might employ the archaeological instrument of stratigraphy, and how archaeologists can adapt their resources to the necessities imposed by the practice of restoration (Quirós-Castillo 2002:33). Equitable solutions must be adjusted in each case; thus communication between archaeologists and architects must be constant. This new relationship should bring about an approach with greater potential for knowledge based on more thoughtful positions vis-à-vis the social context in which the built patrimony was produced. In addition, restoration should echo the construction techniques and materials that for centuries have demonstrated their effectiveness; otherwise, the pursuit of authenticity is at stake.

The protection of the historic patrimony must overcome the destructive nature of its western legacy, which, since before Descartes and the Industrial Revolution, has opposed culture and nature (Criado 1991:28). In restoration, archaeology cannot be a partial partner, but instead should be converted into a central axis, based on both basic and applied investigations, so that restoration can develop from a critical perspective.

The merely reflective character of this communication, concerning a palpable problem in the restoration of the built patrimony that may apply to every part of the world, is aimed at stimulating critical investigations from the perspectives of different disciplines, and at pointing out the reasons why some theoretical and practical positions—despite having demonstrated coherent results or being capable of producing them—have failed to adjust the differences between archaeology and restoration, while older ways of achieving balance (as seen in the practices of Maza, Ramos, and Peña, described above) have been abandoned.

One way of approaching this problem would be to set out cultural particularities to be resolved through conveniently organized management plans. Historical centers are our patrimony, defined by local, heterogeneous idiosyncrasies, but also belonging to humanity. As a key product of human activity, historical centers should retain their authenticity for future generations. In Old Havana, where current work focused on the built patrimony is carried out under economic duress imposed by the U.S. blockade, archaeology demonstrates its importance in civic restoration. Nevertheless, the inescapable conclusion is this: given the new demands and developments in restoring the patrimonial past, archaeology should be a full participant in decisions at all levels.

Acknowledgments

I owe a great many thanks to all the specialists and technicians at the Archaeology Cabinet of the Historian's Office of the City of Havana, especially Roger

Arrazcaeta, Lisette Roura, Beatríz Rodríguez, Sonia Menendez, and Karen Mahe Lugo. For their input and assistance I am also indebted to Gabino La Rosa, Lourdes Domínguez, and Luís G. Lumbreras, as well as Susan Kepecs, L. Antonio Curet, and everyone else who made this volume possible.

Note

1. The Spanish version of the *Charter of Krakow* (*Carta de Cracovia,* 2000) was prepared by the Spanish Institute of Architecture, University of Valladolíd, Spain.

References Cited

Abbot, A.
  1965   *Cartas desde el interior de Cuba.* Consejo Nacional de Cultura, Havana.
  [1829]
Abraira, V., and A. Pérez
  1996   *Métodos multivariantes en bioestadística.* Editorial Centro de Estudios Ramón Areces, S.A., pp. 194–394.
Agorsah, E. K.
  1990   Archaeology of Maroon Heritage in Jamaica. *Archaeology Jamaica* 2:14–19.
  1993   Archaeology and Resistance History in the Caribbean. *African Archaeological Review* 11:175–196.
Alegría, R. E.
  1980   *Cristóbal Colón y el tesoro de los Indios de La Española.* Ediciones Fundación García Arévalo, Santo Domingo.
  1983   *Ball Courts and Ceremonial Plazas in the West Indies.* Publications in Anthropology No. 79. Yale University, New Haven.
Allen, S. J.
  1999   A "Cultural Mosaic" at Palmares? Grappling With the Historical Archaeology of a Seventeenth-Century Brazilian Quilombos. In *Cultura material e arqueología histórica,* edited by P. P. Funari, pp. 141–178. Instituto de Filosofía e Ciências Humanas, Universidade Estadual de Campinas, Brazil.
Álvarez, A., and E. Vento
  1987   Cimarronaje y apalencamiento esclavo en Matanzas. *Espelunca, Órgano Oficial de la Sociedad Espeleológica de Cuba, Havana* 2(1):12–20.
Álvarez, D.
  1977   Carta de Diego Álvarez Chanca. In *El Segundo viaje de descubrimiento,* F. Portuondo, pp. 59–97. Editorial de Ciencias Sociales, Havana.
Angelbello, S. T., and L. Delgado
  2003   La Región Arqueológica Centro-Sur de Cuba: Apuntes para su estudio. *El Caribe Arqueológico* 7:16–23.

Arnold, M.
1991 Antropología social aplicada en organizaciones económicas y participacionales. *Revista Chilena de Antropología* 10:81–95.

Arrazcaeta, R.
2002 Habana Vieja: Arqueología en edificios históricos. *Gabinete de Arqueología* 2:14–23.

Arredondo, C.
2000 Los edentados extintos del cuaternario de Cuba. Ph.D. dissertation, Departamento de Antropología, Universidad de Havana.
2002 Territorial Project Report 0827-I: Tafonomía del depósito arqueológico Solapa de Megalocnus en el Noroeste de Villa Clara, Cuba. Archive of Centro de Estudios y Servicios Ambientales de Villa Clara, Santa Clara.
2005 Territorial Project Report 0827-II: Informe paleontológico sobre depósitos fosilíferos contentivos de restos óseos de vertebrados en oquedades cársicas del Noroeste de Villa Clara. Archive of Centro de Estudios y Servicios Ambientales de Villa Clara, Santa Clara.

Arrom, J. J.
1975 *Mitología y artes prehispánicas de las Antillas*. Siglo XXI Editores, México.

Arrom, J. J., and M. A. García
1986 *Cimarrón. Serie Monográfica No. 18*, Fundación García Arévalo, Santo Domingo.

Azcárate, A.
2002 Intereses cognoscitivos y praxis social en arqueología de la arquitectura. *Arqueología de la arquitectura* 1:55–71.

Barclay, K.
2001 *Scientific Analysis of Archaeological Ceramics: A Handbook of Resources*. Oxbow Books, Oxford.

Bartone, R. N., and A. Versteeg
1997 The Tanki Flip Features and Structures. In *The Archaeology of Aruba: The Tanki Flip Site*, edited by A. Versteeg and S. Rostain, pp. 23–126. Archaeological Museum Aruba and the Foundation for Scientific Research in the Caribbean Region, Oranjestad.

Bashilov, V.
1988 Исследования Поселения Эль-Конвенто (Куба) [Investigations of El Convento Site (Cuba)]. *Archaeological Discoveries 1986*, pp. 527–528. Moscow.

Bashilov, V., and V. Golenko
1992 К Вопросу о Периодизации "Куьтуры Субтаино" в Центральной Части Кубы: По Керамическим Материалам Раскопок Поселения Эль Конвенто [The Problem of the Periodization of Subtaíno Culture in South-Central Cuba: The Ceramic Material from the Site of El Convento]. *Russian Archaeology* 2:240–258 (reprint).

Bate, L. F.
1969 Material lítico: metodología de clasificación. Paper presented at the Quinto Congreso Nacional de Arqueología, La Serena, Chile.
1978 *Sociedad, formación económico social y cultura*. Ediciones de Cultura Popular, México.
1998 *El proceso de investigación en arqueología*. Editorial Crítica, Barcelona.

Bay, L.
1939 Lineamientos de una arquitectura americana. *Revista de arqueología* 1(3):17–22.

Bense, J. (editor)
1999   *The Archaeology of Colonial Pensacola.* University Press of Florida, Gainesville.
2003   *Presidio Santa María de Galve. A Struggle for Survival in Colonial Spanish Pensacola.* University Press of Florida, Gainesville.

Berman, M. J., and C. D. Hutcheson
2000   Impressions of a Lost Technology: A study of Lucayan-Taíno Basketry. *Journal of Field Archaeology* 27(4):417–435.

Binford, L. R.
1962   Archaeology as Anthropology. *American Antiquity* 28(2):217–225.
1981   Behavioral archaeology and the "Pompeii premise." *Journal of Anthropological Research* 37(3):195–208.

Bloch, M.
2004   *Anthropology and Ethnography.* Routledge Press, London.

Bobrinski, A. A., and V. G. Loman
1992   Результаты Технико-Технлогического Анализа Образцов Керамики Поселения Эль Конвенто, Куба [Results of a Technological Analysis of the Ceramic Sample from the Site of El Convento]. *Russian Archaeology* 2:258–269 (reprint).

Bordes, F.
1965   *The Old Stone Age.* World University Library, London.

Boyd, M. F., H. G. Smith, and J. W. Griffin
1951   *Here They Once Stood: The Tragic End of the Apalachee Missions.* University of Florida Press, Gainesville.

Bradley, R. S.
1985   *Quaternary Paleoclimatology: Methods of Paleoclimatic Reconstruction.* Allen & Unwin, Boston.

Brandi, C. M., and G. D'Ossat
1972   *Carta del restauro.* Documento electrónico: http://www.mec.gub.uy /com _patri/ download/ cartas Internacionales.

Bremer, F.
1842   *Resumen del censo de población de la Isla de Cuba a fines del año de 1841.* Imprenta del Gobierno por Su Majestad, Havana.
1980   *Cartas desde Cuba.* Editorial Arte y Literatura, Havana. Comisión de Estadísticas, Cuba.

Brezillion, M. N.
1968   *La dénomination des objets de pierre taillée.* Centre National de la Recherche Scientifique, Université de París.

Bullen, R. P.
1974   Were There Pre-Columbian Cultural Contacts Between Florida and the West Indies: The Archaeological Evidence. *Florida Anthropologist* 27:149–160.

Bullen, R. P., and D. D. Laxon
1954   Some Incised Pottery from Cuba and Florida. *Florida Anthropologist* 7:23–25.

Bunge, M.
1972   *La investigación científica.* Editorial de Ciencias Sociales, Havana.
1999   *Sistemas sociales y filosofía.* Editorial Sudamericana, Buenos Aires.

Bushnell, A. T.
1981   *The King's Coffer: Proprietors of the Spanish Florida Treasury 1565–1702.* University Press of Florida, Gainesville.

Bustamante, R.
 1999   Cartas y convenios internacionales para la conservación del patrimonio cultural. In *Tratado de rehabilitación. Teoría e historia de la rehabilitación*, edited by L. M. Gubert, pp. 321–406. Editorial Munilla-Lería. Madrid.

Caballero, L.
 1996   El análisis estratigráfico de construcciones históricas. *Arqueología de la Arquitectura*, pp. 55–74. Consejo Superior de Investigaciones Científicas, Madrid.

Cabrera, M.
 1978   *Apuntes arqueológicos del Valle de Caujerí*. Cuba Arqueológica, Editorial Oriente, Santiago de Cuba.

Calvera, J., and J. Febles
 1984   *Evidencias arqueológicas de Los Buchillones, Ciego de Avila: Carta Informativa. No. 55*. Departamento de Arqueología.

Calvera, J., J. Jardines, D. Pendergast, E. Graham, A. Bekerman, O. Brito, and M. Martínez
 2001   Informe Final: Investigaciones arqueológicas conjuntas cubano—canadiense en el area de Los Buchillones. Unpublished, Ciego de Avila.

Calvera, J., E. Serrano, M. Rey, I. Pedroso, and Y. Yparraguirre
 1996   El sitio arqueológico Los Buchillones. *El Caribe Arqueológico* 1:59–67.

Cancela, P.
 1952   Algo más sobre la encomienda de Bartolomé de las Casas. *Revista de arqueología y etnología*, No. 15–16, 2da Época, Año VII, pp. 247–258. Havana.

Carniero, R. L.
 1981   The Chiefdom as Precursor to the State. In *Transition to Statehood in the New World*, edited by G. Jones and R. Kautz, pp. 37–79. Cambridge University Press, Cambridge.

Cassá, R.
 1991   Estudio del sitio arqueológico Loma de la Forestal, Holguín. In *Arqueología de Cuba y otras áreas antillanas*, edited by J. Febles and A. V. Rives, pp. 203–246. Editorial Academia, Havana.
 1992   *Los indios de las Antillas*. Editorial Mapfre, Madrid.

Castellanos, N., and A. V. Rives
 1991   Aplicación de los métodos de cluster analysis y de seriación a los estudios ceramográficos. In *Arqueología de Cuba y otras áreas antillanas*, edited by J. Febles and A. V. Rives, pp. 144–162. Editorial Academia, Havana.

Celaya, M., and P. P. Godo
 1998   Guacanayabo, Jagua, y Yucayo: La variación local de la cerámica aborigen de Cuba. Paper presented at the Primer Taller Nacional de Arqueología, Villa Clara.
 2000   "Llora-Lluvia" Expresiones Mítico-Artísticas en la Alfarería Aborigen. *El Caribe Arqueológico* 4:70–84.

Colón, C.
 1961   *Diario de navegación*. Publication of the Comisión Cubana de la Unesco. Tipografía Ponciano, S.A., Havana.

Consejo de Ministros
 1998   *Compilación de textos legislativos*. Consejo Nacional de Patrimonio Cultural. Havana.

Cooper, J.
 2007   Island Interaction in the Prehistoric Caribbean: An Archaeological Case Study from Northern Cuba. Ph.D. thesis, University College, London.

2008 Creating Connections Between Caribbean Islands: An Archaeological Perspective from Northern Cuba. In *British Archaeological Reports Vol. 9, Comparative Island Archaeologies*, edited by J. Conolly and M. Campbell, pp. 179–190.

Cooper, J., and R. Valcárcel
2004 Pre-Hispanic Settlements along the North Coast of Cuba: A Pilot Survey Report from Los Buchillones. *Papers from the Institute of Archaeology* 15:77–81.

Cooper, J., R. Valcárcel, and P. Cruz
2006 Gente en los cayos. Los Buchillones y sus vínculos marítimos. *El Caribe Arqueológico* 9:66–75.

Cosculluela, J. A.
1918 *Cuatro años en la Ciénaga de Zapata: Memorias de un ingeniero*. Impresa y Papelería "La Universal," Havana, Cuba.

Craddock, P. T.
1995 *Early Metal Mining and Production*. Edinburgh University Press, Edinburgh.

Crejo, T.
1976 *La conservación de lugares urbanos. Conservación y restauración de los bienes culturales*. Editorial Pueblo y Educación, Havana.

Crespo, E. F.
2000 *Estudio comparativo biocultural entre dos poblaciones prehistóricas en la Isla de Puerto Rico: Punta Candelero y Paso del Indio*. Doctoral dissertation, Universidad Nacional Autónoma de México.

Criado, F.
1991 *El área Bocelo—Furelos entre los tiempos paleolíticos y medievales*. Xunta de Galicia, Santiago de Compostela.

Cruxent, J. M., and I. Rouse
1969 Early Man in the West Indies. *Scientific American* 221(5):42–52.

Curet, L. A.
1992 House Structure and Cultural Change in the Caribbean: Three Case Studies from Puerto Rico. *Latin American Antiquity* 3(2):160–174.
2009 The Taino Concept from a Sociopolitical Perspective. Paper presented in the symposium "The Politics of Population Reorganization" at the 73rd Annual Meeting of the Society for American Archaeology, Vancouver.

Curet, L. A., S. L. Dawdy, and G. La Rosa (editors)
2005 *Dialogues in Cuban Archaeology*. University of Alabama Press, Tuscaloosa.

Curet, L. A., and J. Oliver
1998 Mortuary Practices, Social Development, and Ideology in Precolumbian Puerto Rico. *Latin American Antiquity* 9(3):217–239.
2004 Island Archaeology and Units of Analysis in the Study of Ancient Caribbean Societies. In *Voyages of Discovery: The Archaeology of Islands*, edited by S. Fitzpatrick, 187–201. Praeger Press, Santa Barbara.

Cusick, J.
1993 *Ethnic Groups and Class in an Emerging Market Economy: Spaniards and Minorcans in Late Colonial St. Augustine*. Ph.D. dissertation, University of Florida, Gainesville.

Dacal, R.
1971 *Ante-proyecto restauración del sitio arqueológico de Lagunas de Limones, en Maisí, Oriente*. Unpublished manuscript, Havana, Cuba, in possession of the author.

1978 *Artefactos de concha en las communidades aborigenes cubanas.* Museo Anthropológico Montané, Havana.
1980 *Informe de visita al sitio arqueológico de Laguna de Limones, Maisí, Guantánamo al Presidente de la Comisión Nacional de Monumentos.* Unpublished manuscript, Havana, Cuba.

Dacal, R., and M. Pino
1968 Excavaciones en la Cueva de Enrique, península de Guanahacabibes. *Serie Pinar del Río* No. 16, Academia de Ciencias de Cuba, Havana.

Dacal, R., and M. Rivero
1996 *Art and Archaeology of Pre-Columbian Cuba.* University of Pittsburgh Press, Pittsburgh.

Davis, D. D.
1996 Revolutionary Archeology in Cuba. *Journal of Archeological Method and Theory* 3:159–188.

Deagan, K. A.
1982 Avenues of Inquiry in Historical Archaeology. In *Advances in Archaeological Method and Theory,* edited by M. Schiffer, pp. 151–178. Academic Press, New York.
1996 Colonial Transformation: Euro-American Cultural Genesis in the Early Spanish-American Colonies. *Journal of Anthropological Research* 52(2):135–160.
2002 *Artifacts of the Spanish Colonies of Florida and the Caribbean, 1500–1800,* Vol. 2: *Portable Personal Possessions.* Smithsonian Institution Press, Washington, D.C.
2004 Reconsidering Taíno Social Dynamics after Spanish Conquest: Gender and Class in Culture Contact Studies. *American Antiquity* 69(4):597–626.
2006 Eliciting Contraband Through Archaeology: Illicit Trade In Eighteenth-Century St. Augustine. *Historical Archaeology* 40(3):98–116.

Deagan, K. A., and J. M. Cruxent
1993 From Contact to Criollos: The Archaeology of Spanish Colonization in Hispaniola. In *The Meeting of Two worlds: Europe and the Americas 1492–1650,* edited by W. Bray, pp. 67–104. Proceeding of the British Academy 81.
2002 *Columbus's Outpost Among the Taínos: Spain and America at La Isabela, 1493–1498.* Yale University Press, New Haven.

Deagan, K. A., and P. Kulst
1998 Reporte preliminar del análisis de laboratorio del Parque Nacional Concepción de la Vega. Temporadas de campo de 1996–1997. On file, University of Florida, Gainesville.

Deagan, K. A., and D. McMahon
1995 *Ft. Mose: Colonial America's Black Fortress of Freedom.* University Press of Florida, Gainesville.

Deagan, K. A., and M. Scardaville
1983 History and Archeology on Hispanic Historic Sites: Impediments and Solutions. *Historical Archaeology* 19:32–37.

Delgado, C. J.
2002a Marxismo y ecología: complejidad de un problema, o ¿un problema de complejidad? *Revista Cubana de Ciencias Sociales* 32:5–12.
2002b *Hacia un nuevo saber. Problemas del enriquecimiento moral del conocimiento humano.* Mecanuscrito. Facultad de Filosofía, Universidad de Havana.

Delle, J. A.
1998   *An Archaeology of Social Space: Analyzing Coffee Plantations in Jamaica's Blue Mountains.* Plenum Press, London.

Delpuech, A., C. L. Hofman, and M. L. P. Hoogland
1999   Excavations at the Site of Anse A La Gourde, Guadeloupe: Organisation, History and Environmental Setting. *Proceedings of the XVIIIth International Congress For Caribbean Archaeology* Vol. XVIII.

Dingwall, E. J.
1931   *Artificial Cranial Deformation.* John Bale and Sons, London, and Danielsson Ltd.

Domínguez, L.
1978   La transculturación en Cuba (s. XVI–XVII). *Cuba arqueológica* I. pp. 33–50. Editorial Oriente, Santiago de Cuba.
1980   Cerámica transcultural en el sitio colonial Casa de la Obrapía. *Cuba arqueológica.* Pp. 15–26. Editorial Oriente No. 2.
1981   Arqueología del sitio colonial Casa de la Obrapia o de Calvo de la Puerta, Habana Vieja. *Santiago* 41:63–82.
1984   *Arqueología colonial cubana: Dos estudios.* Editorial de Ciencias Sociales, Havana.
1991   *Arqueología del centro-sur de Cuba.* Editorial Academia, Havana.
1995   *Arqueología colonial cubana.* Editorial de Ciencias Sociales, Havana.
1998   La ciudad. *Opus Havana* 1:58–63.
1999   El siglo XVI en la arqueología histórica caribeña. *Debates americanos* (7–8):58–66.
2004a Guanabacoa: "Una experiencia india" en nuestra colonización. *Gabinete de Arqueología* 3(3):4–12. Havana.
2004b Online journal published by the Nucleo de Estudios Estratégicos/Arqueología, Universidade Estadual de Campinas, Campinas, Brazil. http://www.historiaehistoria.com.br/materia.cfm?tb=historiadores&ID=9.
2005   Historical Archaeology in Cuba. In *Dialogues in Cuban Archaeology,* edited by L. A. Curet, S. L. Dawdy, and G. La Rosa, pp. 62–71. University of Alabama Press, Tuscaloosa.

Domínguez, L., J. Febles, and A. V. Rives
1994   Las comunidades aborígines de Cuba. In *Historia de Cuba La colonia: evolución socioeconómica y formación nacional, de los orígenes hasta 1867,* edited by M. del Carmen Barcia, G. García, and E. Torres-Cuevas, pp. 5–57. Editora Politica, Havana.

Domínguez, L., and A. V. Rives
1995   Supervivencia o transculturación en el siglo XVI antillano. In *Actas del XV Congreso Internacional de Arqueología del Caribe, San Juan,* edited by R. Alegría and M. Rodríguez, pp. 393–398. Centro de Estudios Avanzados de Puerto Rico y el Caribe, San Juan.

Drennan, R., and C. Uribe (editors)
1987   *Chiefdoms in the Americas.* University Press of America, New York.

Drewett, P.
2003   Feasting at the Ball Game: The Belmont Project, Tortola, British Virgin Islands. *Archaeology International* 6:56–59.

Eidt, R. C.
1973   A Rapid Chemical Field Test for Archaeological Site Surveying. *American Antiquity* 38(2):206–210.

Ellis, G. D.
1977   Hi426: A Late 19th Century Historical Site in the Ybor City Historical District of Tampa, Florida. M.A. thesis, University of South Florida, Tampa.

Elso, E.
1946   Expedición speleo-arqueológica a Punta de la Sierra, Guane, Pinar del Río. Sociedad Espeleológica de Cuba. Archived manuscript, Instituto Cubano de Antropología.

Emerson, M. C.
1999   African Inspirations in a New World Art and Artifact: Decorated Tobacco Pipes from the Chesapeake. In *I, Too, Am America: Archaeological Studies of African-American Life*, edited by T. A. Singleton, pp. 47–82. University Press of Virginia, Charlottesville.

Engels, F.
1972   *The Origin of the Family, Private Property and the State*. Pathfinder Press
[1884] Imprints, New York.

Engerrand, G.
1905   *Nociones sobre las primeras edades*. Publicaciones de la Escuela Moderna, Barcelona.

Ewen, C.R.
2001   Historical Archaeology in the Caribbean. In *Island Lives: Historical Archaeologies of the Caribbean*, edited by P. Farnsworth, pp. 3–21. University of Alabama Press, Tuscaloosa.

Fairbanks, C.
1968   Early Spanish Colonial Beads. *Conference on Historic Sites Archeology Papers* 2:3–22.
1972   The Cultural Significance of Spanish Ceramics. In *Ceramics in America*, edited by I. Quimby, pp. 141–174. University of Virginia Press, Charlottesville.
1974   The Kingsley Slave Cabins in Duval County, Florida. *Conference on Historic Sites Archaeology Papers* 7:62–93.
1984   The Plantation Archaeology of the Southeastern Coast. *Historical Archaeology* 18(1):1–14.

Farnsworth, P. (editor)
2001   *Island Lives: Historical Archaeologies of the Caribbean*. University of Alabama Press, Tuscaloosa.

Febles, J.
1982   *Estudio tecnológico y tipológico del material de piedra tallada de Aguas Verdes, Baracoa y Playita, Matanzas: Posibles relaciones con otras del sudeste de los Estados Unidos*. Editorial Academia, Havana, pp. 312–371.
1988   *Manual para el estudio de la piedra tallada de los aborígenes de Cuba*. Editorial Academia, Havana.
1990   *El protoarcaico de Cuba: distribución espacial, tecnología y tipología de sus industrias de piedra tallada* (unpublished). Editorial Academia, Havana.
1991a Estudio comparativo de las industrias de la piedra tallada de Aguas Verdes (Baracoa) y Playita (Matanzas): Probable relación de estas industrias con otras del SE de los Estados Unidos. In *Arqueología de Cuba y otras áreas antillanas*, edited by M. A. Rodríguez, pp. 312–371. Editorial Academia, Havana.
1991b *Taíno: Arqueología de Cuba*. Personal Database, Havana.

1995 *Taíno: Arqueología de Cuba*. Centro de Antropología, Havana, Cuba. CEDISAC, Havana, Cuba (CD-ROM).

Febles, J., and A. V. Rives
1991 Cluster análisis: Un experimento aplicado a la industria de la piedra tallada del protoarcaico de Cuba. In *Arqueología de Cuba y otras áreas antillanas*, edited by M. A. Rodríguez, pp. 115–124. Editorial Academia, Havana.

Febles, J., and R. Villavicencio
1996 Industria de la piedra tallada del sitio protoagrícola El Dorado, Villa Clara, Cuba. *Carta Informativa*, Academia de Ciencias de Cuba, Havana.

Ferguson, L. G.
1980 Looking for the "Afro" in Colono-Indian Pottery. In *Archaeological Perspectives on Ethnicity in America*, edited by R. Schuyler, pp. 14–42. Baywood Press Farmingdale, New York.

1992 *Uncommon Ground: Archaeology and Early African America, 1650–1800*. Smithsonian Institution Press, Washington, D.C.

Fernández de Oviedo, G.
1992 *Historia general y natural de las Indias*, Vol. I. Biblioteca de Autores Españoles. Ediciones Atlas, Madrid.

Fewkes, J. W.
1904 Prehistoric Culture of Cuba. *American Anthropologist* 6:585–598.

Flannery, K. V.
1973 Archaeology with a Capital "S." In *Research and Theory in Current Archaeology*, edited by C. L. Redman, pp. 47–53. Wiley, New York.

Florida Department of State
2006 *Florida Cuba Heritage Trail*. Division of Historical Resources. Tallahassee. http://dhr.dos.state.fl.us/services/trails/cht/.

Forde, C. D.
1965 *Habitat, economía y sociedad: Introducción geográfica a la etnología*. Oikos-Tau Editions, Barcelona.

Francovich, R., and L. Bianchi
2002 L´archeologie dell´elevato come archeologia. *Arqueología de la arquitectura* 1:101–111.

Franklin, M., and L. McKee (editors)
2004 African Diaspora Archaeologies: Present Insights and Expanding Discourses. *Historical Archaeology* 38(1).

Funari, P. P.
1999 Etnicidad, identidad y cultura material. Un estudio del Cimmarón, Palmares, Brasil, siglo XVII. In *Sed Non Satiata. teoría social en la arqueología latinoamericana contemporánea*, edited by A. Zarankin and F. A. Acuto, pp. 77–96. Tridente Editions, Buenos Aires.

2006 Conquistadors, Plantations, and Quilombo: Latin America in Historical Archaeological Context. In *Historical Archaeology*, edited by M. Hall and S. W. Silliman, pp. 210–229. Blackwell Publishing, Malden, MA.

Gadamer, H. G.
1975 *Truth and Method*. Seabury Press, New York.

Gamble, C.
1983 Culture and Society in the Upper Palaeolithic of Europe. In *Hunter-Gatherer*

Economy in Prehistory, edited by C. N. Bailey, pp. 201–211. Cambridge University Press, Cambridge.
1990   *El poblamiento paleolítico de Europa.* Editorial Crítica S.A., Barcelona.
Gándara, M.
1992   El análisis de posiciones teóricas: Aplicaciones a la arqueología social. *Boletín de antropología americana* No. 27, México. pp. 5–20.
Garcell, J.
2002   Arqueología en un refugio de cimarrones: Cueva del negro. *El Caribe arqueológico* 6:44–48.
García, G.
2002   *La esclavitud desde la esclavitud.* Editorial de Ciencias Sociales, Havana.
García, J. A.
1938   Asiento Yayal. *Revista de arqueología* 1:44–57.
1940   Asiento El Pesquero. *Revista de arqueología* 4:56–60.
1941   Asientos taínos localizados en el cacicato de Baní. *Revista de arqueología* 5:18–22.
1947   La transculturacíon indo-española en Holguín. *Notas del Museo García Fera de Holguín.* Cuaderno 6. (re-issued in *Academia de la Historia,* signature 12, capitulo 593, May 31, 1951). Holguín.
1949   La transculturación indo-española en Holguín. *Revista de Arqueología y Etnología* Año IV, No. 8-9:195–205.
García y Grave de Peralta, F.
1938   Excursiones arqueológicas. *Revista de arqueología y etnología* 1(1):20–31.
Godo, P. P., G. Baena, A. Menéndez, and A. Morffis
1987   Industria de la piedra tallada en Punta del Vizcaíno, Caibarién, Villa Clara. *Carta informativa* Época II, No. 100, Academia de Ciencias, Havana.
Goggin, J. M.
1968   Spanish Majolica in the New World. *Yale University Publications in Anthropology,* No. 72. Yale University Press, New Haven.
Gold, R.
1969   *Borderland Empires in Transition: The Triple-Nation Transfer of Florida.* Southern Illinois University Press, Carbondale.
González, A., and I. Avello
1946   Asiento Cantabria: Descubrimiento del residuario de cultura alfarera mas occidental de Cuba. *Revista de Arqueología y Etnología,* 2da Epoca, Año I, No. 3:11–27. Havana.
Gower, J. C.
1971   A General Coefficient of Similarity and Some of Its Properties. *Biometrics* 2(4):857–872.
Griffin, J. W.
1943   The Antillean Problem in Florida Archaeology. *Florida Historical Quarterly* 22:86–91.
1949   The Historic Archaeology of Florida. In *The Florida Indian and His Neighbors,* edited by J. Griffin, pp. 45–54. Rollins College Inter-American Center, Winter Park, Florida.
1978   End Products of Historic Sites Archaeology: Symposium on the Role of Archaeology in Historical Research. (1958). In *Historical Archaeology: A Guide*

References Cited / 173

        to *Substantive and Theoretical Contributions*, edited by R. Schuyler, pp. 20–22. Baywood Press, Farmingdale, N.J.
1990   Changing Perspectives on the Spanish Missions of La Florida. In *Columbian Consequences, Volume II: Archaeological and Historical Perspectives on the Spanish Borderlands East*, edited by D. H. Thomas. pp. 399–408, Smithsonian Institution Press, Washington, D.C.

Griffin, J. W., and H. G. Smith
1948   *The Goodnow Mound, Highlands County, Florida*. Contributions to the Archaeology of Florida No. 1, Florida Park Service, Tallahassee.

Guarch, J. M.
1970   Excavaciones arqueológicas en Cueva Funche, Guanahacabibes, Cuba. *Serie espeleológica* No. 10, Academia de Ciencias de Cuba, Havana, pp. 1–20.
1972   *Excavaciones en el extremo oriental de Cuba. Serie Arqueológica No. 1*. Academia de Ciencias de Cuba, Instituto de Arqueológica, Havana
1978   *El Taíno de Cuba, Ensayo de reconstrucción etno-histórica*. Instituto de Ciencias Sociales, Havana.
1987   *Arqueología de Cuba: Métodos y sistemas*. Editorial de Ciencias Sociales, Havana.
1988   Sitio arqueológico El Chorro de Maíta. *Revista cubana de ciencias sociales* 17:162–183.
1990   *Estructura para las comunidades aborigines de Cuba*. Ediciones Holguín, Holguín.
1994   *Yaguajay, Yucayeque, Turey*. Publicigraf, Holguín.
1996   La muerte en las Antillas: Cuba. *El Caribe arqueológico* 1:12–25.

Guarch, J. J.
1991   Sistema para el levantimiento topográfico y la planigrafía de los sitios arqueológicos. In *Arqueología de Cuba y otras áreas antillanas*, edited by J. Febles and A. V. Rives, pp. 102–109. Editorial Academia, Havana.

Guarch, J. M., C. Rodríguez, and R. Pedroso
1987   Investigaciones preliminares en el sitio El Chorro de Maíta. *Revista de historia* 3: 25–40.

Guerrero, J. G.
1999   Contacto indohispánico temprano en Santo Domingo: Una lectura histórica y arqueológica. *El Caribe arqueológico* 3:102–108.

Gutiérrez, A., and R. Iglesias
1996   Identificación y análisis de los restos de fauna recuperados en los Conventos de San Francisco y Santo Domingo de Quito, siglos XVI–XIX. *Revista española de antropología americana* 26:77–100. Universidad Complutense, Madrid.

Haidar, M.
1998   A Consideration of Depositional Process in the Urban Archaeological Record: A Case Study from Ybor City, Florida. Master's thesis, University of South Florida.

Handler, J. S.
1983   An African Pipe from Slave Cemetery in Barbados, West Indies. In *The Archaeology of the Clay Tobacco Pipe: America*, edited by P. Davey, pp. 245–253. British Archaeological Reports, International Series, No. 175. Oxford.

Harrington, M. R.
1921 *Cuba Before Columbus.* 2 vols. Indian Notes and Monographs, Museum of the American Indian, Heye Foundation, New York.
1925 *Cuba Before Colombus.* Colección de Libros Cubanos, Vol. I, Chapter XXXII. Cultural S.A., Havana.
1935 *Cuba antes de Colón.* Translated by A. del Valle and F. Ortíz. Colección de Libros Cubanos, Vol. XXXII, Vol. 1, Cultural S.A., Havana.

Harris, E. C.
1979 *Principles of Archaeological Stratigraphy.* Academic Press, London.
1991 *Principios de estratigrafía arqueológica.* Editorial Crítica, Barcelona.
2004 Estratigrafía de estructuras en pie. *Gabinete de arqueología* 3:79–87.

Harris, M.
2000 *Teorías sobre la cultura en la era postmoderna.* Editorial Crítica. Barcelona.

Haviser, J. B. (editor)
1999 *African Sites: Archaeology in the Caribbean.* Markus Weiner Publishers, Princeton, NJ.

Hayden, B., and A. Cannon
1983 Where the Garbage Goes: Refuse Disposal in the Maya Highlands. *Journal of Anthropological Archaeology* 2(3):117–163.

Helms, M. W.
1993 *Craft and the Kingly Ideal: Art, Trade, and Power.* University of Texas Press, Austin.

Hernández, I.
2005 Puerto Príncipe en el Chorrito. Continuación de una investigación inconclusa. *Gabinete de arqueología* 4:199–200.
2006 Arqueología en Pueblo Viejo de Nuevitas: problemáticas actuales y perspectivas. *Cuaderno de Historia Principeña 5,* Oficina del Historiador de la Ciudad de Camagüey.

Herrera, R.
1946 Tres notas para la arqueologia indocubana. *Revista de arqueologia y etnologia 1.*
1964 *Estudio de las hachas antillanas: Creacíon de indices axiales para las petaloides.* Empresa Consolidada de Artes Gráficas, Havana, Cuba.

Hofman, C., M. L. P. Hoogland, and A. L. van Gijn (editors)
2008 *Crossing the Borders: New Methods and Techniques in the Study of Archaeological Materials from the Caribbean.* University of Alabama Press, Tuscaloosa.

Hughen, K. A., M. G. L. Baillie, E. Bard, J. W. Beck, C. J. H. Bertrand, P. G. Blackwell, C. E. Buck, G. S. Burr, K. B. Cutler, P. E. Damon, R. L. Edwards, R. G. Fairbanks, M. Friedrich, T. P. Guilderson, B. Kromer, G. McCormac, S. Manning, C. B. Ramsey, P. J. Reimer, R. W. Reimer, S. Remmele, J. R. Southon, M. Stuiver, S. Talamo, F. W. Taylor, J. van der Plicht, and C. E. Weyhenmeyer
2004 Marine04 Marine Radiocarbon Age Calibration, 0–26 Cal Kyr BP. *Radiocarbon* 46(3):1059–1086.

Hughes, J., and W. Sharrock
1999 *La filosofía de la investigación social.* Fondo de Cultura Económica. México, D. F.

Hutcheson, C.
2001 Reweaving the Strands: Continued Exploration into the Basketry Technology

of Prehistoric Bahamians. *Proceedings of the XVIIIth International Congress for Caribbean Archaeology* 18:185–198.

Irving, W. N.
1971 Recent Early Man Researches in the North. *Arctic Anthropology* 8(2):68–82.

Iturralde-Vinent, M., and R. D. E. MacPhee
1999 Paleogeography of the Caribbean Region: Implications for Cenozoic Biogeography. *Bulletin of the American Museum of Natural History* 238.

Iturralde-Vinent, M., R. D. E. MacPhee, D. Franco, R. Rojas, W. Suárez, and A. Lomba
2000 Las Breas de San Felipe: A Quaternary Fossiliferous Asphalt Seep Near Martí, Matanzas Province, Cuba. *Caribbean Journal of Science* 36(3–4):300–313.

Izquierdo, G., and A. Rives
1993 Lista tipológica de la industria de la concha en las comunidades aborigenes de Cuba y Las Antilles. Report submitted to the Departament of Archaeology, Centro de Antropologia, Academia de Ciencias de Cuba.

Izquierdo, G., and R. Sampedro
2002 Útiles de concha y unidades habitacionales de las comunidades aborigenes de Cuba. *El Caribe arqueológico* 6:71–76.

Jacobus, A. L.
1996 Louças cerâmica no sul do Brasil no século XVIII: O registro de viamâo como estudo de caso. *Revista do CEPA*, Santa Cruz do Sul 20(23):7–58.

Jardines, J., and J. Calvera
1999 Estructuras de viviendas aborígenes en Los Buchillones. *El Caribe arqueológico* 3:44–52.

Jiménez, A.
1979 Estudio del esqueleto 01 de las excavaciones de la Villa de la Concepción. *Boletín del Museo del Hombre Dominicano* 12:262–276.

Jiménez, O., M. M. Condis, and E. García
2005 Vertebrados postglaciales en un residuario fósil de *Tyto alba* Scopoli (Aves: Tytonidae) en el occidente de Cuba. *Revista mexicana de mastozoología* 9:85–109.

Johnson, S.
2001 Casualties of Peace: Tracing the Historic Roots of the Cuban Diaspora, 1763–1804. *Colonial Latin American Historical Review* 10(1):91–125.

Jouravleva, I.
2002 Origen de la alfarería de las comunidades protoagroalfareras de la región central de Cuba. *El Caribe arqueólogico* 6:35–43.

Keegan, W. F.
1992 *The People Who Discovered Columbus: The Prehistory of the Bahamas*. University of Florida Press, Gainesville.

Kelso, W. M., and B. Straube
2004 *Jamestown Rediscovery 1994–2004*. The Association for the Preservation of Virginia Antiquities.

Kepecs, S.
2002 Saving Old Havana. *Archaeology* 55(2):42–47.

Kepecs, S., and R. T. Alexander (editors)
2005 *The Postclassic to Spanish-Era Transition in Mesoamerica: Archaeological Perspectives*. University of New Mexico Press, Albuquerque.

Knight, V. J., and J. E. Worth
  2007   A Cuban Origin For Glades Pottery? A Provocative Hypothesis Revisited. Online paper, University of South Alabama Anthropology Department. http://www.as.ua.edu/ant/Faculty/knight/Cuban%20Origin%20Glades%20Pottery.
Kozlowski, J.
  1974   *Preceramic Cultures of the Caribbean.* Prace Archeologiczne, Cracovia, No. 20.
  1975   Las industrias de la piedra tallada de Cuba en el contexto del Caribe. In *Serie arqueológica* No. 5, pp. 5–20. Editorial Academia, Havana.
Kozlowski, J., and B. Ginter
  1975   *Técnica de la talla y tipología de los instrumentos líticos.* Editorial Pueblo y Educación, Havana.
La Rosa, G.
  1984   Elementos para la construcción histórica de los palenques. *Bohemia* 76(33), Havana.
  1988   *Los palenques del oriente de Cuba: Resistencia y acoso.* Editorial Academia, La Habana.
  1990   Refugios cimarrones en el Pan de Matanzas. In *Carta informativa* no. 6, Época III, Academia de Ciencias de Cuba, Havana.
  1991a La Cueva de la Cachimba: Estudio arqueológico de un refugiode cimarrones. In *Estudios Arqueológicos,* pp. 57–84. Editorial Academia, Havana.
  1991b *Los paleneques del oriente de Cuba: Resistencia y acoso.* Editorial Academia, Havana.
  1995   *Arqueología en sitios de contrabandistas.* Editorial Academia, Havana.
  2001   La ciencia arqueológica en Cuba: Retos y perspectivas en los umbrales del siglo XXI. *Revista Cubana de Antropología* 8:36–46.
  2003a *Runaway Slave Settlements in Cuba: Resistance and Repression.* University of North Carolina Press, Chapel Hill.
  2003b La orientación este de los entierros aborígenes en cuevas de Cuba: Remate de una fábula. *Latin American Antiquity* 14(2):143–157.
  2005   Subsistence of Cimarrones: An Archaeological Study. In *Dialogues in Cuban Archaeology,* edited by L. A. Curet, S. L.Dawdy, and G. La Rosa, pp. 163–180. University of Alabama Press, Tuscaloosa.
La Rosa, G., and O. Ortega
  1990   Refugios cimarrones en el Pan de Matanzas. In *Carta informativa* No. 6, Epoca III, Academia de Ciencias de Cuba, La Habana.
Landers, J. G.
  2004   Una comunidad del siglo XVIII en el exilio: los floridanos en Cuba. *Del Caribe* 44:53–61.
Las Casas, B. de
  1875   *Historia de las Indias.* Vol. 3. Imprenta de Miguel Ginesta, Madrid.
  1951   *Historia de las Indias.* 2 vols. Fondo de Cultura Económica, Mexico City.
  1965   *Historia de Las Indias.* Fondo de Cultura Económica, México.
Le Paige, G.
  1971   *Industrias líticas de San Pedro de Atacama.* Editorial Orbe, Argentina.
Lightfoot, K.
  1995   Culture Contact Studies: Redefining the Relationship between Prehistoric and Historical Archaeology. *American Antiquity* 60(2):199–217.

Little, B. J.
1996   People with History: An Update on Historical Archaeology in the United States. In *Images of the Recent Past*, edited by C. Orser, pp. 42–78. Altamira, London.

López, F.
2002   La noción de patrimonio entre lo local y lo global, una mirada al patrimonio cultural arqueológico. *Revista de arqueología americana* 21:155–169.

Loven, S.
1935   *Origins of the Tainan Culture, West Indies*. Elanders Boktryckeri Aktiebolag, Goteborg, Sweden.

Lumbreras, L. G.
1974   *La arqueología como ciencia social*. Ediciones Histar, Lima, Peru.

Lyon, Eugene
2006   The Fate of the South Florida Indians. Paper presented at the Historic St. Augustine Research Institute, Flagler College, St. Augustine, Florida.

MacNeish, R.
1976   Early Man in the New World. *American Scientist* 64(3):316–327.

MacPhee, R. D. E., C. Flemming, and D. P. Lunde
1999   Last Occurrence of the Antillean Insectivoran Nesophontes: New Radiometric Dates and Their Interpretation. *American Museum Novitiates* 3261, pp. 1–19.

MacPhee, R. D. E., M. Iturralde, and O. Jiménez
2007   Prehistoric Sloth Extinctions in Cuba: Implications of a New "Last" Appearance Date. *Caribbean Journal of Science* 43(1):94–98.

Marrero, L.
1972   *Cuba: Economía y Sociedad*, Vol. 1. Editorial San Juan, Puerto Rico.

Marrinan, R. A.
1995   Archaeology in Puerto Real's Public Sector: Building B. In *Puerto Real: The Archaeology of a Sixteenth-Century Spanish Town in Hispaniola*, edited by K. Deagan, pp. 167–196. University of Florida Press, Gainesville.

Martínez, A. G.
1991   Algunos aspectos significativos de la cerámica aborigen del sitio Ojo de Agua, Municipio de Abreus, Provincia de Cienfuegos, Cuba. In *Arqueología de Cuba y otras áreas antillanas*, edited by J. Febles and A. V. Rives, pp. 281–303. Editorial Academia, Havana.

Martínez, F.
1963   *Superposición cultural en Damajayabo, Oriente de Cuba*. Editorial Ciencia y Técnica, Havana.
1968   *Superposición cultural en Damajayabo*. Editorial Ciencia y Técnica, Instituto del Libro, Havana.

Martinón-Torres, M., R. Valcárcel, J. Cooper, and T. Rehren
2007   Metal, Microanalysis and Meaning: A Study of Metal Objects Excavated from the Indigenous Cemetery of Chorro de Maíta, Cuba. *Journal of Archaeological Science* 34:194–204.
2008   Diversifying the Picture: Indigenous Responses to European Arrival in Cuba. *Archaeology International* 10:37–40.

Maza, A.
1952   La Iglesia Parroquial Mayor de San Juan Bautista de Remedios: Indicaciones

[1944] sobre su valor artístico e histórico y la necesidad de su conservación. *Revista de arqueología y etnología* 13-14:287-331.

McGuirre, R. H., and R. Paynter
1991 *The Archaeology of Inequality.* Blackwell, Oxford.

Mesa, I., J. Jardines, and J. Calvera
1994 Estudio preliminar de la cerámica del sitio arqueológico "Los Buchillones," provincia de Ciego de Avila. In *Estudios arqueologicos,* edited by J. Febles, L. Dominguez, F. Ortega, G. La Rosa, A. Martinez, and A. V. Rives, pp. 66-79. Editorial Academia, Havana.

Miguel, O.
1949 Descubrimiento y excavación de un montículo funeral en el potrero "El Porvenir." *Revista de arqueología y etnología* 8-9:110-118.

Mira, E.
1997 *El indio antillano: repartimiento, encomienda y esclavitud (1492-1542).* Muñoz Moya, Seville.

Morales, L.
1989 Análisis de artefactos líticos procedentes de la región central de Cuba. Paper presented at the Fourth International Meeting of Aboriginal Archaeology Yaguajay 1996, Sancti Spíritus, Cuba.

Morales, L., R. Villavicencio, and C. Arredondo
2004 Territorial Project Report 0841: Estudio para la interpretación de las industrias de piedra tallada del Noreste de Villa Clara. Archive of Centro de Estudios y Servicios Ambientales de Villa Clara, Santa Clara.

Morales, L., R. Villavicencio, and N. Gómez
2005 Territorial Project Report 0856: Estudio del período de las comunidades aborígenes del municipio de Ranchuelo, Villa Clara, Cuba. Archive of Centro de Estudios y Servicios Ambientales de Villa Clara, Santa Clara.

Morales, L., R. Villavicencio, and A. Sueiro
2008 Territorial Project Report 0853: Estratigrafía de las comunidades aborígenes más tempranas del Noreste de Villa Clara. Archive of Centro de Estudios y Servicios Ambientales de Villa Clara, Santa Clara.

Morales, O., R. Herrera, F. Royo, A. González, I. Avello, and A. Leiva
1947 Cayo Ocampo, historia de un cayo: Estudio de una de las isletas de la Bahía de Cienfuegos, determinando el emplazamiento del poblado indio que encontraron los Españoles. *Revista de arqueología y etnología,* 2da Epoca, Año II, Nos. 4-5:55-123. Havana.

Morales, O., and R. Pérez
1945 El período de transculturación indo-hispánica: Contribuciones del Grupo Guamá. *Revista de arqueología y etnología* 4-6:5-37. Havana.

Moreira, L. J.
2003 Hubo Cacigazgos en la Mayor de las Antillas? *Cataúro: Revista Cubana de Antropología,* Año 5, No. 8:144-158.

Morejón, Y.
1978 La arqueología en Triunvirato. *Bohemia* 43:92-93.

Morin, E.
1996 Por una reforma del pensamiento. *El correo de la UNESCO* XLIX:10-14.

Mormino, G. R.
2005 *Land of Sunshine, State of Dreams. A Social History of Modern Florida.* Gainesville, University Press of Florida, Gainesville.

Mormino, G. R., and G. E. Pozzetta
 1998 *The Immigrant World of Ybor City: Italians and Their Latin Neighbors in Tampa, 1885–1985.* University Press of Florida, Gainesville.
Moscoso, F.
 1986 *Tribu y clases en el Caribe antiguo.* Ediciones de la Universidad Central del Este, Santo Domingo.
Müller-Beck, H., J. Weinig, L. Morales, R. Villavicencio, E. Guarch, and J. Jardines
 2008 International Project Report: El poblamiento más temprano de Cuba. Centro deEstudios y Servicios Ambientales de Villa Clara (CESAM)—Centro de Investigaciones y Servicios Ambientales y Tecnológicos de Holguín (CISAT)—Pro-Arch Co. of Igolstad—Eberhard Karls Universität Tübingen.
Museo Nacional de Cuba
 1990 *La Habana, salas del Museo Nacional de Cuba.* Editorial Cubana, Havana.
Núñez, A.
 1948 *Mayarí: Descripción general.* Sociedad Espeleológica de Cuba, Havana.
O'Shea, J.
 1984 *Mortuary Variability. An Archaeological Investigation.* Academic Press, New York.
Olazagasti, I.
 1997 The Material Culture of the Taino Indians. In *The Indigenous People of the Caribbean,* edited by S. Wilson, pp. 131–139. University Press of Florida, Talahassee.
Oliver, J. R.
 1998 *El centro ceremonial de Caguana, Puerto Rico: Simbolismo iconográfico, cosmovisión y poder caciquil taíno en Borinquén.* BAR International Series 727. British Archaeological Reports, Oxford.
 2002 Gold Symbolism among Caribbean Chiefdoms: Of Feathers, Cibas, and Guanín Power among Taíno Elites. In *Precolumbian Gold: Technology, Style and Iconography,* edited by C. McEwan, pp. 196–219. British Museum Press, London.
 2003 An Interpretive Analysis and Discussion of the Río Cocal-1 Community of Sabana Seca, Puerto Rico. In *Archaeological Survey and Evaluation of Sites at NSWC Sabana Seca, Vol. IV, Parts I–II: Evaluation of the Prehistoric Río Cocal-1 Site,* edited by R. C. Goodwin, J. R. Oliver, D. D. Davis, J. Brown, S. Sanders, and M. Simmons, pp. 337–402. Submitted by R. Christopher Goodwin & Associates to the U.S. Department of the Navy, Atlantic Division, Naval Facilities Engineering Command, Norfolk, VA. On file at the State Historic Preservation Office, San Juan, Puerto Rico.
Orser, C. E., Jr.
 1990 Archaeological Approaches to New World Plantation Slavery. In *Archaeological Method and Theory,* Vol. 2, edited by M. Schiffer, pp. 111–154. University of Arizona Press, Tucson.
 1992 *In Search of Zumbi: Preliminary Archaeological Research at the Serra da Barriga, State of Alagoas, Brazil.* Midwestern Archaeological Research Center, Illinois State University, Normal.
 2000 *Introducción a la arqueología histórica.* Editorial Tridente, Buenos Aires.
Orser, C. E., Jr. (editor)
 2001 *Race and the Archaeology of Identity.* University of Utah Press, Salt Lake City.
Orser, C. E., Jr., and P. P. Funari
 2001 Archaeology and Slave Resistance and Rebellion. *World Archaeology* 33(1):61–72.

Ortega, E.
1982 *Arqueología colonial de Santo Domingo*. Editorial Taller, República Dominicana.

Ortega, E., and C. Fondeur
1978 *Estudio de la cerámica del periodo indohispano en la antigua Concepción de la Vega*. Editora Taller, Santo Domingo.

Ortíz, F.
1935 *Historia de la arqueología indocubana*. Colección de Libros Cubanos, Vol. 33. Cultural, S.A., Havana.
1940 *Contrapunteo cubano del tabaco y el azúcar*. Jesús Montero, Havana.
1943 *Las cuatro culturas indias de Cuba*. Biblioteca de Estudios Cubanos, Vol. 1.
1983 *Contrapunteo cubano del azúcar y el tabaco*. Editorial de Ciencias Sociales, Havana.
1995 *Cuban Counterpoint. Tobacco and Sugar*. Translated by Harriet de Onís. Duke University Press, Durham.

Ostapkowicz, J. M.
1997 To Be Seated with "Great Courtesy and Veneration": Contextual Aspects of the Taíno Duho. In *Taíno: Pre-Columbian Art and Culture from the Caribbean*, edited by F. Bercht, E. Brodsky, J. A. Farmer, and D. Taylor, pp. 56–67. Monacelli Press, New York.

Padilla, R., and M. Celaya
2003 Classification of the Regional Aboriginal Ceramic Production and Distribution in the Central Regional of Cuba Based on INAA. In *Nuclear Analytical Techniques in Archaeological Investigations*, pp. 119–134. Technical Reports Series 416. International Atomic Energy Agency, Vienna. HTTP://www-pub.iaea.org/MTCD/publications/PDF/TRS416_webpdf.

Pagan-Jiménez, J. R., and J. R. Oliver
2006 Starch Residues on Lithic Artefacts from Two Contrasting Contexts in Central Puerto Rico: Cueva de los Muertos and Vega Nelo Vargas. In *Society of American Archaeology: New Methods and Techniques in the Study of Material Culture from the Caribbean*. San Juan, Puerto Rico.

Palov, M. Z.
1999 Useppa's Cuban Fishing Community. In *The Archaeology of Useppa Island*, edited by W. H. Marquardt, pp. 149–169. Institute of Archaeology and Paleoenvironmental Studies, Monograph 3. University of Florida, Gainesville.

Parker, S. R.
1999 *The Second Century of Settlement in Spanish St. Augustine, 1670–1763*. Ph.D. dissertation (History), University of Florida, Gainesville.

Parker Pearson, M.
2003 *The Archaeology of Death and Burial*. Sutton Publishing, Phoenix Mill.

Peguero, L.A.
2001 Las plazas ceremoniales como espacio ritual de las culturas prehistóricas del Caribe: Su posible vinculación a otros contextos culturales. *Boletín del Museo del Hombre Dominicano* 28:29–61, Santo Domíngo.

Peña, A.
1987 La investigación arqueológica en la restauración de la casa natal de Calixto García. *Revista de Historia* 3: 59–64.

Pendergast, D., J. Calvera, J. Jardines, E. Graham, and O. Brito
2003   Construcciones de madera en el mar: Los Buchillones, Cuba. *El Caribe Arqueológico* 7:24–32.
Pendergast, D., E. Graham, J. Calvera, and J. Jardines
1999   Houses in the Sea: Excavation and Preservation at Los Buchillones, Cuba. In *Enduring Records: The Environmental and Cultural Heritage of Wetlands*, edited by B. Purdy, pp. 71–82. University Presses of Florida, Gainesville.
2002   The Houses in Which They Dwelt: The Excavation and Dating of Taino Wooden Structures at Los Buchillones, Cuba. *Journal of Wetland Archaeology* 2:61–75.
Pérez, J.
1972   *Desaparición de la población indígena cubana.* Universidad de la Habana 196–197:68–83.
Pérez, R.
1943   *Mounds, caneyes, cerritos o lometones.* Imprenta Pérez Sierra, Havana.
Peros, M. C.
2005   *Middle to Late Holocene Environment Change and Archaeology on the North Coast of Central Cuba.* Ph.D. thesis, University of Toronto.
Persons, A. B., R. Valcárcel, V. J. Knight, V. James, L. Pérez, and J. E. Worth
2007   Archaeological Investigations at El Chorro de Maíta. Holguín Province, Cuba. 2007 season. On file, University of Alabama, Tuscaloosa.
Pichardo, E.
1976   Diccionario provincial casi-razonado de voces y frases Ubanas. Editorial de
[1836]   Ciencias Sociales, La Habana.
Pichardo, F.
1934   *El Camagüey Precolombino.* J. Montero, Havana.
1945   *Los indios de Cuba en sus tiempos históricos.* Imprenta el siglo XX. Academia de Ciencias, Havana.
1990   *Caverna, costa y meseta.* Editorial de Ciencias Sociales, Havana.
Pichardo, H.
1971   *Documentos para la historia de Cuba*, Vol. I. Editorial de Ciencias Sociales, Havana.
Piel-Desruisseaux, J. L.
1989   *Instrumental prehistórico: Forma, fabricación, utilización.* Ediciones Masson, S.A., España.
Pino, M.
1990   *Actualización de fechados radiocarbónicos de sitios arqueológicos de Cuba hasta diciembre de 1993.* Departament de Arqueología, Centro de Antropología. Editorial Academia, Havana, Cuba.
Plog, S., F. Plog, and W. Wait
1978   Decision Making in Modern Surveys. In *Advances in Archaeological Method and Theory*, Vol. 1, edited by M. Schiffer, pp. 383–421. Academic Press, New York.
Prat, J.
1947   *El Pre-Barroco en Cuba: Una escuela criolla de arquitectua morisca.* Diputación de Barcelona, La Habana.
Pupo, R.
1990   *La actividad como categoría filosófica.* Editorial de Ciencias Sociales. Havana.

Quirós-Castillo, J.
2002   Arqueología de la arquitectura en España. *Arqueología de la arquitectura* 1:28–29.
Ramírez, R., and L. Morales
2001   Comunidades aborígenes en Villa Clara. In *Historia de la provincia de Villa Clara*, unpublished manuscript. Instituto de Historia, Havana.
Ramos, A.
1988   La investigación arqueológica en los inmuebles coloniales. *Documentos* 1:3–23.
Rankin, A.
1980   La cerámica del sitio arqueológico El Convento. In *Cuba arqueológica II*, pp. 115–138. Editorial Oriente, Santiago de Cuba.
Reimer, P. J.
2005   Marine Reservoir Correction Database. http://radiocarbon.pa.qub.ac.uk/marine/ ed.
Reimer, P. J., M. G. L. Baillie, E. Bard, A. Bayliss, J. W. Beck, C. J. H. Bertrand, P. G. Blackwell, C. E. Buck, G.S. Burr, K. B. Cutler, P. E. Damon, R. L. Edwards, R. G. Fairbanks, M. Friedrich, T. P. Guilderson, A. G. H. Hogg, K. A. B. Kromer, G. McCormac, S. Manning, C. B. Ramsey, R. W. Reimer, S. Remmele, J. R. Southon, M. Stuiver, S. Talamo, F. W. Taylor, J. van der Plicht, and C. E. Weyhenmeyer
2004   IntCa104 Terrestrial Radiocarbon Age Calibration, 0–26 Cal Kyr BP. *Radiocarbon* 46(3):1029–1058.
Renfrew, C., and P. Bahn
1993   *Arqueología: Teoría, métodos y práctica*. Ediciones Akal, Barcelona.
Rey, E., and F. G. García
1988   Hipótesis sobre el poblamiento temprano de Cuba a partir de un estudio paleoclimático del cuaternario. In *Revista de Estudios Arqueológicos* 2–21.
Reyes, J. M.
1997   Estudios dietarios de cinco sitios "apropriadores ceramistas" del suroriente cubano. *El Caribe arqueológico* 2:41–49.
Rivero, M., C. Rodríguez, and M. Montero
1990   Estudio de un cráneo europoide encontrado en el sitio aborigen de El Chorro de Maíta, Yaguajay, Banes, Provincia de Holguín, Cuba. *Revista de historia* 1:64–92.
Rives, A., L. Domínguez, and M. Pérez
1987   *Carta informativa No. 76*. Departamento de Arqueología, Academia de Ciencias de Cuba, La Habana.
1991   Los documentos históricos sobre las encomiendas y las experiencias indias de Cuba y las evidencias arqueológicas del contacto indohispánico. In *Estudios arqueológicos 1989*, edited by J. Febles, L. Domínguez, J. M. Guarch, A. Martínez, and A. Rives, pp. 26–35. Editorial Academia, Havana.
Rives, A., L. Domínguez, J. Tomé, M. Pérez, J. Pose, and Y. Zaldívar
1987   *Carta informativa No. 84*. Departamento de Arqueología, Academia de Ciencias de Cuba, La Habana.
Rivet, P., and H. Arsandoux
2005   *La Metallurgie en Amerique Precolombienne*. Musée del'Homme, Paris.
[1946] *Taínos y Caribes: Las culturas aborígenes antillanas*. Punto y Coma, San Juan.

Rodríguez, B., and I. Hernández
2006   La arqueología de la arquitectura en el centro histórico de la Habana Vieja: Un caso de estudio. *Gabinete de arqueología* 5:4–15.
Rodríguez, C.
2003   Estimación de la estatura de los esqueletos del cementerio aborigen de Chorro de Maíta, Holguín, Cuba. *El Caribe arqueológico* 7:86–92.
Rodríguez, M.
1876   *Naturaleza y civilización de la Grandiosa Isla de Cuba,* Vol. 1. J. Noguera Press, Madrid.
Rodríguez, M. E.
2000–   La encomienda de Bartolomé de Las Casas y Pedro de Rentería en Jagua (in
2002   5 parts). *Ariel, la Revista cultural de Cienfuegos* Año III, No. 2:40–47; Año IV, No. 1:20–26; Año IV, No. 2:57–63; Año V, No. 1:52–64; Año V, No. 2:59–63.
2004   *Historia de Cienfuegos: Aborígenes de Jagua.* Ediciones Mecenas, Cienfuegos, Cuba.
Rodríguez, R., E. Babilonia, L. A. Curet, and J. Ulloa
2008   The Pre-Arawak Pottery Horizon in the Antilles: A New Approximation. *Latin American Antiquity* 19:47–63.
Rodriguez, R., and J. R. Pagan-Jiménez
2006   Primeras evidencias directas del uso de plantas por los grupos agroalfareros de Cuba suroriental. Paper presented at the Annual Meeting of the Society of American Archaeology, San Juan, Puerto Rico.
Romero, L. E.
1981   Sobre las evidencias arqueologicas de contacto y transculturación en el ambito Cubano. *Santiago* 44:77–108. Havana.
Rosario, L., J. Jardines, and C. Rodríguez
2003   Estudio arqueozoológico en Los Buchillones: Economía y medio ambiente. Unpublished manuscript on file at Centro de Investigaciones y Servicios Ambientales y Tecnológicos. Ministerio de Ciencia Technología y Medio Ambiente.
Rouse, I.
1941   *Culture of the Fort Liberté Region.* Yale University Publications in Anthropology No. 24, Yale University Press, New Haven.
1942   *Archaeology of the Maniabon Hills, Cuba.* Yale University Publications in Anthropology No. 21, Yale University Press, New Haven.
1949   The Southeast and the West Indies. In *The Florida Indian and His Neighbors,* edited by J. W. Griffin, pp. 117–137. Inter-American Center, Rollins College, Winter Park, Florida.
1958   Archaeological Similarities between the Southeast and the West Indies. In *Florida Anthropology,* edited by C. Fairbanks, pp. 3–14. *Florida Anthropological Society Publications* No. 5, Tallahassee.
1992   *The Taínos: Rise and Decline of the People Who Greeted Columbus.* Yale University Press, New Haven.
Rousseau, P. L., and P. Díaz
1919   *Memoria descriptiva: historia y biografía de Cienfuegos.* El Siglo XX, Havana.
Samson, A. V. M., and M. L. P. Hoogland
2007   Residencia taína: Huellas de asentamientos en El Cabo, República Dominicana. *El Caribe arqueológico* 10:93–103.

San Pedro, R., G. Izquierdo, and R. Villavicencio
2001 Tecnología y tipología en la tradición paleolítica de Villa Clara: Una primera Interpretación. In *El Caribe arqueológico* No. 5, pp. 52–61. Publicaciones de la Casa del Caribe, Santiago de Cuba.

Sanjurjo, J.
1950 Descubimiento arqueológico en el "Abra" de Castellón, Cumanayagua, Cienfuegos. *Revista de arqueología y etnología,* 2da Epoca, Año V, Nos. 10–11:11–12.

Sannen, P.
2006 Theoretical Approaches to the Study of Mortuary Practice and their Application to Selected Burial Assemblages from the Caribbean. Master's thesis, Universidad de Leiden.

Sarmiento, G.
1992 *Las primeras sociedades jerárquicas.* Colección Científica, Instituto Nacional de Antropología e Historia, México, D.F.

Schiffer, M.
1972 Archaeological Context and Systemic Context. *American Antiquity* 156–65
1976 *Behavioral Archaeology.* Academic Press, New York.

Schinkel, K.
1992 The Golden Rock Features. In *The Archaeology of St. Eustatius: The Golden Rock Site,* edited by A. Versteeg and K. Schinkel, pp. 143–212. Publication of the St. Eustatius Historical Foundation No. 2, St. Eustatius.

Schmidt, P. R., and T. C. Patterson
1995 Introduction: From Constructing to Making Alternative Histories. In *Making Alternative Histories,* edited by P. R. Schmidt and T. C. Patterson, pp. 1–24. School of American Research Press, Santa Fe.

Schmidt, S.
1975 Problemas actuales del estudio de las fuentes históricas. *Lecturas escogidas de metodología.* Compiled by A. Plasencia, pp. 125–173. Editorial Ciencias Sociales, Havana.

Schuyler, R. L.
1978a Historical and Historic Sites Archaeology: Basic Definitions and Relationships. In *Archaeology: Guide to Substantive and Theoretical Contributions,* pp 27–32. Bay Wood Publishing Company, Farmingdale, New York.
1978b Subfields of Historical Archaeology. Introduction to Part 2 of *Historical Archaeology: A Guide to Substantive and Theoretical Contributions,* edited by R. Schyler, pp. 33–35. Baywood Press, Farmingdale, N.J.

Siegel, P. E., and K. P. Severin
1993 First Documented Prehistoric Gold-Copper Alloy Artifact from the West Indies. *Journal of Archeological Science* 20(1):67–79.

Singleton, T. A.
2001 Slavery and Spatial Dialectics on Cuban Coffee Plantations. *World Archaeology* 33(1):98–114.
2005 An Archaeological Study of Slavery at a Cuban Coffee Plantation. In *Dialogues in Cuban Archaeology,* edited by L. A. Curet, S. L. Dawdy, and G. La Rosa, pp. 181–199. University of Alabama Press, Tuscaloosa.

Singleton, T. A. (editor)
1985 *The Archaeology of Slavery and Plantation Life.* Academic Press, New York.

1999   *"I, Too, Am America" Archaeological Studies of African-American Life.* University of Virginia Press, Charlottesville.
Smathers Libraries (University of Florida)
    2001   UF to Rescue Cuban National Archives. *Chapter One* (Newsletter) 2001. http://www.uflib.ufl.edu/pio/Summer2001ChapOne.pdf#search=%22Bruce%20Chappell%20cuba%22.
Smith, H. G.
    1956   *The European and the Indian: European-Indian Contacts in Georgia and Florida.* Florida Anthropological Society, *Publication* 4, and Florida State University, Department of Anthropology, *Notes in Anthropology* 2. Tallahassee.
Sotolongo, P. L.
    1998   Matematización, hermenéutica y postmodernismo. In *Modernidad, postmodernidad: Pensar en Cuba,* pp. 132–164. Editorial Ciencias Sociales, Havana.
South, S.
    1977   *Method and Theory in Historical Archaeology,* Academia Press, New York.
Sued-Badillo, J.
    1989   *La mujer indígena y su sociedad.* Editorial Cultural, San Juan.
Tabío, E.
    1984   Nueva periodización para el estudio de las comunidades aborigines de Cuba. *Islas* 78:37–57. Santa Clara, Cuba.
Tabío, E., and J. M. Guarch
    1966   *Excavaciones en Arroyo del Palo, Mayarí, Oriente, Cuba.* Departamento de Antropología de la Academia de Ciencias de Cuba, Havana.
Tabío, E., and E. Rey
    1966   *Prehistoria de Cuba.* Departamento de Antropología, Academia de Ciencias de Cuba, Havana.
    1979   *Prehistoria de Cuba.* Editorial de Ciencias Sociales, Havana, Cuba.
    1985   *Prehistoria de Cuba.* Editorial de Ciencias Sociales, Havana, Cuba.
Tepaske, J.
    1964   *The Governorship of Spanish Florida, 1700–1763.* Duke University Press, Durham.
Tixier, J.
    1961   *Typologie de l'epipaléolithique du Maghreb,* Vol. I. Arts et Métiers Graphiques, París.
Tomé, J.
    1994   Análisis de perforaciones cónicas en algunas muestras de concha. In *Estudios arqueológicos,* edited by J. Febles, L. Dominguez, F. Ortega, G. La Rosa, A. Martinez, and A. Rives, pp. 59–65. Editorial Academia, Havana.
Tomé, J., and A. Rives
    1987   *Carta informativa No. 83.* Departamento de Arqueología, Academia de Ciencias de Cuba, Havana, p. 1.
Torres, D.
    2004   La arqueología cubana en la encrucijada: La teoría o la empiria. *El Caribe arqueológico* No. 8, pp. 2–7. Santiago de Cuba.
    2006   *Tainos: Mitos y realidades de un pueblo sin rostro.* Asesor Pedagógico, México.
    2008   Taínos en Cuba, ¿quimera o realidad? Paper presented in the Symposium "The Taínos: Myth, Invention or Reality" organized by L.A. Curet for the 73rd Annual Meeting of the Society for American Archaeology, Vancouver.

Torres, D., R. Dacal , and M. Capablanca
2001   Evaluación del patrimonio arqueológico aborigen del Municipio Maisí, Guantánamo. Paper presented at the Fifth International Conference on Cultural Patrimony: Context and Conservation, CENCREM, Havana.
Trigger, B.
1993   *Historia del pensamiento arqueológico*. Editorial Crítica, Barcelona
Trujillo, H.
2008   *Nueva propuesta de geosistemas para la provincia de Villa Clara*. Empresa Geocuba Villa Clara-Sancti Spíritus, Santa Clara.
Ulloa, J.
2002   "Arquelogía y rescate de la prescencia aborígen en Cuba y el Caribe." *Kacike*, http://www.kacike.org/.
2005   Approaches to Early Ceramics in the Caribbean: Between Diversity and Unilineality. In *Dialogues in Cuban Archaeology*, edited by L. A. Curet, S. L. Dawdy, and G. La Rosa, pp. 103–124. University of Alabama Press, Tuscaloosa.
Ulloa, J., and R. Valcárcel
2002   Cerámica temprana del centro-sur del Oriente de Cuba. Viewgraph-Taraxcum, S.A., Santo Domingo.
Uyemura, K.
1967   The Artistic Works of Ivan Gundrum with Particular Reference to His Reproductions of Clay Objects from the Florida Gulf Coast Indians. Master's thesis, Florida State University, Tallahassee.
Valcárcel, R.
1997   Introducción a la arqueología del contacto indo-hispánico en la Provincia de Holguín, Cuba. *El Caribe arqueológico* 2:64–77.
1999   Banes Precolumbino: Jerarquía y sociedad. *El Caribe arqueológico* 3:84–94.
2002a   *Banes Precolumbino: La ocupación agricultora*. Ediciones Holguín, Holguín.
2002b   Reporte de composición metálica de objetos asociados a entierros en el sitio arqueológico El Chorro de Maíta. On file, Departamento Centro Oriental de Arqueología, Holguín.
Valcárcel, R., J. Cooper, J. Calvera, O. Brito, and M. Labrada
2006   Postes en el mar: Excavación de una estructura constructiva aborigen en Los Buchillones. *El Caribe arqueológico* 9:76–88.
Valcárcel, R., M. Martinón-Torres, J. Cooper, and T. Rehren
2007   Oro, *guanines* y latón: Metales en contextos aborígenes de Cuba. *El Caribe arqueológico* 10:116–131.
Valcárcel, R., A. B. Persons, V. J. Knight, and L. Pérez
2007   Trabajos arqueológicos en El Chorro de Maíta, 2007. On file, Departamento Centro Oriental de Arqueología, Centro de Investigaciones y Servicios Ambientales y Tecnológicos (CISAT), Ministerio de Ciencias, Tecnología y Medio Ambiente de Cuba (CITMA), Holguín.
Valcárcel, R., and C. Rodríguez
2005   El Chorro de Maíta: Social Inequality and Mortuary Space. In *Dialogues in Cuban Archaeology*, edited by L. A. Curet, S. L. Dawdy, and G. La Rosa, pp. 125–146. University of Alabama Press, Tuscaloosa.
Vargas, I.
1990   *Arqueología ciencia y sociedad*. Editorial Abre Brecha, Caracas.

Vázquez, M.
1837 El mayordomo de un intenio. Origen del mal desempeño que se observan en estas plazas, y algunas refleciones a los señores hacendados. Palmer, La Habana.

Vega, B.
1988 Los metales y los aborígenes de La Hispaniola. In *Santos, shamanes y zemíes*, pp. 31–56. Fundación Cultural Dominicana, Santo Domingo.

Veloz, M.
1977 *Indigenous Art and Economy of Santo Domingo*. Ediciones Cohoba, Santo Domingo.
1991 *Panorama histórico del Caribe precolombino*. Banco Central de la República Dominicana, Santo Domingo.

Veloz, M., I. Vargas, M. Sanoja, and F. Luna
1976 *Arqueología de Yuma, Republica Dominicana*. Editora Taller, Santo Domingo.

Venegas, H.
1980 Consideraciones en torno a la economía remediana colonial. *Revista Islas* No. 67, pp. 16–27. Universidad Central de Las Villas, Santa Clara.

Versteeg, A., and K. Schinkel
1992 *The Archaeology of St. Eustatius: The Golden Rock Site*. Publication No. 2, Historical Foundation St. Eustatius, y No. 130, Foundation for Scientif Research in the Caribbean Region, St. Eustatius, Antillas Holandesas.

Villaverde, C.
1961 *Excursión a Vueltabajo*. Consejo Nacional de Cultura, La Habana.
[1891]
1982 *Diario del Rancheador*. Editoral Letras Cubanas, Le Habana.

Villavicencio, R.
1995 Fundamentación de una hipótesis sobre el poblamiento más temprano del centro-norte de Cuba. Paper presented at the Fourth International Meeting of Aboriginal Archaeology Yaguajay 1996, Sancti Spíritus, Cuba.
2000 *¿Hachas de mano en Cuba?* Colección Ensayo, Editorial Capiro, Santa Clara, Villa Clara, Cuba.

Villavicencio, R., L. Morales, and N. A. Gómez
2003 Territorial Project Report 0840: Entorno y población paleolítica en las Alturas del Noroeste de Villa Clara. Archives of Centro de Estudios y Servicios Ambientales de Villa Clara, Santa Clara.

Villoro, L.
2001 *El pensamiento moderno: Filosofía del Renacimiento*. Fondo de Cultura Económica, México, D. F.

Wickham, D.
2006 Opinion: U.S. Pushes Foolish Policy of "Baseball, Sí, Academics, No." *USA Today*, March 6, 2006. Online, http://www.usatoday.com/news/opinion/columnist/wickham/2006-03-06-wickham-edit_x.htm.

Wood, J. J.
1974 Computer Program for Hierarchical Cluster Analysis. In *Newsletter of Computer Archaeology*, No. 9, pp. 2–13.

Worth, J.
2004a Cuban Parish Records Reveal Immigrant Calusa Indians. Friends of the Randell Research Center *Newsletter* 2(4):1.

2004b Report on Cuban Fishing Industry. Documents Reviewed and Discovered in the Archivo Nacional de Cuba in Havana, April 2004. Report submitted to P.F. Miller, Jr., and the Useppa Island Historical Society, April 30, 2004.

Wright, I. A.
1916 *The Early History of Cuba, 1492–1586.* Macmillan Co., New York.

Contributors

Jorge Calvera, a member of the Cuban Ministry of Science, Technology, and the Environment, has conducted investigations in diverse parts of Cuba for over 40 years. He currently directs the project "Archaeology of Turiguano and northern Ciego de Avila, Cuba" and has carried out many investigations at the site of Los Buchillones.

Jago Cooper, Leverhulme Early Career Fellow at the School of Archaeology and Ancient History at the University of Leicester, England, directs the Archaeology of Climate Change in the Caribbean project, a collaboration between the University of Leicester and the Cuban Ministry of Science, Technology, and Environment. His doctoral research focused on island interaction in northern Cuba.

L. Antonio Curet is an associate curator at The Field Museum of Natural History in Chicago. His main interest is the study of social and cultural change, specifically in the pre-Columbian Caribbean and Mesoamerica. Most recently, he has been doing household archaeology at the earliest ceremonial center in the Caribbean, the site of Tibes, Ponce, Puerto Rico. His recent publications include a book, *Caribbean Paleodemography: Population, Culture History, and Sociopolitical Processes in Ancient Puerto Rico* (2005), and two edited volumes: *Dialogues in Cuban Archaeology* (with S. L. Dawdy and G. La Rosa, 2005) and *Tibes: People, Power, and Ritual at the Center of the Cosmos* (2009), all published by The University of Alabama Press.

Kathleen Deagan is Distinguished Research Curator of Archaeology and the Lockwood Professor of Florida and Caribbean Archaeology at the University of Florida's Florida Museum of Natural History. Her research has focused on the archaeology of the Spanish colonial period in Florida and the Caribbean. She is the author of more than 70 scientific papers and eight books, including *Archaeology at La Isabela* (with J. M. Cruxent, Yale University Press, 2002), and *Artifacts of the Spanish Colonies* (2 vols., Smithsonian Press, 2002).

Lourdes Domínguez, tenured investigator of the Archaeological Cabinet of the Office of the City Historian, Havana, has been carrying out archaeological investigations in Cuba since 1968. Her research spans a substantial range of Cuban archaeology, although her main focus is historical archaeology in Old Havana. She is an adjunct professor at multiple institutions including the University of Havana, the University of Campinas, São Paulo, the Center for Advanced Studies of Puerto Rico and the Caribbean, and the Dominican Museum of Man. She is also a Fellow at the Foundation for Research Support of the State of São Paulo (FAPESP). Her most recent book, *Particularidades arqueológicas*, was published in 2010 by Editorial Boloña, Havana.

Iosvany Hernández Mora currently serves as director of the Archaeological Cabinet of the City Historian's Office in Camagüey, Cuba. His current archaeological project, in Nuevitas Bay, Camagüey, explores Santa María del Puerto del Príncipe, the first Spanish village in the region. His recently published articles include "Rodolfo Payarés and the practice of historical archaeology in Cuba: Fundamental questions" (*Cuaderno de Historia Principeña* No. 7, 2009) and "Puerto Príncipe en el Chorrito: Investigando sus vestigios materiales" (*Revista Senderos* No. 9, 2009).

Susan Kepecs, honorary fellow in the Department of Anthropology, University of Wisconsin-Madison, has studied and written about historical archaeology in Old Havana, though her main geographic focus is northeast Yucatan, Mexico. She specializes in world systems theory and longue durée political-economic analysis. Her recent publications include two edited volumes, *Colonial/Postcolonial Change in Mesoamerica: Archaeology as Historical Anthropology*, co-edited with Rani Alexander, in preparation for the School for Advanced Research Press, and *The Postclassic to Spanish-Era Transition in Mesoamerica: Archaeological Perspectives* (S. Kepecs and R. T. Alexander, editors), University of New Mexico Press, 2005.

Vernon James Knight Jr. is Professor of Anthropology at the University of Alabama. His research centers on social, political, and religious organization in late prehistoric and early historic indigenous societies of the New World. With Roberto Valcárcel, he is currently co-directing a project at the site of El Chorro de Maíta, Holguín Province, Cuba. His latest book is *Mound Architecture at Moundville: Architecture, Elites, and Social Order* (University of Alabama Press, 2010).

Gabino La Rosa Corzo, of the History Section of the Union of Writers and Artists of Cuba, has published over 50 articles in academic journals published in Cuba, Colombia, Spain, the Dominican Republic, and the United States. Among his books are *Los cimarrones de Cuba* (Editorial de Ciencias Sociales, Havana, 1988); *Los palenques del oriente de Cuba* (Editorial Academia, Havana, 1991); *Costumbres funerarias de los aborígenes de Cuba* (Editorial Academia, Havana, 1995); *Arqueología en sitios de contrabandistas* (Editorial Academia, Havana,1995); and *Cazadores de esclavos* (with M. González, Fundación Fernando Ortíz, 2004). *Runaway Slave Settlements in Cuba*, a translation of *Los palenques del oriente de Cuba*, was published by the University of North Carolina Press (2003). Dr. La Rosa is co-editor, with L. A. Curet and S. L. Dawdy, of *Dialogues in Cuban Archaeology* (2005).

Marcos Martinón-Torres is a senior lecturer of archaeological science and material culture at the Institute of Archaeology, University College London. He is co-editor, with Thilo Rehren, of *Archaeology, History and Science: Integrating Approaches to Anciente Materials*, a University College London Institute of Archaeology Publication (2009, Left Coast Press).

Lorenzo Morales Santos, of the Center for Environmental Studies and Services of the Cuban Ministry of Science, Technology, and Environment, specializes in the archaeology of early human occupation in Cuba. His work is included in "The Earliest Settlement in Cuba," a forthcoming, collaborative publication based on an international project carried out by Cuban researchers and colleagues from the Pro-Arch Company of Ingolstadt, Germany, and Eberhard Karls Universität Tübingen, Baden-Württemberg, Germany.

Thilo Rehren is a professor of archaeological materials and technologies at the Institute of Archaeology, University College London. He is co-editor, with Marcos Martinón Torres, of *Archaeology, History and Science: Integrating Approaches to Anciente Materials*, a University College London Institute of Archaeology Publication (2009, Left Coast Press). Dr. Rehren is also the editor of the *Journal of Archaeological Science*, and current president of the Society for Archaeological Sciences.

Daniel Torres Etayo is head of the archaeology department of Cuba's National Center for Conservation, Restoration, and Museology. He specializes in the late pre-Columbian agricultural societies of eastern Cuba. He is the author of the book, *Taínos: Mitos y realidades de un pueblo sin rostro* (Asesor Pedagógico, S.A., México, 2006).

Roberto Valcárcel Rojas, investigator at the Cuban Ministry of Science's Department of Central-Eastern Archaeology in Holgúin, is director of the project "Study of Hispano-aboriginal interaction at El Chorro de Maíta, Cuba." This project is an integral part of his doctoral research at the University of Leiden in Holland. Valcárcel is the author of several books, including *Banes precolombino: La ocupación agricultora* (Ediciones Holguín, 2002), and *Cerámica temprana en el centro del oriente de Cuba* (with J. Ulloa), Editora Arcograf Dominicana, Santo Domingo (2002).

Index

Page numbers in italics refer to figures and tables.

Abbot, Abriel, 128, 142n10
Abra de Castellón, El, 27, 33, 38
Abraira, V., 54
Academia de Ciencias, 20
African American archaeology, 21
African archaeology, 6
aglets (lacetags), 113, *115*–18, 119, 122, 124–25
Agorsah, E. K., 127
agroalfarero sites (agro-ceramic), 12, 26, *108,* 109; and Arawakan expansion model, 40, 42, 43, 110; Banes district, 37, 100; developmental model of, 31; Domínguez and, 38, 46n6; in eastern Cuba, 30; Loma del Convento, 31; objections to nomenclature, 45n2; pottery clay composition at, 38–39; sites in Jagua Bay, *28*; in south-central Cuba, 28; Tabío and, 45, 109
agujetas (lacetags), 113, *115*–18, 119, 122, 124–25
Alberti, Celso Pasos, 90–98
Alcalá, 114, 117
Alegría, R. E., 86, 117
Allen, S. J., 135
Alturas del Centro, 129
Alturas del Noroeste, 64
Alturas del Norte, 129

Álvarez, A., 139
Álvarez, Diego, 117, 119
American Indians, transculturation and acculturation with Spaniards, 25
Ames, Kenneth, 3
Angelbello, S. T., 28, 98
anthropomorphic pottery vessel rim adornos, 29
apropiadores pretribales, 69n1
Arawakans, 12, 109; expansion, 26, 31, 40–43; migration, 9
arc designs, 39
archaeohistory, 6
Archaeological Census of Cuba, 28
archaeological refuse, 76
archaeology: and architecture, 145; chronological order of, 151; and restoration, 158. *See also* Cuban archaeology
"Archaeology Behind the Blockade," 1
Archaic-with-ceramics, 43
architecture and archaeology, 145
Archivo General de Indias, Seville, 45
Archivo Nacional, 20
argillites, 50
Arimao River basin, 27, 29, 30, 39, 40
Arnold, M., 149

Arqueología Social Latinamericano (ASL), 10, 71, 73
Arrazcaeta, Roger, 146
Arredondo, Carlos, 47, 50, 52, 59, 64
Arrom, J. J., 118, 135
Arsandoux, H., 118
Art and Archaeology of Pre-Columbian Cuba (Dacal and Rivero), 2
Atajadizo, El, Dominican Republic, 120
authenticity, and restoration, 152–53
Avello, I., 27
Azcárate, 151

Bacín Verde, 111
Bahamas, basketry-impressed griddles *(burens)*, 104
Bahn, P., 53
Baldwin, Tammy, 2
Banes district, 29; agricultural-ceramic sites, 37, 110; objects of personal adornment, 44
Baní, "provincias indias" of, 110
Bantu artifacts, 136
Barajagua, 120
Barclay, K., 100
Bartone, R. N., 92
Bashilov, Vladimir, 28, 32, 33–34, 38, 46n3
Bate, Luis F., 10, 60, 69n1, 73, 85, 88n1
beaked axes, 59
beaks, 62
Bense, J., 20
Berman, M. J., 104
Bianchi, L., 156
Biblioteca Nacional, 20
Binford, L. R., 8
bitter manioc, 31
blade cores, 60
Bloch, M., 6
Bobrinski, A. A., 38
Bordes, F., 65
Boyd, M. F., 18
bracelets, 113
Bradley, R. S., 61
Brandi, C. M., 152
brass: in extended burials at El Chorro de Maíta, 121, 122–23; indigenous use of, 118–19; and Indo-Hispanic contact, 119–22
Breas de San Felipe, 52
Bremer, Frederika, 128–29, 132, 142n7

Brezillion, M. N., 54
Bronce, El, Puerto Rico, 94
Brookfield Charles, *19*
built patrimony: and archaeology, 148, 149–52; historical edifices as multistrata totalities, 144; intervention in, 143–44; and minimal intervention, restoration, and archaeology, 148–49; restoration and rehabilitation of, 150–51
Bullen, R. P., 17, 27
Bunge, M., 148, 149
burenes (griddles), 32, 93; double-edged, 100
burial positions: extended, 11, 120–23; flexed, 113, 120, 121, 123; "Taino" sites, 120
burins, 62
Bush, George W., 2
Bush, Jeb: "Travel to Terrorist States" law, 24–25
Bushnell, A. T., 18
Bustamante, R., 144, 152, 153

Cabagán, 38
Caballero, L., 156
Cabo, El, Dominican Republic, 37
Cabrera, M., 70
"cachimbas," 136
cacicazgos (chiefdoms), 43, 70, 73, 74–75, 87, 88n5
Caibarién, 60, 61
Calle San Ignacio, Havana: building No. 314, 157–58; building No. 602, *154, 155*; building Nos. 314 and 414, 145; building Nos. 350 and 356, 158
Calvera, Jorge, 10, 32, 90–98
Canal San Nicolás, 50
Canarreo, 39–40, *41*
Cannon, A., 76
Cantabria: "Cantabria culture," 34; pottery assemblage, 33
Caoba *(Swietenia mahagoni)*, 96
Caribe Arqueológica, El, 15
Carniero, R. L., 43
Carreras, Raquel, 88n7
Casa de la Reina, Dominican Republic, 88n9
"casimbas" (karst sinkholes), 50, 52, 61, 64
Cassá, R., 119
cassava-based agriculturalist societies, 100
cassava bread, 32
Castellanos, N., 30, 38, 46n6

Index / 195

cattle remains, 139
Caunao River drainage, 39
caves, sites of escaped slaves, 129
Cayo Contrabando, 97; ceramics, 100; maps of sites with contemporaneous radiocarbon determination with Los Buchillones, *103*; paste mineralogy, 100; radiocarbon dating, 102
Cayo Conuco, 54
Cayo Guillermo, 97, 98
Cayo Hijo de Guillermo Este, 97, 98–100, 102, 104; maps of sites with contemporaneous radiocarbon determination with Los Buchillones, *103*; paste mineralogy, 100; radiocarbon dating, 102; shell artifacts from Cave 1, *101*; shell debitage, 102; shell species from top stratigraphic layers of excavations in Caves 1 and 3, 98, *99*, 100
Cayo Hijo de Guillermo Oeste, 97, 98, 100
Cayo Ocampo, 27, 29, 38, 40
Ceiba Mocha, 22
Celaya, M., 28, 39, 43, 46n7
cemetery, at El Chorro de Maíta, 111–25
"cemis," 29
Centro Avanzado de Estudios Puertorrique-ños y del Caribe, 23
ceramics: African motifs on those made by slaves, 136; Cayo Contrabando, 100; Cayo Hijo de Guillermo Este, 100; Chican Ostionoid subseries, 110; chronology of in Cuba, 100; differences between interior and coastal sites, 32; at escaped slave sites, 134–35; Los Buchillones, 100–102; Meillacan ostionoid subseries, 110; Saladoid, 120; south-central Cuba, 27; variations in generated by European contact, 109
ceremonial plazas: Cuban, 77–78, 86–87; of Greater Antilles, 86–87; Laguna de Limones, 77, 79, 82, 86
chalcedonies, 50, 57
Chappell, Bruce, 20–22
Charcón, El, 54
Charter of Architectural Survey (Bustamante), 144
Charter of Krakow, 144, 149, 153
Charter of Venice, 144, 152
Chican Ostionoid subseries, 84, 110, 120
Chicoid pottery, 42

chiefdoms, in Cuba, 43–44, 70
Chorro de Maíta, 11
Chorro de Maíta, El: brass and Indo-Hispanic contact at, 106–25; domesticated pig bones *(Sus scrofa)*, 111; plan of, *112*; reuse of European objects according to native symbolic codes, 119
Chorro de Maíta cemetery, *108*, 111–15; body adornment objects, 113; brass tubes (lace-tags), 113, *115*–18, 119, 122, 124–25; burial position variations, 111; confluence of European with indigenous practices, 123; European metal materials, 107; extended burial positions, 115, 120–21, 123; flexed-position burials, 113, 121, 123; fronto-occipital tabular oblique cranial deformation, 113, 114; ornament from burial No. 25, *115*; persistence and change, 122–24; post-Columbian indigenous elites, 11, 123–24; presumed pre-Columbian origin of, 121; radiocarbon dates of skeletons, 113, 121–22; skeleton No. 25, 117–18, 119, 121–22, 123; skeleton No. 57, 113, *114*, 119, 124; strong post-Columbian use, 122
Christian extended burial position, 120, 123–24
Chuchita 1 (Quemado de Güines) 54, 68; complete cycle of stone tool production, 65; extinct species found in karst sinkhole at, 64–65
Church of San Felipe Neri, Old Havana, section of recent excavation in, *147*
Ciego de Avila province, 10, 89; indigenous ceramic sherds, 100; map of Cuba showing, *91*
Cienaga Oriental de Zapata, 29
Cienfuegos (city), 26
Cienfuegos Bay, 61
Cienfuegos province, 26, *51*
cimarrones. *See* escaped slaves; escaped slave sites
cimarrón pottery, 135
clay cones *(hormas)*, 136–37
Codakia orbicularis valves, 99
Cold War, 25
collagen-method dating, 34–36, 46n5
collections research, 38–39
collective property, establishment of, 74
Colón, C., 117

colonial archaeology, 145
Columbia Plain, 34; mayolica pottery, 111
Comunidades neoliticas (Neolithic communities), 109
Comunidades tribales agroceramistas (Agriceramic tribal communities). *See* agroalfarero sites (agro-ceramic)
Concepción de la Vega, Hispaniola, 111, 117
conucos, 43
Cooper, Jago, 8, 10, 11, 90, 94, 102
cores, 60, 65, 68
Corralillo, 50, 62, 63
Cosculluela, J. A., 40
coup de point, 65
Courí, Dominican Republic, 47
Craddock, P. T., 116
cranial deformation: El Chorro de Maíta cemetery burials, 113, 114; as ethnic identifier of agricultural, ceramic-producing groups, 122
Crejo, T., 148
creolization, 126
Crespo, E. F., 119, 120
Criado, F., 160
Cruxent, J. M., 47, 117, 123
crystraline quartz, 50
Cuba: conservation of built patrimony in, 143–44; development of national science, 88n2; development of social complexity in, 73; indigenous peoples of Indo-Euro contact period, 109–11; Indo-Hispanic contact in, 26, 34, 44–45, 107–11, 123; law of protection of patrimony, 149; studies of shell point technology, 99. *See also* agroalfarero sites (agro-ceramic); Cuban archaeology
Cuba and Florida: connections in historical archaeology, 16–25; migrations of people between, 17–18; shared administrative context, 18
Cuban Academy of Sciences, 6, 13, 78, 79; Institute of Social Sciences, 29–30
Cubanacan, "provincias indias" of, 110
Cuban archaeology: basis for understanding relevance of archaeology for restoration, 143; decentralized position in decision-making in Old Havana, 158–59; dialectical materialism, 42; disjuncture of historical archaeology in, 156; effect of U.S. isolationist policies on, 2–5; framed as historical science, 6; and Marxist theory, 4; methodological advances in urban historical archaeology, 4–5; methodological problems, 75–77; new theoretical focus on social complexity, 70–71; prehispanic archaeology, 5–7; theoretical and methodological framework, 11, 71–77
Cuban condor, 52
Cuban Ministry of Sciences, Technology and Environment (CITMA), 90; Center for Archaeology, 80
Cuban Revolution of 1959, 25
Cuban shell artifact classification methods, 98
Cueva Berovides, 52
Cueva Caleta, 52
Cueva de la Cachimba, 136
Cueva del Puerco, 61
cultural variant Jagua, 28
Curet, L. A., 4, 12, 70, 76, 90, 92, 94
Cusick, J., 23

Dacal, Ramón, 1, 47, 79, 80, 98, 104
Damajayabo, Granma province, 36
Damují River, 39, 61
Davis, Dave, 5, 6, 7
Dawdy, Shannon Lee, 1
"Daytona Conference" group, 1948, *19*
Deagan, Kathleen A., 4, 9, 18, 21, *22*–24, 44, 107, 116, 117, 123, 124
debitage, 60, 65, 102
Delgado, C. J., 149, 160
Delgado, L., 28
Delle, J. A., 127
Delpuech, A., 90
dendograms, 53, 54
denticulates, 65
Department of Archaeology, Holguín, 111
Dialogues in Cuban Archaeology (Curet, Dawdy, and La Rosa), 1, 2, 5
Díaz, P., 40
dog remains, 135, 139
Domínguez, Lourdes, 16, 18, 22, 23, 26, 29, 42, 74, 104, 110, 151; classificatory methodology, 107; *Comunidades neoliticas* (Neolithic communities), 45n2, 109; and El Yayal, 114; excavations at Loma del

Convento, 30–32, 37; and historical archaeology in Cuba, 5, 7, 20–21, 24; "Homage to Dr. Betty Meggers," 9, 13, *14*, 15,; "La Cuidad," 7; on regional centralization in Jagua area, 44; on Seboruco industry, 60; seriation of south-central agroalfarero site assemblages, 46n6; and transculturation, 8; work on pottery technology of south-central agroalfarero sites, 38, 135

Dominican Republic: Casa de la Reina, 88n9; ceremonial plazas, 86; Courí, 47; El Atajadizo, 120; El Cabo, 37; La Isabella, 117, 120; Mordán industry, 60; Padre Las Casas, 86; Palero, 86

D'Ossat, 152

Drennen, R., 70, 88n5

Drewett, P., 90

duhos, 93

Duke, Luly, 3

ear spools, 113

Eidt procedure, 81

electron microscopy, 116

Ellis, G. D., 23

Elso, Eladio, 135

Emerson, M. C., 136

empiricist-historicist framework, 73

En Bas Saline, Haiti, 44

encomienda, 26, 44; archaeology of, 44; in Baní, 110; indigenous resistance to, 45; of Las Casas, 9, 26, 29, 39–40, *41*, 45

energetic frameworks, 50, 69

energy dispersive spectrometry, 116

Engels, F.: notion of primitive communism, 6–7; *The Origin of the Family, Private Property and the State*, 6

Engerrand, G., 54, 59

escaped slaves: use of firearms, 139. *See also* escaped slave sites

escaped slave sites, 21; archaeology of, 126–29; artifacts and objects of wood and vegetable fiber, 138; botijas, 132, 138; clay cones *(hormas)*, 136–37; containers for liquids, 130, 137–38; containers for solid foods, 134–37; demijohns, 132, 137–38, 142n5; dependence on slave-based haciendas, 128–29; dietary remains, 139; faunal species, by number of sites, *140*; flints, 139; general location of sites, *130*; glass bottles, 137; glazed ceramic pots, 134–35; gourd (güira) remains, 138, 142n7; grès stoneware flasks, 132, 137; hearths, 130; inaccessibility of, *133*, 141; locally produced pots and plates, 135–36; metal tools and utensils, 138–39; percentages of artifacts and tool types, by category, *134*; seasonal refuges in caves and rockshelters, 127, 129; settlements at higher elevations, 127; shackles, 139; site characteristics, 129–33, *131–32*; sites in Havana-Matanzas uplands, 126, 127; studies of, 127; tobacco pipes, 135, *136*, 138; tools for resistance, 133–39; *trébedes*, 134; unexpected objects, 142n10

Espenshade, Christopher, 94

Etapa Agroalfarera (Agriceramic stage), 109

Etayo, Daniel Torres, 10

ethnoarchaeological studies, and archaeological refuse, 76

ethnohistory, 6

Euclidian distance measures, 54

European metals, 107

Evans, Clifford, 13

Ewen, C. R., 151

expedient solution, 57

extended burial position, 11; and brass artifacts, 121, 122–23; El Chorro de Maíta cemetery, 120–21; and European influence, 120–21

Fairbanks, Charles, 16, *19*–21

Farallones de Seboruco, quartzite macroliths, 47–48

Farnsworth, P., 127

Fase Agricultores (Agricultural phase), 109

faunal analysis, *85*, 139, *140*

Febles, J., 17, 28, 45n2, 47, 50, 53, 57, 59, 60, 90, 95

Feingold, Russ, 2

Feminias, Cancela, 40

Ferguson 1980, 135

Ferguson, L. G., 127

Fernández de Oviedo, G., 109

Fewkes, J. W., 17

Flake, Jeff, 3

flake tools, 60, 65–66
Flannery, K. V., 4
flexed-position burials, 113, 120, 121, 123
flintknapping, 58
flints, 50
Florida: Glades culture, 27; migrations to Cuba during eighteenth century, 24; postrevolutionary Cuban population, 24; Spanish colony until 1821, 18
Fondeur, C., 111
Fort Mose, Florida, 21
Francovich, R., 156
Franklin, M., 21
fugitive slaves. *See* escaped slaves; escaped slave sites
Funari, P. P., 127, 128, 135
funerary practices. *See* burial positions; Chorro de Maíta cemetery

Gabinete de Arqueología, Oficina del Historiador de la Ciudad de La Habana, 7, 8, 21, 145, 146; section of recent excavation in church of San Felipe Neri, Old Havana, *147*
Gadamer, H. G., 151
Gamble, C., 50, 57
Gannon, Michael, 21, *22*
García, Calixto, 145, 157
García, F. G., 60
García, J. A., 18, 44, 104, 110, 114, 115
García, M. A., 118, 135
García y Grave de Peralta, F., 142n9
General Conference of the Organization of the United Nations for Education, Science and Culture, 144
geotechnical recording methods, 156
giant tortoise, 52
Glades culture, south Florida, 27
Godo, P. P., 28, 39, 43, 46n8, 61
Goggin, John, 16, *19*, 20; *Spanish Majolica in the New World*, 19
gold, among indigenous peoples in Greater Antilles, 118
Gold, R., 18
Golenko, Viktor, 28, 32, 33–34, 38
Gómez, Néstor, 47
González, A., 27
gourd (güira) remains, 138, 142n7

Gower, J. C., 53
Graham, Elizabeth, 90
Greater Antilles: "arc of," 77; "cacicazgos," 70; ceremonial plazas, 86; gold among indigenous peoples, 118
"Great Wall of San Lucas," 78
griddles. *See burenes* (griddles)
Griffin, John W., 17–20
Grupo Guamá, 19, 20, 27
Guamuhaya, 27
guanín, 118, 123, 125n2
Guantánamo province, 78
Guarch, José M., 6, 28, 30, 42, 47, 79, 86, 95, 109; "Cultural Variant Bayamo," 46n8; and Laguna de Limones, 10, 87; shell classification, 98; use of term *Fase Agricultores* (Agricultural phase), 109; work in El Chorro de Maíta, 111, 113–14, 116, 120, 121
Guayacán *(Guaiacum sp.)*, 96
Guerrero, J. G., 120
Gundrum, Ivan, 20
Gutiérrez, A., 139
Gutiérrez, Luis, 2
Guzmán, Gonzalo de, 110

"Habana Vieja" (Arrazcaeta), 146
hafted harpoon point, 100
Haidar, M., 23
Haiti, Republic of, 77
Halbirt, Carl, 21
hammerstones, 65
handaxe: comparison, Tecas and Seboruco, 59; partial biface, Jibá industry, Northwest Villa Clara, 65
hand hammers, 99
Handler, J. S., 136
hand picks, 99
Harrington, Mark R., 5, 42, 52, 78, 82
Harris, Edward C., 8, 143–45, 149, 150
Harris matrix, 8, 143–46, 153; versus stratigraphic excavation, 146
Harty, Maura, 3
Havana. *See* Calle San Ignacio, Havana; Old Havana
Havana province, 1817, 141n2
Haviser, J. B., 127
Hayden, B., 76
hen remains, 139

Hernández Mora, Iosvany, 8, 11, 145, 146, 151, 153, 155, 156
Herrera, René, 5, 16, 17, 19, 27
Hispaniola, 42, 109–10; Concepción de la Vega, 111; Ostionoid societies, 74; regional *cacicazgos*, 43; "Taino" sites, 31
historical archaeology, 7–9, 145; advances in urban, 4–5; approach to fugitive slaves, 126, 127; as archaeology of historic sites, 150; connections between Cuba and Florida, 16–25; critique of documentary sources generated in centers of colonial power, 127; expansion in Florida and Cuba since 1980s, 23; lack of unified criteria for practice, 150; Lourdes Domínguez and, 5, 7, 20–21, 24
historical materialism, 71, 88n1
Holguín province: Department of Archaeology, 111; Levisa I, 60; Mayarí, 60; sites showing Indo-Hispanic transculturation, 44
holistic studies, 154
Hoogland, M. L. P., 37
hormas, 136–37
household effigies, 93
house structure, indigenous house, Los Buchillones, 90–94
Hughen, K. A., 96
Hughes, J., 159
Hurt, Wesley, *19*
Hutcheson, C. D., 104
hutia, 32

Iglesias, Fé, 22, 139
incised decoration, 33
Indo-Hispanic contact, 26, 44–45, 107–11, 123; at Chorro de Maíta, 106–25; and extended burial position, 120–21; at Loma del Convento, 34, 40; and transculturation, 44; and use of brass ornaments, 119–22
inferential analysis, 6
Institute of Social Sciences, Academy of Sciences of Cuba, 29–30
IntCa104 atmospheric calibration curve, 96
intercommunal parentage links, 74
interfaces, 146, 147
International Association for Caribbean Archaeology, 23

International Charter for the Administration of the Archaeological Patrimony (Bustamente), 144, 156
Irving, W. N., 60
Isabella, La, Dominican Republic, 117, 120
Iturralde-Vinent, M., 50, 52
Izquierdo, G., 60, 98, 99

Jacobus, A. L., 135
Jagua Bay, 26–29; migration history of people of, 39
Jamestown, Virginia, 117
jaragua *(Acrosynanthus trachyphyllus)*, 84
Jardines, J., 90
Jardines del Rey Archipelago, 89; islands with archaeological evidence for indigenous human activity, 97–98; map of Cuba showing, *91*
Jibá industry, Northwest Villa Clara, 54, 62–66; fine-grained chalcedonies, 68; flake-blade cores, 65, 68; partial biface handaxe, 66; raw materials, 65; spatial correlation with wooded zone, 63; toolmaking techniques, 65; tool types, 65–66
Jiménez, A., 120
Jiménez, O., 125
Johnson, Sherry, 18, 20, 24
Jouravleva, I., 100, 135
Journal of Archaeological Science, 2
jutía rat remains, 139

Kacike, 7
Kalunga (palenque), 128, 137, 138
Keegan, W. F., 110
Keistler, Woody, *22*
Kelso, W. M., 117
Kepecs, S., *4, 8*
Knight, Judith, 2, 17
Knight, Vernon James, 8, 9–10, 17, 20, 110, 122
Kozlowski, Janus, 47
Kulst, P., 117

labor drafts, 44–45
lageniform, 65
Laguna de Limones, 10; ceremonial plaza, 77, 79, 80, 82, 86; Dacal's work at, 79, 80, 82; excavation in Mound No. 3, 84; explorations in perimetral zones, 84; faunal re-

mains identified at, *85*; habitation area, 82, 84; hierarchical phase of tribal socioeconomic formation, 85, 87; machine leveling of, 80; new investigations at, 80–85; phosphate contamination, 82, 87; previous work at, 78–80; principal structural components of, *81*; regional location of, *72*; in regional perspective, 77–80; social complexity, 86; Tabío and Guarch's work at, 79, 80, 82; "Taíno zone" site, 86; topographic maps of, 80; vectoral map showing direction of rainwater flow, *83*

Lanaluze, Victor: "Corte de Caña," 142n5

Landers, Jane, 18, 20, 24

land tortoise remains, 135, 139

La Rosa Corzo, Gabino, 151; African motifs on ceramics made by slaves, 136; and the archaeology of slave resistance, 5, 11, 21, 126–42; and Cuban-Florida historical archaeology, 22; and Cuban historical archaeology, 7; *Dialogues in Cuban Archaeology*, 1; *Runaway Slave Settlements in Cuba: Resistance and Repression*, 2, 21; and study of Los Buchillones site, 90

Las Auras (hacienda), 29

Las Casas, Bartólome de: encomienda, 9, 26, 29, 39–40, *41*, 45; *Historia de las Indias*, 39–40, 43, 77, 84; on indigenous interest in brass, 119

Latin American Antiquity, 2

Latin American archaeology, 6

Latin American Social Archaeology (Arqueología Social Latinamericano [ASL]), 10, 71, 73

Latin American Studies Association, 2

Laxon, D. D., 27

Leal, Eusebio, 20

Le Paige, G., 59

Levallois tradition, 65

Levisa I, Holguín province, human bone site, 60

Levisa river basin, 47

Lightfoot, K., 107

Limones II, 84, 87

Limones III, 84, 87

Lindsey, David, 3

Little, B. J., 126

"llora-lluvia" ("cries-rain"), 46n8

Loma del Convento, 10; archaeological background, 27–29; Bobrinski and Loman study, 38–39; bronze navigator's compass, *35*; collagen-method dating, 34–36; and Cuban archaeology, 26–46; Cuban-Soviet excavation of, 32–35, *36–37*; degree of hierarchization, 31; differences in pottery designs, 31–32; discovery and fieldwork, 1974–1988, 29–38; economic interdependence with coastal sites, 32; evidence of early Indo-Hispanic contact, 34, 40; Ford diagrams of modes of pottery decoration by horizon, 34; historical research, 39–40; Horizon III deposit, 37; location of Las Casas's Canarreo, 26, 29, 39–40, *41*, 45; map of mounded middens, *30*; radiocarbon dating, 30, 34; as regional center, 31, 39, 44; as Spanish encomienda, 39–40, 45; Structure I, *36, 37*; Structure II, 37

Loma del Grillo, 141n1

Loman, V. G., 38

looters, 78, 79

López, F., 148, 150

Lores, Abigail, 79, 80

Los Buchillones, 10, 88n7, 89–90; artifacts, 93; basketry-impressed griddles *(burens)*, 104; ceramics, 100–102; chronology, 95–96; indigenous house, 90–94; intensive woodworking, 90; island and marine environment interaction, 90, 96, *97*, 98, 102; known archaeological sites contemporaneous with, 102, *103*; map of Cuba showing, *91*; maps of sites with contemporaneous radiocarbon determination with, *103*; paste mineralogy, 100; paucity of evidence for direct Indo-Hispanic interaction, 104–5; plan of site extent, *95*; radiocarbon dating, 95–96, 104; recent archaeological research, 90–98; regional interaction, 104; settlement size and location, 94; shell artifacts from, *101*; shell debitage, 102; shell species from top stratigraphic layers of excavations in D2-1 and F1-1, 98–100, *99*; structure D2-6, *93*–94; Taíno period assemblage, 95; wooden posts, 92–93

Los Palmares, Brazil, 128

Loven, S., 42, 43
Lumbreras, Luis, 10
Lyon, Eugene, 20, 24

MacNeish, R., 60
MacPhee, R. D. E., 50, 52
macroblades, 60, 61
macroflakes, 60
Main Church of San Juan Bautista de Remedios, Villa Clara province, 145, 156
Maisí, 77, 78
majá boa constrictor, 139
Malpáez, beaked axe made on limestone bedrock, *59*
Manacas River, *63*
Maniabón Hills, 107
manioc horticulture, 42
Manucy, Albert, *19*
Máquina, La, 78
Marine04 calibration curve, 96
maroons. *See* escaped slaves; escaped slave sites
Marrero, L., 27, 40
Marrinan, R. A., 117, 120
Martínez, A. G., 28
Martínez, F., 36, 48
Martinón-Torres, Marcos, 2, 11, 116, 117
Marxist theory, 73, 88n1, 88n3
Masío, El, 38
massive core tools, 60
mass suicide, 45
Matanzas province, 50, 60
Mayarí, Holguín province, 60
Mayarí river basin, 47
Maza y Santos, Aquiles: "Iglesia Parroquial Mayor de San Juan Bautista de Remedios: Indicaciones [1944] sobre su valor artístico e histórico y la necesidad de su conservación," 145, 157, 160
McGuire, R. H., 126
McKee, L., 21
McMahon, D., 21
Megalocnus rodens, 52
Megalocnus sp. (Giant Caribbean ground sloth), 10, 52, 63; molar fragment, Solapa Alta, *63*
Meggers, Betty Jane, 3, *4,* 13, *14,* 15; pan-Latin and pan-Carribean perspective, 9

Meillacan ostionoid subseries, 27, 42, 110, 120
Melado, 111
Mendoza, Ariadna, 8
Mesa González, I., 90, 100, 104
microliths, 58
microtopography, 80
middle-range societies, 70, 71
Miguel, O., 120
minimal intervention, principle of, 148–49
minimum number of individuals (MNI), 96, 98
Ministry of Sciences, Technology and Environment (CITMA): Center for Technological Applications and Nuclear Development, 116; collaborative archaeological investigations of Los Buchillones, 90; Department Central-East of the Center for Archaeology, 80
Mira, E., 110
modeled decoration, 33
Monte Cristo, 77
Moráles, Oswaldo Patiño, 16, 19, 27
Morales Santos, Lorenzo, 10, 18, 44, 59, 61, 63, 107
Mordán industry, Dominican Republic, 60
Moreira, L. J., 43, 70, 74
Morejón, Y., 145
Morin, E., 149
Mormino, G. R., 17, 23
Morro Castle, Havana Bay, 145
Moscoso, F., 123
Mousterian industry, Middle Paleolithic, 62, 65
Müller-Beck, H., 57
Muscovy duck remains, 139

Nara Conference, 152–53
National Museum of Natural History, 13, 14
necklaces, 113
"neolithic stage," 45n2
neutron activation analysis, 39
New Archaeology, 4
nonegalitarian societies, 70
Northwest Villa Clara Project, 48–50; Casimbas 2, 61; cluster analysis results, 53–54; dendograms showing early tradition tool groups, *56*; early tradition, 69; Jibá industry, 62–66; link to hunter-gatherer groups,

48–50; Middle Pleistocene, 50; Pleistocene/Holocene transition, 50; principal locations of early tradition sites in, *51*; relationships among early human inhabitants, Late Pleistocene fauna, and remnant Pleistocene fauna, 52–53; Seboruco industry, 47, 59–62 (*See also* Seboruco industry, Northwest Villa Clara); spatial energetic framework, 50–53; Tecas industry, 54–59, 67, 68 (*See also* Tecas industry); technological and typological values applied in cluster analysis of artifacts of early tradition in, *55*; techno-typological order of early stone tool industries of, *67*; three industrial groups in early tradition, 53–54
number of individual elements (NIE), 98
Núñez, Antonio, 59, 80

Obama, Barack, 2
Oficina del Historiador de la Ciudad de la Habana, 20; Gabinete de Arqueología, 7, 8, 21, *145–47*
Ojo de Agua, 28
Olazagasti, I., 104
Old Havana: archaeological practice in, 153–56; decentralized position of archaeology in decision-making about, 158–59; multidisciplinary collaborations in, 8; restoration plans, 7, 159; work on built patrimony hindered by U.S. blockade, 160
Oliva reticularis shells, 100
olive jars, 111
Oliver, J. R., 37, 70, 100, 113, 118, 119
opals, 50
Opus, 7
Orser, C. E., Jr., 21, 127, 150
Ortega, E., 111, 142
Ortega, O., 137, 138
Ortíz, Fernando, 4, 42; *Cuban Counterpoint,* 8; and transculturation, 8, 18, 25, 44, 107
O'Shea, J., 53
Ostapkowicz, J. M., 104
Ostionoid societies, Hispaniola, 74
overshot (outrrepassé) blades, 65

Padilla, R., 39, 43, 46n7
Padre Las Casas, Dominican Republic, 86
Pagan-Jiménez, J. R., 100

Palacio de los Capitanes Generales, 17
Palacio de los Condes de Cañongo, 158
palenques, 128, 137, 138
Paleolithic-type traditions, 69n1
Palero, Dominican Republic, 86
Palmetto Grove, San Salvador, 104
Palo Hincado, Puerto Rico, 86
Palov, M. Z., 23
Papeles Procedentes de Cuba, The East Florida Papers, 23–24
parietal test pits, 157
Parker, S. R., 18
Parocnus brownii, 52
partial bifaces, 65
patrimonial models, 149
Patterson, T. C., 6
Payares, Adolfo, 20
Paynter, R., 126
Peebles, Christopher, 53
Peguero, L.A., 88n9
Peña, Angela, 145, 158, 160
Pendergast, David, 90, 96
Pérez, A., 54
Pérez, J., 45
Pérez, R., 18, 44, 107, 142n7
perforators, 62, 65
Peros, M. C., 93, 94
Persons, A. B., 122
phosphate contamination, 82, 87
photogrammetry, 156
Pichardo, E., 5, 18, 77, 123
Piedras Toscamente Esféricas (PTE). *See* Roughly Spherical Stones (Piedras Toscamente Esféricas [PTE])
Piel-Desruisseaux, J. L., 57, 65
Pigeon Creek, San Salvador, 104
Pinar del Rio province, 42, 135, 138
Pino, M., 47
placer gold, 27
planimetry, 156
Playa Blanca, Puerto Rico, 94
Pleistocene crocodile, 52
Pleistocene megaspecies, 64
Plog, S., 4
poststructuralism, 4
pottery: Baní style, 27; "Cantabria style" ("early Taíno"), 27; Columbia Plain, 111; Loma del Convento, 33–37; shift from rep-

resentational to decorative motifs, 43; talismans, 29
Pozzetta, G. E., 23
Prat, José, 16, 20, 157
pre-agroceramic, 69n1
preforms, 65
Price, R., 135
primitive communism, 6-7
"Problem of the Periodization of Subtaíno Culture in South-Central Cuba, The" (Bashilov and Golenko), 33
Protoagrícola sites, 43
proto-Archaic, 69n1
Pueblo Viejo, 77, 86, 87; regional location of, *72*
Puerto Real, Haiti, 21, 117, 120
Puerto Rico, 110; ceremonial plazas, 86; structures at Taíno sites, 94; "Taino" sites, 31
punctiforms, 60, 65
Punta Alegre, 94
Punta del Muerto, 54, 60, 61
Punta de Maisí, 78
Pupo, R., 149

quartzites, 50
Quemado de Güines, 50, 62; extinct species found in karst sinkhole, Chuchita 1, 64-65
Quirós-Castillo, J., 156, 159, 160

rabots, 62
radiocarbon dating: Los Buchillones, 95-96; problem of chronological definition of entire region based on one date, 77
rafter hooks, 93
Ramírez, R., 59
Ramos, A., 145, 150, 157-59
Rancho Club site, 35
Rankin Santander, Alfredo, 29-31; Loma del Convento work, 31, 34, 37; survey of lower Arimao, 40
reducciones, 45
Rehren, Thilo, 11
Reimer, P. J., 96
Renfrew, C., 53
Rentería, Pedro de, 39
resource exploitation, 63, 65, 89, 98, 102
restoration: and authenticity, 152-53, 155; defined, 153

Restoration Charter of 1972, 152
Rey, Estrella, 4, 6, 30, 43, 77; on Cuban ceremonial plazas, 86-87; and Laguna de Limones, 10; *Prehistory of Cuba* (with Tabío), 88n4; on Seboruco-Mordán industry, 60
Reyes, J. M., 98
Rivera, David, 25
River Maya, 78
Rivero, Manuel, 2, 111
Rives, A. V., 23, 38, 45n2, 46n6, 53, 98, 107, 109
Rivet, A., 118
Robiou-Lamarche, Sebastian, 104
rockshelters, 129
Rodríguez, Beatríz, 145, 153, 155, 156
Rodríguez, C., 42, 113, 118, 121, 123, 125n1, 125n3
Rodríguez, Miguel, 77
Rodríguez, Pino, 35
Rodríguez, R., 42, 45n2, 100
Rodríguez Matamoros, Marcos E., 27, 34, 35-36, 39-41
Romero, L. E., 21
Rosario Pérez, L., 96, 98
Roughly Spherical Stones (Piedras Toscamente Esféricas [PTE]), 58-59, 61, 68
Rouse, Irving, 5, 19; *Archaeology of the Maniabon Hills, Cuba*, 29, 44, 107, 111; and Chican Ostionoid subseries, 84, 110, 120; on Cuban-Florida contact, 17, 27; Florida research, 16; and Meillacan ostionoid subseries, 110, 120; and social complexity in Cuba, 6; studies in El Chorro de Maíta, 111; on the Tainos, 95; work in Courí in the Dominican Republic, 47
Rousseau, P. L., 40
Royal Ontario Museum, 90

Sabana, Puerto Rico, 86
Sagua Grande River, 50, *63*
Sagua la Grande, 50, 54, 60, 62
Saladoid ceramics, 120
Sampedro Hernández, R., 60, 99
Samper, Juanita Saenz, 113
Samson, A. V. M., 37
San José de las Lajas, 142n3
Sanjurjo, J., 27
San Lucas, *72*, 87

San Pedro, R., 59
Santa Elena, South Carolina, 117
Sarmiento, G., 73
Scardaville, M., 24
Schiffer, M., 4, 8
Schinkel, K., 76, 92
Schmidt, P. R., 6, 150
Schuyler, Robert, 18, 150
scrapers, 58, 65, 99
Seboruco industry, Northwest Villa Clara, 47, 59–62; beaked axe on thick flint macroblade, *59*; Clactonian-like technical variation, 62; dynamic relation between technology and spatial frameworks, 61; flake-blade artifacts, 66, 68; macroblade tradition, 68; oldest lithic tradition in Cuba and Caribbean, 54, 60; toolmaking techniques and tool types, 62; use of quartzites, 62
Seboucoid population, migration routes, 60, 61
Seven Years' War, 18
Severin, K. P., 118
Sevilla, Luis Bay, 143
Sharrock, W., 159
shell artifacts: from Cayo Hijo de Guillermo Este, 98, *99*, 100, *101*, 102; classification methods, 98; decorative jewelry, 100; *Oliva reticularis* shells, 100; shell hammers, 90, 99
shell point technology, 99
side scrapers, 65
Siegel, P. E., 118
Sierra de Escambray, 27, 29
Sierra de Esperón, 141n1
Sierra de la Güira, 138
Singleton, T. A., 7, 9, 20, 21, 23, 127
Sitiecito, 54
slave hunters' diaries, 129
slave resistance, 21, 128
slaves: on sugar plantations, 137. *See also* escaped slaves; escaped slave sites
Smith, Hale, 16, 18, *19*, 20
Smithsonian Institution, 13
social complexity: development of in Cuba, 73; new theoretical focus of Cuban archaeology, 70
social differentiation, 75

Society for American Archaeology, San Juan, Puerto Rico, 1
sociohistorical processes, theory of, 71
sociopolitical complexity, rise of, 43–44
Solapa Alta: molar fragment, *Megalocnus* sp. (Giant Caribbean ground sloth), *63*; silex artifacts, 63
Solapa de la Rinconá, 138
Sotolongo, P. L., 148
South, S., 150
south-central Cuban sites, attempt to seriate, 38
Spanish: pressure to modify indigenous practices, 122; *repartimiento*, 44. *See also* encomienda; Indo-Hispanic contact
Spanish majolica, 34
St. Augustine, Florida, 117; administered from Havana during Spanish domination, 17; archaeological preservation ordinance, 21; emigration of residents to Cuba after English takeover, 18
star decoration, *136*
stone tool industries, 47; of the Caribbean, and opportunism, 57; map of principal regions with evidence of in Cuba, *49*; previous studies, 47–48. *See also* Northwest Villa Clara Project; tools
stratigraphic analysis, 8, 145–46, *147*, 156
Straube, B., 117
Strombus costatus shell hammer, 99
Strombus gigas gastropods, 99
Strombus sp. points, 99
structural archaeology, 145
"Study of the Aboriginal Ceremonial Plazas of the Eastern Extreme of Cuba, 77
Sued-Badillo, J., 124

Tabío, Ernesto, 4, 6, 30, 43, 77, 109; on Cuban ceremonial plazas, 86–87; and Laguna de Limones, 10, 78–79; *Prehistory of Cuba* (with Rey), 88n4; on Seboruco-Mordán industry, 60; use of term *Etapa Agroalfarera* (Agriceramic stage), 45, 109; work at Laguna de Limones, 78–79
"Taino" sites, 5, 12, 78, 95; burial positions, 120; Chican Ostionoid subseries, 84; configuration of middens, 82; Hispaniola and Puerto Rico, 31; ritual gear, 42

Tairona pectoral ornaments, 113
Tecas industry, 54–59; artifact types, 58–59; atypical flakes with usewear, 59; beaked axe made on limestone bedrock, 59; controversial identification, 66; Malpáez beaked axes, 59; natural or atypical forms, 68; raw materials, 57; resemblance of artifacts to Lower Paleolithic tools, 57; Roughly Spherical Stones (Piedras Toscamente Esféricas [PTE]), 58–59, 61, 68; stratigraphic position at Chuchita 1, 68; tendency toward opportunism, 57; tool-making techniques, 57–58
Tepaske, J., 18
Terebra taurinum, 84
thrown projectiles, 59
Tibisí reeds, 138, 142nn8–9
Tixier, J., 65
tobacco pipes, at escaped slave sites, 135, *136*, 138
Tomé, J., 98, 109
tools: cortex, 57, 59; flake, 60, 65–66; flint-knapping, 58; handaxe comparison, Tecas and Seboruco, 59; Jibá industry, 65–66; microliths, 58; Northwest Villa Clara, *56*, *67*; for resistance at escaped slave sites, 133–39; Roughly Spherical Stones (Piedras Toscamente Esféricas [PTE]), 58–59, 61, 68; scrapers, 58; Seboruco industry, 62; Tecas industry, 57–58; thermal fracture, 58; thrown projectiles, 59. *See also* stone tool industries
topographical recording methods, 156
Torres, D., 12, 110; and Laguna de Limones, 10, 70–88; use of term *Communidades tribales agroceramistas* (Agriceramic tribal communities), 109
"tradition," 53–54
transculturation, 8, 16, 18, 25, 44, 107
transculturation studies, 11
trash middens, 76
"traspatio archaeology," 7
tribal revolution, 73–74
tribal societies, developmental phases, 74, 85, 87
Trigger, B., 148
Triunvirato sugar mill, Matanzas, 145
Trujillo, H., 50
turey, 119

Ulloa, Jorge, 7, 42, 45n2, 100
units of analysis and units of observation, 76
University of Florida P. K. Yonge Library of Florida History, 23
urban archaeology, 4–5, 7, 148
Uribe, C., 70, 88n5
U.S. blockade of Cuba, 6, 11; denial of entry visas to Cuban academics, 24; hindrance of work on built patrimony in Old Havana, 160
Uyemura, K., 20

Valcárel Rojas, Roberto, 8, 42, 45n2, 70, 74, 105; Banes district work, 29, 37–38, 44, 110; on early ceramics in Cuba, 100; El Chorro de Maíta work, 106–25, 125n3; Los Buchillones work, 10, 11, 90, 94, 96, 104; on sociopolitical complexity, 44; survey of Jardines del Rey Archipelago, 97
Valdespino, Rafael, 145
Vargas, Iraida, 73, 75
Vásquez, M., 137
Vega, B., 119
Velázquez, Diego, 27, 39, 40
Velóz, M., 120
Velóz formation, 50, 61, 65, 70, 74, 104
Venegas, H., 50
Vento, E., 139
Versteeg, A., 76, 92
Villaverde, Cirilo, 129–30, 132, 139
Villavicencio, Raúl, 47, 59, 65
Viñales, Pinar del Rio, 142n3

Waring, Antonio, *19*
wedges, 62
Western Lithic co-Tradition, 60
Wickham, DeWayne, 2
wild pig remains, 135, 139
Willey, Gordon, *19*
Wisconsin Age, 60
Wolfson Archaeological Science Laboratories, Institute of Archaeology, University College of London, 116
Wood, J. J., 53
wooden artifacts, 138
wooden posts: Laguna de Limones, 84; Los Buchillones, 92–93
wooden vessels, 93

Worth, John E., 17, 20, 23, 24
Wright, I. A., 45
Wurdemann, J. G., 128

Xancus angulatus shell hammer, 90, 99
X-ray fluorescence, 116

Yaguajay: indigenous sites with early European materials, 110; map of, *108*
Yale University Caribbean program, 19
Yayal, El, 114, 120

zigzag motifs, 33, 38, 39